Constantin-François Volney

Travels through Syria and Egypt, in the Years 1783, 1784, and 1785

Vol. I

Constantin-François Volney

Travels through Syria and Egypt, in the Years 1783, 1784, and 1785
Vol. I

ISBN/EAN: 9783744756860

Printed in Europe, USA, Canada, Australia, Japan

Cover: Foto ©Andreas Hilbeck / pixelio.de

More available books at **www.hansebooks.com**

TRAVELS

THROUGH

SYRIA AND EGYPT.

VOL. I.

TRAVELS

THROUGH

SYRIA AND EGYPT,

IN THE YEARS 1783, 1784, AND 1785.

CONTAINING

The prefent Natural and Political State of thofe Countries, their Productions, Arts, Manufactures, and Commerce; with Obfervations on the Manners, Cuftoms, and Government of the TURKS and ARABS.

ILLUSTRATED WITH COPPER PLATES.

BY M. C—F. VOLNEY.

TRANSLATED FROM THE FRENCH.

IN TWO VOLUMES.

VOL. I.

THE SECOND EDITION.

LONDON:

PRINTED FOR G. G. J. AND J. ROBINSON, PATER-NOSTER-ROW.

MDCCLXXXVIII.

PREFACE.

OCTOBER, 1786.

FIVE years ago, being still young, a small inheritance, which fell to me, put me in possession of a sum of money. The difficulty was, how to employ it. Some of my friends advised me to enjoy the capital, others to purchase an annuity; but, on reflection, I thought the sum too inconsiderable to make any sensible addition to my income, and too great to be dissipated in frivolous expences. Some fortunate circumstances had habituated me to study; I had acquired a taste, and even a passion for knowledge, and this accession to my fortune appeared to me a fresh means of gratifying my inclina-

VOL. I.   A   tion,

tion, and opening a new way to improvement. I had read, and frequently heard repeated, that of all the methods of adorning the
mind, and forming the judgment, travelling is the moſt efficacious; I determined,
therefore, on a plan of travelling, but to
what part of the world I ſhould direct my
courſe remained ſtill to be choſen : I wiſhed
the ſcene of my obſervations to be new, or
at leaſt brilliant. My own country, and
the neighbouring nations, ſeemed to me
either too well known, or too eaſy of acceſs :
the riſing States of America, and the ſavages,
were not without their temptations; but
other conſiderations determined me in favour
of Aſia. Syria, eſpecially, and Egypt, both
with a view to what they once have been,
and what they now are, appeared to me a
field equally adapted to thoſe political and
moral obſervations with which I wiſhed to
occupy my mind. " Thoſe are the coun-
" tries," ſaid I, " in which the greater part of
" the opinions that govern us at this day
" have had their origin. In them, thoſe
" religious ideas took their riſe, which have
" operated ſo powerfully on our private
                        .   " and

" and public manners, on our laws, and
" our focial ftate. It will be interefting,
" therefore, to be acquainted with the
" countries where they originated, the cuf-
" toms and manners which gave them birth,
" and the fpirit and character of the nations
" from whom they have been received as
" facred: to examine to what degree this
" fpirit, thefe manners, and thefe cuftoms,
" are altered or retained; to afcertain the
" influence of climate, the effects of the
" government, and the caufes of the va-
" rious habits and prejudices of thefe coun-
" tries; in a word, to judge from their pre-
" fent ftate, what was their fituation in for-
" mer times."

On the other hand, confidering the political circumftances of the Turkifh empire,
for the laft twenty years, and reflecting on
their poffible confequences, it appeared to
me equally curious and ufeful to acquire
correct notions of its internal government,
in order to form a juft eftimate of its real
power and refources. With thefe views I
fet out for Egypt, about the end of 1782.
After continuing feven months at Cairo,

A 2   finding

finding too many obftacles to a proper examination of the interior parts of the country,
and too little affiftance in learning Arabic,
I determined to proceed into Syria. The
more tranquil ftate of that province correfponded better with my intentions. Eight
months refidence among the Drufes, in an
Arabian convent, rendered the Arabic fa-
miliar to me, and enabled me to travel
through all Syria during a whole year. On
my return to France, after an abfence of
near three years, imagining my refearches
might prove of fome utility, I refolved to
publifh a few obfervations on the prefent
ftate of Syria and Egypt; and I was confirmed in this refolution by the difficulty
attending travelling in thofe countries, which
have, therefore, but feldom been vifited, and
are but imperfectly known. Travellers, in
general, have directed their refearches more
to examine their antiquities, than their prefent fituation; and almoft all, haftily paffing
through them, have been deficient in the
two principal means of acquiring knowledge,
time, and the language of the country.
Without poffeffing the language, it is impoffible

fible to appreciate either the genius or the character of a nation. Interpreters can never fupply the defect of a direct communication. And without continuing a fufficient time, no traveller can form an accurate judgment, for the novelty of every thing around us naturally confounds and aftonifhes. The firft tumult muft fubfide, and the objects which prefent themfelves be repeatedly examined, before we can be certain the ideas we have formed are juft. To fee well is an art which requires more practice than is commonly imagined.

On my return to France, I found that a late traveller * had anticipated me, with refpect to *Egypt*, by a firft volume of *Letters* on that country. He has fince publifhed two others; but, as the field is extenfive and fertile, there ftill remain fome novelties to glean ; and on fubjects already treated, the world may poffibly not be averfe to hear two witneffes.

Syria, though not lefs interefting than Egypt, is undoubtedly a more novel fubject. What has been already written on it by fome

---

* M. Savary.

A 3   travellers,

travellers, is now grown obfolete, and, at beft, very imperfect. I had at firft determined to relate only what I myfelf had feen; but, defirous, for the fatisfaction of my readers, to complete my defcription of that province, I was unwilling to deprive myfelf of the obfervations of others, when, from what I had feen myfelf, I could not doubt their veracity.

In my relation, I have endeavoured to maintain the fpirit with which I conducted my refearches into facts; that is, an impartial love of truth. I have reftrained myfelf from indulging any fallies of the imagination, though I am no ftranger to the power of fuch illufion over the generality of readers; but I am of opinion that travels belong to the department of hiftory, and not that of romance. I have not therefore defcribed countries as more beautiful than they appeared to me; I have not reprefented their inhabitants more virtuous, nor more wicked than I found them, and I have perhaps been enabled to fee them fuch as they really are, fince I have never received from them either benefits or injuries.

As

As to the form of this work, I have not followed the method usual in books of travels, though, perhaps, the moft fimple. I have rejected, as too prolix, both the order and the details of an itinerary, as well as all perfonal adventures; I have only exhibited general views, as better calculated to combine facts and ideas, and from a defire of faving the time of the reader, amid the prodigious fucceffion of new publications. To render more clear my geographical obfervations on Egypt and Syria, I have annexed maps of thofe two countries. That of Egypt, for the Delta, and the defert of Sinai, is laid down from the aftronomical obfervations of M. Niebuhr, who travelled for the King of Denmark, in 1761: they are the lateft, and moft accurate, yet publifhed. The fame traveller has afforded me great affiftance in the map of Syria, which I have completed from that of Danville, and my own obfervations. To conclude, I have no doubt but the lovers of the ancient arts will thank me for accompanying with a drawing the defcription I have given of the two moft

beautiful

beautiful remains of antiquity in Afia, the Ruins of Palmyra, and thofe of the Temple of the Sun at Balbec ; and I have reafon to believe that the admirers of the modern arts will fee with pleafure the execution of the two engraved plates of thofe monuments.

CONTENTS

CONTENTS

OF THE

FIRST VOLUME.

CHAP.

Page

The

STATE

STATE OF SYRIA.

TRAVELS

MEDITERRANEAN SEA

SYRIA

DESERT OF ARABIA

DESERT OF AFRICA

SAID or UPPER EGYPT

MAP
of
EGYPT.

TRAVELS

IN

EGYPT AND SYRIA.

STATE of EGYPT.

CHAP. I.

Of Egypt in general, and the City of Alexandria.

IT is in vain that we attempt to prepare ourselves, by the perufal of books, for a more intimate acquaintance with the cuftoms and manners of nations; the effect of narratives upon the mind, will always be very different from that of objects upon the fenfes. The images the former prefent, have neither correctnefs in the defign, nor livelinefs in the colouring; they are always indiftinct, and leave but a fugitive impreffion, very eafily effaced. This we more particularly experience, when we are ftrangers to the objects to be laid before us; for the imagination, in that cafe, finding no terms of comparifon ready formed, is compelled to collect and compose new ideas; and, in this operation, ill directed, and haftily executed, it is difficult not to confound the traits, and disfigure the forms. Ought we then to be astonished, if, on beholding the things themselves, we are unable to discover any resemblance between the originals and the copies, and if every impression bears the character of novelty?

Such is the situation of a stranger who arrives, by sea, in Turkey. In vain has he read histories and travels; in vain has he, from their descriptions, endeavoured to represent to himself the aspect of the countries, the appearance of the cities, the dresses, and manners of the inhabitants: he is new to all these objects, and dazzled with their variety: every idea he has formed to himself vanishes, and he remains absorbed in surprize and astonishment.

No place is more proper to produce this effect, and prove the truth of this remark, than Alexandria in Egypt. The name of this city, which recalls to memory the genius of one of the moft wonderful of men; the name of the country, which reminds us of so many great events; the picturesque appearance of the

the place itfelf; the fpreading palm-trees; the terraced houfes, which feem to have no roof; the lofty flender minarets, all announce to the traveller that he is in another world. A variety of novel objects prefent themfelves to every fenfe; he hears a language whofe barbarous founds, and fharp and guttural accents, offend his ear; he fees dreffes of the moft unufual and whimfical kind, and figures of the ftrangeft appearance. Inftead of our fmooth fhaved faces, our fide curls, our triangular hats, and our fhort, and clofe dreffes, he views, with aftonifhment, tanned vifages, with beards and muftachios, large rolls of ftuff wreathed round their bald heads; long garments, which, reaching from the neck to the feet, ferve rather to veil than clothe the body, pipes of fix feet long, with which every one is provided, hideous camels, which carry water in leathern facks, and affes, faddled and bridled, which lightly trip along with their riders in flippers; he obferves their markets ill fupplied with dates, and round flat little loaves; a filthy drove of half ftarved dogs roaming through the ftreets, and a kind of wandering phantoms, which, under a long drapery of a fingle piece, dif-

cover

cover nothing human, but two eyes, which shew that they are women. Amid this croud of unusual objects, his mind is incapable of reflexion; nor is it until he has reached his place of residence, so desirable on landing after a long voyage, that, becoming more calm, he reflects on the narrow, ill paved streets, the low houses, which, though not calculated to admit much light, are still more obscured by lattice work, the meagre and swarthy inhabitants, who walk bare-footed, without other clothing than a blue shirt fastened with a leathern girdle, or a red handkerchief, while the universal marks of misery, so manifest in all he meets, and the mystery which reigns around their houses, point out to him the rapacity of oppression, and the distrust attendant upon slavery.

But his whole attention is soon attracted by those vast ruins which appear on the land side of the city. In our countries, ruins are an object of curiosity. Scarcely can we discover, in unfrequented places, some ancient castle, whose decay announces rather the desertion of its master, than the wretchedness of the neighbourhood: in Alexandria, on the contrary, we no sooner leave the New Town, than we are astonished aftonifhed at the fight of an immenfe extent of ground overfpread with ruins. During a walk of two hours, you follow a double line of walls and towers, which form the circumference of the ancient Alexandria. The earth is covered with the remains of lofty buildings deftroyed; whole fronts crumbled down, roofs fallen in, battlements decayed, and the ftones corroded and disfigured by faltpetre. The traveller paffes over a vaft plain, furrowed with trenches, pierced with wells, divided by walls in ruins, covered over with ancient columns, and modern tombs, amid palm-trees, and nopals *(a)*, and where no living creature is to be met with, but owls, bats, and jackalls. The inhabitants, accuftomed to this fcene, behold it without emotion; but the ftranger, in whom the recollection of ancient ages is revived by the novelty of the objects around him, feels a fenfation, which not unfrequently diffolves him in tears, infpiring reflexions which fill his heart with fadnefs, while his foul is elevated by their fublimity.

I fhall not here repeat the defcriptions, given by all travellers, of the remarkable an-

(*a)* Vulgarly called *raquette*, the cochineal tree.

tiquities

tiquities of Alexandria. The reader will find in Norden, Pocock, Niebuhr, and in the Letters lately publifhed by M. Savary, every neceffary detail on the baths of Cleopatra, the two obelifks that bear her name, the catacombs, the refervoirs, and the Pillar, improperly called Pompey's *(b)* Pillar. Thefe names are majeftic; but the originals by no means correfpond with the figures we have feen of them. The pillar alone, from its loftinefs, its prodigious circumference, and the folitude with which it is furrounded, impreffes a genuine fentiment of refpect and admiration.

At prefent, Alexandria is the emporium of a confiderable commerce. It is the harbour for all the commodities exported from Egypt by the Mediterranean, except the rice of Damietta. The Europeans have eftablifhments there, where factors difpole of their

(b) It ought for the future to be called the Pillar of Severus, fince M. Savary has proved it was erected in honour of that Emperor. Travellers differ with refpect to the dimenfions of this column ; but the calculation the moft generally admitted at Alexandria, makes the height of the fhaft, with the capital, 96 feet, and the circumference 28 feet, 3 inches.

merchan-

merchandize by barter. Veffels are conftantly to be met with there from Marfeilles, Leghorn, Venice, Ragufa, and the dominions of the Grand Seignor; but it is dangerous to winter there. The new port, the only harbour for the Europeans, is clogged up with fand, infomuch that, in ftormy weather, fhips are liable to bilge; and, the bottom being alfo rocky, the cables foon chafe and part, fo that, one veffel driving againft a fecond, and that againft a third, they are perhaps all loft. Of this there was a fatal inftance fixteen or eighteen years ago, when two-and-forty veffels were dafhed to pieces on the mole, in a gale of wind, from the north-weft, and numbers have been fince loft there at different times. The old port, the entrance to which is covered by a neck of land called the Cape of Figs (c), is not fubjedt to this inconvenience; but the Turks admit no fhips into it but thofe of Muffulmen. It will, perhaps, be afked, in Europe, why do they not repair the New Port? The anfwer is, that, in Turkey, they deftroy every thing, and repair nothing. The old harbour will be deftroyed, likewife,

(c) *Ras el-tin,* pronounced *teen.*

as

as the ballaft of veffels has been continually thrown into it for the laft two hundred years. The fpirit of the Turkifh government is to ruin the labours of paft ages, and deftroy the hopes of future times, becaufe the barbarity of ignorant defpotifm never confiders to-morrow.

In time of war, Alexandria is of no importance; no fortification is to be feen; even the Pharos, with its lofty towers, cannot be defended. It has not four cannon fit for fervice, nor a gunner who knows how to point them. The five hundred Janifaries, who fhould form the garrifon, reduced to half that number, know nothing but how to fmoke a pipe. It is fortunate for the Turks that the Franks find their intereft in preferving this city. A fingle Ruffian or Maltefe frigate would fuffice to lay it in afhes; but the conqueft would be of no value. A foreign power could not maintain itfelf there, as the country is without water. This muft be brought from the Nile by the Kalidj, or canal of twelve leagues, which conveys it thither every year at the time of the inundation, and fills the vaults or refervoirs dug under the ancient city, which muft ferve till the next year. It is evident,

evident, therefore, that were a foreign power to take poffeffion, the canal would be fhut, and all fupplies of water cut off.

It is this canal alone which connects Alexandria with Egypt; for, from its fituation without the Delta, and the nature of the foil, it really belongs to the deferts of Africa; its environs are fandy, flat and fterile, without trees and without houfes, where we meet with nothing but the plant *(d)* which yields the Kali, and a row of palm-trees, which follows the courfe of the *Kalidj* or canal.

We do not really enter Egypt until we arrive at Rofetta, called by the natives *Rafhid:* there the fands peculiar to Africa end, and a black, fat, and loamy foil, the diftinguifhing characteriftic of Egypt, begins: there, alfo, for the firft time, we behold the waters of the celebrated Nile, which, rolling between two fteep banks, confiderably refembles the Seine between Auteuil and Paffy. The woods of palm-trees, on each fide, the orchards, watered by its ftreams, the lemon, the orange, the banana, the peach, and other trees, by their perpetual verdure, render Rofetta aftonifhingly delightful,

(d) Glafs-wort, called by the Arabs *el-kali,* from whence the name of the falt *al-kali.*

and

and its beauties appear ſtill more charming by its contraſt with Alexandria, and the ſea we have juſt left ; and from hence to Cairo, every objeſt tends to increaſe the effeſt.

As we aſcend the river we begin to acquire ſome general idea of the ſoil, the climate, and productions of this celebrated country. Nothing more reſembles its appearance than the marſhes of the lower Loire, or the plains of Flanders ; inſtead however of the numerous trees and country houſes of the latter, we muſt imagine ſome thin woods of palms and ſyca-mores, and a few villages of mud-walled cottages, built on artificial mounds. All this part of Egypt is ſo level, and ſo low, that we are not three leagues from the coaſt when we firſt diſcover the palm-trees, and the ſands on which they grow; from thence, as we proceed up the river, the declivity is ſo gentle, that the water does not flow faſter than a league an hour. As for the proſpeſt of the country, it offers little variety ; nothing is to be ſeen but palm-trees, ſingle, or in clumps, which become fewer in proportion as you advance : wretched villages of mud-walled huts, and a boundleſs plain, which at different ſeaſons is an ocean of freſh water, a

miry

miry morafs, a verdant field, or a dufty
defart; and on every fide an extenfive and
foggy horizon, where the eye is wearied
and difgufted; till at length, towards the
junction of the two branches of the river, the
mountains of Grand Cairo are difcovered in
the eaft, and to the fouth-weft, three detached
maffes appear, which, from their triangular
form, are known to be the Pyramids. We
now enter a valley which turns to the fouthward, between two ridges of parallel eminences. That to the eaft, which extends to
the Red Sea, merits the name of a mountain
from the fteepnefs of its afcent, and that of a
defart from its naked and favage afpect (e);
but the weftern is nothing but a ridge of rock,
covered with fand, which has been very properly termed a natural mound, or caufeway.
To defcribe Egypt in two words, let the
reader imagine, on one fide, a narrow fea and
rocks; on the other, immenfe plains of fand,
and, in the middle, a river flowing through a
valley of one hundred and fifty leagues in
length, and from three to feven wide, which,
at the diftance of thirty leagues from the fea,
feparates into two arms, the branches of

(e) Called in Arabic *mokattam*, or *hewn mountain*.

which

which wander over a country where they meet no obftacles, and which is almoft without declivity.

The prevailing tafte for natural hiftory, now, to the honour of the prefent age, become fo general, demands doubtlefs fome details on the nature of the foil, and the minerals of this extenfive country. But, unfortunately, the manner of travelling here is ill adapted to favour fuch refearches. It is not the fame in Turkey as in Europe : with us, travels are agreeable excurfions ; there, they are difficult and dangerous undertakings, efpecially for Europeans, whom the fuperftitious natives believe to be forcerers, come to difcover by magic, treafures which the Genii have concealed under the ruins. This ridiculous, but deep rooted opinion, added to perpetual wars and difturbances, deprives the traveller of fecurity, and prevents every difcovery. No one dares even walk alone in the fields ; nor can he procure any body to accompany him. We are confined therefore to the banks of the river, and a route frequented by every one, which can afford no new information. It is only by comparing what we have feen ourfelves with the obfervations

vations made by others that some general ideas can be acquired.

After having made this comparison, we shall find reason to conclude that the basis of all Egypt, from Asouan, (the ancient Syene) to the Mediterranean, is a continued bed of calcareous stone, of a whitish hue, and somewhat soft, containing shells analogous to those found in the two neighbouring seas *(f)*. This quality is discoverable in the Pyramids, and in the Lybian rock on which they stand. The same kind of stone is likewise to be found in the Cisterns, in the Catacombs of Alexandria, and in the projecting shelves upon the coast. We also find it in the Eastern mountain, in the latitude of Cairo, and the materials with which that city is built. It is this calcareous stone, in short, which forms the immense quarries that extend from Sawadi to Manfalout, for the space of upwards of twenty-five leagues, according to the testimony of Father Sicard. That missionary informs us, also, that marble is found in the

(f) These shells consist principally of echini, volutes, bivalves, and a species in the form of lentils. See Shaw's Travels.

valley

valley of *Carts (g)*, at the foot of the mountains bordering on the Red Sea, and in the
mountains to the north-eaft of Afouan.   Between that place and the Cataract are the principal quarries of red granite; but there muft
be others lower down, for, on the oppofite
fhore of the Red Sea, the mountains of Oreb,
of Sinaï, and their dependencies *(h)*, at two
days journey towards the north, are formed
of it.   Not far from Afouan, to the north-
weft, is a quarry of ferpentine ftone, employed
in its native ftate by the inhabitants to make
veffels which will ftand the fire.   And, in
the fame parallel, on the Red Sea, was formerly a mine of emeralds, all traces of which
are now loft.   Copper is the only metal of
this country mentioned by the ancients.   The
road to Suez is the part of it where the greateft
quantity of what are called Egyptian flints, or
pebbles, is found, though the bottom. be of
a calcareous ftone, hard and fonorous; there
likewife thofe ftones are found, which, from
their form, have been taken for petrified

(g) See Savary's Letters, Vol. I. page 437.
(h) The former is grey, fpotted with black, and fometimes red.

wood.

wood. In fact, they do refemble logs cut flanting at the ends, and full of fmall holes, and might eafily be taken for petrefactions; but chance throwing in my way a confiderable quantity of thefe, in the road of the Haouatat Arabs *(i)*, I carefully examined them, and am convinced they are real minerals *(k)*.

The two lakes of Natron, defcribed by Father Sicard, are more interefting objects; they are fituated in the defart of Shayat, or St. Macarius, to the weft of the Delta. Their bed is a fort of natural trench, three or four leagues long, by a quarter wide, the bottom of which is hard and ftony. It is dry for nine months in the year, but, in winter, there oozes from the earth a water of a reddifh violet colour, which fills the lake to the height of five or fix feet; the return of the great heats caufing this to evaporate, there remains a bed of falt two feet thick, and very hard, which is broken with

(i) Each tribe has its particular road, to avoid difputes.

(k) Befides, there do not exift ten trees in this defart, and it feems incapable of producing any.

bars

bars of iron. Thirty thoufand quintals are procured from them every year. This phenomenon, which indicates a foil impregnated with falt, is common throughout all Egypt. In every part of it, on digging, a brackifh water is found, containing natron, marine falt, and a little nitre. Even when the gardens are overflowed, for the fake of watering them, the furface of the ground, after the evaporation and abforption of the water, appears glazed over with falt; and this foil, like that of the whole continent of Africa and Arabia, feems either to be compofed of falt, or to produce it.

In the midft of thefe minerals of various qualities, in the midft of that fine and reddifh coloured fand peculiar to Africa, the earth of the valley through which the Nile flows, difcovers properties which prove it of a diftinct clafs. Its blackifh colour, its clayey, cementing quality, demonftrate its foreign origin; and, in fact, it is brought by the river from the heart of Abyffinia; as if Nature had determined artfully to form an habitable ifland in a country to which fhe had denied every thing. Without this fat and

and light mud, Egypt never could have produced any thing; that alone feems to contain the feeds of vegetation and fecundity: and thefe again are owing to the river, by which it is depofited.

C H A P. II.

Of the Nile, and the enlargement of the
Delta.

THE whole phyfical and political exiftence of Egypt depends upon the Nile ; that
alone provides for the greateft neceffity of
animal life, the want of water, fo frequently,
and fo diftrefsfully, experienced in warm climates. The Nile alone, without the aid of
rain, every where fupplies vegetation with
moifture, the earth, during the three months
inundation, imbibing a fufficient quantity
of water for the reft of the year. Were it
not for this overflowing, only a very fmall part
of the country could be cultivated, and even
that would require prodigious labour ; it is
with reafon, therefore, this river has been
ftiled the fource of plenty, of happinefs, and
of life itfelf. Had Albuquerque, the Portu-
guefe, been able to execute his project, of
turning its courfe from Ethiopia into the
Red

Red Sea *(l)*, this country, now so rich, would have become a savage desert, surrounded by solitudes. When we reflect on the use man makes of his powers, how little reason have we to regret that Nature has granted him no more!

It is with reason, therefore, that the Egyptians have always professed, and still retain, a religious veneration for the Nile *(m)*; but an European must be pardoned, if, on hearing them boast its beauty, he smiles at their ignorance. Never will these troubled and muddy waters have for him the charm of transparent fountains and limpid streams; never, except from some extraordinary excitement, will a swarthy Egyptian woman, driping from these yellow and muddy waters, remind him of the bathing Naiads. For six months of the year the water of the river is so thick that it must have time to settle be-

(*l*) See Savary's Letters. T.

(*m*) They called it *holy*, *blessed*, *sacred*; and, on the appearance of the new waters, that is, on the opening of the canals, mothers are seen plunging their children into the stream, from a belief that these waters have a purifying and divine virtue, such as the antients attributed to every river.

C 2   fore

fore it can be drunk *(n)*: and, during the three months which precede the inundation, reduced to an inconfiderable depth, it grows heated, becomes green, fœtid, and full of worms, and it is neceffary to have recourfe to that which has been before drawn and preferved in cifterns.   At all times, people of delicacy take care to perfume it, and cool it by evaporation *(o)*.

Travellers and Hiftorians have written fo much on the Nile, and its phænomena, that

(n) Bitter almonds are made ufe of, for this purpofe, with which the veffel is rubbed, and the water then becomes really light and good. But nothing but thirft, or prejudice, could induce any perfon to give it the preference to that of our fountains and large rivers, fuch as the Seine, and the Loire.

(o) Earthen veffels, unglazed, are kept carefully in every apartment, from whence the water continually tranfpires; this tranfpiration produces the more coolnefs in proportion as it is more confiderable; for which reafon, thefe veffels are often fufpended in paffages where there are currents of air, and under the fhade of trees.   In feveral parts of Syria they drink the water which has tranf-pired; in Egypt they drink that which remains; befides, in no country is fo much water ufed.   The firft thing an Egyptian does, on entering a houfe, is to lay hold of the *kolla*, (the pitcher of water) and take a hearty draught of it; and, thanks to their perpetual perfpiration, they feel no inconvenience from the practice.

I was

I was at firſt inclined to think the ſubject exhauſted; but, as ideas vary reſpecting
the moſt invariable facts; frequently, while
there remains nothing new to ſay, there is
ſtill ſomething to correct. Such appears to
·me to be the caſe, with ſome opinions of
M. Savary, in the Letters he .has lately
publiſhed. The poſitions he endeavours to
eſtabliſh concerning the enlargement, and
riſe of the Delta, are ſo different from the
concluſions I have deduced from the facts
and authorities he quotes that I think it my
duty to ſubmit our contradictory opinions to
the tribunal of the public. This diſcuſſion
ſeems to me the more neceſſary, as a reſidence
of two years, upon the ſpot, gives a weight
to the teſtimony of M. Savary, which would
ſoon become authority: let us ſtate the queſ-
tions, and treat, in the firſt place, of the ex-
tenſion, or enlargement of the Delta.

A Greek hiſtorian, to whom we are in-
debted for almoſt all our knowledge of ancient Egypt, and whoſe authority every day's
obſervation confirms, wrote thus, two-and-
twenty centuries ago: " That part of Egypt
" frequented by the Greeks, (the Delta) is an
" acquired land, the gift of the river, as is all

" the

" the marſhy country, along its banks, for
" three days ſail up the Nile *(p)*."

The reaſons he alleges in ſupport of this
aſſertion prove that it was not founded on
prejudice. " In fact," adds he, " the ſoil of
" Egypt, which is a black and fat mud, is
" abſolutely different, both from that of
" Africa, which is a red ſand, and that of
" Arabia, which is clayey and ſtoney.—This
" mud is brought from Ethiopia, by the
" Nile.—And the ſhells found in the deſert
" ſufficiently prove that the ſea formerly
" extended farther into the country."

Herodotus, however, though he admits
this encroachment of the river, ſo conformable to probability, has not determined its
proportions. Theſe M. Savary has imagined
himſelf able to ſupply; let us examine his
reaſoning.

" While it encreaſed it height, Egypt *(q)*,
ſays he, " augmented in length likewiſe;
" to prove which, among ſeveral facts which
" hiſtory has preſerved, I ſhall ſelect only
" one. During the reign of Pſammeticus,

(p) Herodot. lib. 2. p. 105. edit. Weſling.

(q) See Letters on Egypt, Vol. I. p. 17. of the Engliſh
Tranſlation, Second Edit.

" the

" the Milefians, with thirty ſhips, landed at
" the mouth of the Bolbitine branch, at
" prefent the branch of Rofetta, where they
" fortified themſelves, and built a city,
" which they called Metelis, (Strabo, lib. 17.)
" now named Faoüa, but which, in the
" Coptic vocabularies, is ſtill called Meffil.
" This city, which was formerly a fea-port,
" ſtands, at preſent, nine leagues fiom the
" ſhore; which fpace the Delta has length-
" ened, from the age of Pfammeticus to the
" prefent."

Nothing fo accurate at firſt fight as this
reafoning; but, on recurring to the original,
M. Savary's authority, we find, that the principal fact is wanting; the following is a literal
tranflation of the text of Strabo *(r)*.

" Beyond the Bolbitine mouth, is a low
" fandy cape, called the horn of the Lamb,
" which ſtretches pretty far (into the fea);
" beyond that, the watch-tower of Perfeus,
" and the wall of the Milefians; for the
" Milefians, in the reign of Cyaxares, King
" of the Medes, cotemporary with Pfamme-
" ticus, King of Egypt, arriving at the Bol-

(r) Strabonis Geograph. Interp. Cafaubon. Edit. 1707.
Lib. 17. p. 1153.

" bitine

" bitine mouth, with thirty veffels, landed
" there, and erected the work which bears
" their name. Some time after, having ad-
" vanced into the Saitic Nome, and van-
" quifhed Inarus, in a naval battle, they
" founded the city of Naucratis, a little above
" Schedia. Beyond the wall of the Mile-
" fians, as we approach the Sebennytic
" mouth, are lakes, one of which is named
" the Butic."

Such is the paffage of Strabo, relative to
the Milefians; no mention is made of Metelis,
of which not even the name is to be found in
his whole work. Danville (s) has copied it
from Ptolemy, who does not afcribe it to the
Milefians: and unlefs M. Savary can prove
the identity of Metelis, and the Milefian wall,
by refearches made upon the fpot, his conclufions ought not to be admitted.

He is of opinion, too, that Homer affords
him a fimilar teftimony in thofe paffages
wherein he fpeaks of the diftance of the ifle
of Pharos from Egypt (t); the reader fhall

(s) See the excellent Memoir of Danville, on Egypt,
in 4to. 1765, p. 77.
(t) See Savary's Letters, p. 17.

judge,

judge, whether this is better founded. I quote the tranflation of Madame Dacier *(u)*, which, though lefs brilliant, is more literal than any other, and our bufinefs is with the literal. Menelaus is made to fpeak thus:

" In the Egyptian fea, oppofite the Nile, " there is a certain ifland, called Pharos; dif-" tant from one of the mouths of that river " about as far as a veffel can fail in one day " before the wind."—and, foon after, Proteus fays to Menelaus: " Inflexible deftiny does " not permit you to revifit your dear coun-" try—until you fhall have returned again " into the river Egyptus, and offered un-" blemifhed hecatombs to the immortals."

" He faid," refumes Menelaus, " and my " heart was feized with grief and fadnefs, be-" caufe this God commanded me to return " into the river Egyptus, the way to which " is difficult and dangerous."

From thefe paffages, and efpecially from the former, M. Savary would infer that the Pharos, which, at prefent joins the main land, was at that time very remote from it; but when Homer fpeaks of the diftance of this

(*u*) Odyff. lib. 4.

ifland,

ifland, he does not mean its diftance from the
fhore oppofite, as that traveller has tranflated
him; but from the land of Egypt, and the
river Nile. In the fecond place, by a day's
fail, we muft not underftand the indefinite
fpace, which the veffels, or, more properly
fpeaking, the boats, of the ancients could
pafs through in a day; the Greeks ufed this
expreffion to denote a certain fixed diftance of
five hundred and forty ftadia. Herodotus *(x)*,
who clearly afcertains this fact, gives us an
example of it, when he fays that the Nile
has encroached upon the fea the whole extent
of country for three days fail up the river;
and the fixteen hundred and twenty ftadia,
arifing from this computation, agree with the
more accurate meafure of fifteen hundred
ftadia, which he gives us in another place, as
the diftance of Heliopolis from the fea. Now,
taking, with Danville, the five hundred and
forty ftadia for twenty-feven thoufand toifes,
or near half a degree *(y)*, we fhall find this
meafure is the diftance of the Pharos from
the Nile; it extends exactly to two-thirds of
a league above Rofetta, a fituation where we

(x) Herod. lib. 11. p. 106 and 107.
(y) This is only 1,300 toifes too much.

have

have reafon to place the city which gave name to the Bolbitine mouth; and it is re- markable that it was this which the Greeks frequented, and where the Milefians landed, a century and a half after Homer. It is, therefore, far from being proved, that the increafe of the Delta, or of the Continent, was fo rapid as has been imagined; and, if we were difpofed to maintain it, we fhould ftill have to explain how this fhore, which has not gained half a league from the days of Alexander, fhould have gained eleven in the far fhorter period from the time of Menelaus to that conqueror *(z)*.

A more fatisfactory eftimate of this en- croachment might have been deduced from the dimenfions of Egypt, given by Hero- dotus: the following are his words. " The

---

(z) It may be objected Homer is not exact when he fays the Pharos was oppofite the Nile; but, in his excufe, it may be urged, that when he calls Egypt the extremity of the world, he cannot mean to fpeak with precifion. We muft alfo obferve, that the Canopic branch ran formerly by the lakes, opening itfelf a paffage near Abou- kir; and if, as the view of the country leads me to think, it paffed even to the weft of Aboukir, which muft have been an ifland, Homer, might fay, with reafon, that the Pharos was oppofite the Nile.

4 " breadth

" breadth of Egypt, along the fea-coaft, from
" the Gulph of Plinthine, to the Lake Ser-
" bonis, near Mount Cafius, is three thou-
" fand fix hundred ftadia ; and its length,
" from the fea to Heliopolis, fifteen hundred
" ftadia."

Let us confine ourfelves to this laft meafure, which alone concerns the prefent difpute. Danville has proved, with that fagacity which was peculiar to him, that the
ftadium of Herodotus is equivalent to between fifty and fifty-one French toifes ; and
taking it at the latter eftimation, the fifteen
hundred ftadia are equal to feventy-fix thoufand toifes, which, after the rate of fifty-feven
thoufand to a degree, gives one degree and
near twenty minutes and a half. Now, from
the aftronomical obfervations of M. Niebuhr,
who travelled for the King of Denmark, in
1761 (a), the difference of latitude between
Heliopolis, (now called Matarea) and the
fea, being one degree twenty-nine minutes,
at Damietta, and one degree twenty-four at
Rofetta, there is a difference, on one fide, of

(a) See *Voyage en Arabie*, by C. Niebuhr, in 4to.
tom. 1. which muft be diftinguifhed from his *Defcription
de l'Arabie* ; 2 vol. in 4to.

three

three minutes and a half, or a league and a half
encroachment; and eight minutes and a half,
or three leagues and a half, on the other; that
is to say, the ancient shore answers to eleven
thousand eight hundred toises below Rosetta,
which corresponds very nearly to the sense
in which I understand the passage in Homer,
while, on the branch of Damietta, it falls
nine hundred and fifty toises below that
city. It is true that, in measuring immediately on the map, the line of the shore
will be found about three leagues higher on
the side of Rosetta, and falls on Damietta
itself, which is occasioned by the angle produced by the difference of longitude. But,
in that case, Bolbitinum, mentioned by Herodotus, is not within its prescribed limits;
and it is no longer true that Busiris (Abou-
sir) was situated, as Herodotus has told
us (b), in the middle of the Delta. It must
not be denied that the relations of the ancients, and the knowledge we have of the
country, are not sufficiently precise exactly
to determine the successive encroachments.

(b) Lib. ii. p. 123.

In order to reafon accurately, refearches fimilar to thofe of the Comte de Choifeul, on the
Meander *(c)*, would be neceffary; the
ground fhould be dug into, but fuch labours
require means and opportunities which few
travellers poffefs; and a greater difficulty than
all is, that the fandy foil, which forms the
lower Delta, undergoes great changes every
day. Thefe are not entirely owing to the
Nile and the fea; the wind itfelf is a very
powerful agent, which fometimes choaks up
the canals, and drives back the river, as it
has done at the Canopic branch. At others,
it amaffes the fand, and buries the ruins, fo
that their very remembrance is loft. M.
Niebuhr relates a remarkable inftance of
this. While he was at Rofetta, in 1762,
he difcovered, by chance, under the fandy
hillocks, to the fouthward of that city, feveral
ancient ruins, and, among others, twenty
fine marble columns of Grecian workmanfhip,
without being able to learn any tradition
even of the name of the place *(d)*. This
appears to me to have been the cafe with the

(c) See Voyage Pittorefque de la Grèce, tom. 2.
(d) This fituation agrees very well with that of Bolbitinum.

whole

whole of the adjacent defert. This tract, formerly interfected by large canals, and filled with towns, prefents nothing but hillocks of a yellowith fand, very fine, which the wind heaps up at the foot of every obftacle, and which frequently buries the palmtrees; wherefore, notwithftanding the induftrious refearches of Danville, we cannot be certain he is right in the fituations he has affigned to feveral ancient places.

M. Savary has been much more exact in what he has cited concerning one of the changes the Nile has undergone (e), by which it appears, that river formerly flowed entirely through Lybia, to the fouth of Memphis. But the relation of Herodotus himfelf, on whofe authority this depends, is not without difficulties. When that hiftorian, therefore, afferts, after the priefts of Heliopolis, that Menes, the firft king of Egypt, dammed up the elbow, formed by the river, two leagues and a quarter (one hundred ftadia) above Memphis (f), and dug a new channel, to the eaftward of that city, does it not follow that Memphis was at that time fituated in

(e) Letter i. p. 12.
(f) Herodot. ii, lib. 2.

a barren

a barren defert, far diftant from any water?
And how improbable is fuch an hypothefis!
Can we literally believe in thefe immenfe
works of Menes, who is fuppofed to have
founded a city which is mentioned as exifting
before his time; who is imagined to have
dug canals and lakes, thrown bridges over
rivers, and erected palaces, towers and temples; and all this in the earlieft age of the
nation, and the infancy of all the arts? Is
not this Menes himfelf an hiftorical chimæra, and are not all the relations of the
priefts, concerning this remote antiquity,
wholly mythological? I am inclined to think
therefore, that the turning the courfe of the
Nile, by Menes, was no more than a diver-
fion of fome fmaller branch, to increafe the
inundation of the Delta; and this conjecture
feems the more probable, fince, notwithftanding the teftimony of Herodotus, this
part of the valley, feen from the Pyramids,
prefents nothing which could have been an
obftruction to the courfe of the river. Befides, I cannot but think that M. Savary
prefumes too much, when he makes the
great channel, called *bahr bela ma*, or river
without water, terminate at the mound
before-

before-mentioned, above Memphis, and fup-
pofes it to have been the ancient bed of the
Nile. Every traveller, cited by Danville,
places that termination at the Lake of Fayoum, of which it appears a more natural
continuation *(g)*. To have proved this pofition, he fhould have vifited the places themfelves, and I never heard, at Cairo, that M.
Savary advanced farther to the fouthward,
than the Pyramids of Djiza. The formation
of the Delta, which he deduces from this
alteration, is equally repugnant to probability; for, in this fudden change, why fhould
we imagine, the " enormous weight of the
" waters, difcharging themfelves into this
" gulph *(h)*, would repel thofe of the fea?"
The meeting of two maffes of fluid produces nothing but a mixture, from which a
common level foon refults; if we imagine
the water increafed, we can only expect
that more land will be covered. It is true,

(g) In fact, we fhall be more inclined, from an in-
fpection of the map, to believe that this was the ancient
courfe of the river: as for the petrefactions of mafts and
whole veffels, mentioned by Father Sicard, thofe, to gain
credit, ought to be attefted by more enlightened travellers
than that miffionary.

(h) Letters on Egypt, vol. I. page 13.

M. Savary adds, " the fand and mud car-
" ried along by the Nile, were accumulated,
" and the Delta, very inconfiderable at firft,
" rofe from the fea, by encroaching on its
" limits." But how does an ifland rife out
of the fea? Running waters level much more
than they heap up. This leads us to the
queftion of the elevation.

C H A P.

CHAP. III.

Of the Rife of the Delta.

HERODOTUS, on whofe authority this hypothefis is founded, has not very fatisfactorily explained the fact, but he has a paffage of which M. Savary has availed himfelf to draw certain pofitive conclufions; the following is his reafoning:

" In the time of Mœris, who lived five
" hundred years before the Trojan war *(i)*,
" eight cubits were fufficient to overflow the
" whole Delta *(Herodot. lib. 2.)*; fifteen
" were neceffary in the age of Herodotus;
" under the Roman empire, fixteen; under
" the Arabs, feventeen: eighteen cubits is
" the ftandard of abundance at this day; and
" the Nile fometimes rifes to two-and-twenty.
" Thus, in the fpace of 3284 years, we
" fee the Delta has rifen fourteen cubits."

True, if we admit the facts as they are ftated; but, on a careful examination, we

(i) Letter I. p. 13.

D 2

fhall

ſhall find circumſtances which invalidate both the premiſes and concluſion. Let us firſt cite the text of Herodotus:

"The Egyptian prieſts," ſays that author *(p)*, " report that in the reign of King " Mœris, the Nile inundated the Delta, if it " only roſe to eight cubits. At preſent it does " not overflow it unleſs it attain ſixteen, or " at leaſt fifteen. Now, from the death of " Mœris to this time, nine hundred years " have not yet elapſed."

Let us calculate from theſe materials.

From Mœris to Herodotus   -   900 years,

From Herodotus to the year 1777,

    two thouſand two hundred and

    thirty-ſeven, or if he will   -   2,240

                Total, - 3,140

Why this difference of one hundred and forty-four years excefs in the calculation of M. Savary? Why does he uſe other numbers than thoſe of his author? But let us paſs over the chronology.

In the time of Herodotus, ſixteen cubits were neceſſary, or at leaſt fifteen, to overflow

(p) Lib. ii. p. 109.

                             the

the Delta. .The fame number was fufficient in the time of the Romans : fifteen and fix-teen are invariably the meafure.

" Before the time of Petronius," fays Stra-bo *(q)*, " plenty was not known in the Del-
" ta unlefs the Nile rofe to fourteen cubits.
" But this Governor obtaining by art what
" nature denied, under his prefecture, plenty
" has been known at twelve." The Arabs tell us the fame. A book in Arabic ftill exifts which contains a table of all the rifings of the Nile, from the firft year of the Hegira (A. D. 622), down to the year 875, (A. D. 1470); and this work afcertains that, in the lateft times, as often as the Nile has fourteen cubits depth in its channel, there is a harveft fufficient for the year; that, if it reaches fixteen, there is fufficient for two years; but when it falls fhort of fourteen, or exceeds eighteen, famine enfues; which correfponds exactly with the account of Herodotus. The book I quote is Arabic, but its contents are in every one's hands, who choofes to confult the word *Nile* in the Bibliotheque Orientale of D'Herbelot, or the Extracts from Kalkafendas, in Dr. Shaw's Travels.

(q) Lib. xvii.

D 3

Nor

Nor is the meafure of thefe cubits uncertain.
Fréret, Danville, and M. Bailli have proved
that the Egyptian cubit, being invariably
twenty-four digits, is equal to twenty and a
half French inches *(r)*; and the prefent cubit,
called *Draa mafri,* is precifely divided into
twenty-four digits, and contains twenty and
a half of our inches. But the columns with
which the rife of the Nile is meafured, have
undergone an alteration which we muſt not
omit to notice.

" In the earlier ages, and while the Arabs
" governed Egypt," fays *Kalkafendas,* " they
" perceived that when the Nile did not at-
" tain the ftandard neceffary for plenty, every
" one was anxious to lay in fufficient pro-
" vifion for the year, which occafioned great
" inconveniencies. Complaints of this were
" made to the Caliph Omar, who gave orders
" to Amrou to enquire into the matter ; and
" he reported as follows:—Having made
" the refearches you commanded, we have
" found that when the Nile rifes to fourteen

(r) I have meafured feveral of them with a *pied de Roi,*
ſtandard foot of copper ; but I found they all varied from
one to three lines. The *Draa ſtambouli* is of twenty-eight
digits, or twenty-four inches, wanting one line.

" cubits,

" cubits, it produces a fufficient harveft for
" the year; when it attains fixteen cubits,
" we have plenty; but that at twelve and
" eighteen dearth enfues. We alfo find that
" the cuftom of making known the height
" of the waters by proclamation, is produc-
" tive of many irregularities, and is very
" difadvantageous to commerce."

Omar, to remedy this abufe, was, perhaps,
inclined to abolifh thefe proclamations; but
that not being practicable, he devifed an ex-
pedient, fuggefted by Aboutaaleb, to produce
the fame effect. Until then the meafuring
column, called the *Nilometer (s)*, had been
divided into cubits of twenty-four digits
each; Omar ordered this to be deftroyed, and
fubftituting another in its place, which he
erected in the ifland of Raouda, he commanded that the twelve lower cubits fhould
confift of twenty-eight digits, inftead of twenty-four, while the upper remained of the
ufual number; hence, when the rife of the
Nile appeared, by the column, to be twelve
cubits, it was really fourteen; for thefe twelve
cubits being each four digits too long, there

(s) In Arabic, *Mekias*, or *Meafure.*

D 4 was

was an excefs of forty-eight digits, or two
cubits.   Therefore, when fourteen cubits,
the meafure of a fufficient harveft, were pro-
claimed, the inundation was really at the
height for plenty, and the multitude, always
eafily deceived by words,. never fufpected the
impofition.   But this alteration could not
efcape the Arabian hiftorians, who tell us
the columns of the Said, or Upper Egypt,
continued to be divided by twenty-four digits ; that the height of eighteen cubits (old
ftyle), was always injurious ; and that nineteen was very rare, and almoft a prodigy *(t)*.

Nothing therefore is lefs certain than the
progreffive changes here alleged, and which
are rendered improbable by a known fact,
which is, that in the long period of eighteen
centuries, the rife of the Nile never varied.
How does it happen then that it is fo different
at prefent ?   How can it fo foon have altered

(t) Dr. Pocock, who has feveral good obfervations on
the Nile, has entirely miftaken the meaning of the text
of Kalkafendas ; from an obfcure paffage he has been led
to conclude, that the Nilometer, in the time of Omar,
was only twelve cubits, and this error has led him into a
number of falfe conjectures. *Pocock's Travels*, vol. 1.
253.

from

from fifteen to twenty-two cubits, fince the
year one thoufand four hundred and feventy-
three? This problem is, in my opinion, eafy
of folution; not from phyfical changes, but
from other circumftances. It is not the Nile
but the column and meafures which have varied. The myftery in which the Mekias is enveloped by the Turks, has prevented the greater
part of travellers from difcovering the truth;
but Pococke, who obtained a fight of it in
1739, relates that the fcale of cubits was inac-
curate and unequal. He even obferves it appeared to him to be new, a circumftance which
may lead us to imagine the Turks, in imitation
of Omar, have made fome recent alteration.
In fhort there is a fact which removes every
doubt, for M. Niebuhr (u), whom the
world would not eafily fufpect of falfehood or
miftake, having meafured, in 1762, the marks
of the inundation, on a wall at Djiza (Giza),
found that, on the firft of June, the Nile had
fallen twenty-four French feet. But twenty-
four feet, reduced to cubits, at the rate of
twenty inches and a half each, give precifely
fourteen cubits one inch. It is true there

(u) *Voyage en Arabie*, tom. I. p. 102.

ftill

ftill remains eighteen days decreafe; but by eftimating that at half a cubit, agreeable to what has been obferved by Pococke *(x)*, we have only fourteen cubits and a half, which correfponds exactly with the antient calculation.

There is another affertion of M. Savary's to which, likewife, I cannot fubfcribe without reftriction.—" Since I have been in *Egypt*," fays he, Letter I. p. 15, " I have twice " made the tour of the Delta; I have even " croffed it by the canal of Menouf. The " river, though full to the brim, in the great " branches of Rofetta and Damietta, and " thofe which run through the interior parts " of the country; only overflowed the " land where it lay low, or where banks had " been raifed to ftop its waters, and throw " them over the rice fields." Hence he concludes, " that the prefent pofition of the " Delta is the beft poffible for agriculture; " fince, ceafing to be overflowed, this ifland " has a yearly gain of the three months dur-

(*x*) The 17th of May, eleven pikes (or cubits) of the column were above the water, and the 3d of June eleven and a half: in feventeen days therefore there was a difference of half a cubit. *Pocock's Travels*, vol. I. p. 256.

" ing

" ing which the Thebais is inundated."
It muſt be confeſſed that nothing can be
more extraordinary than this gain. If the
Delta has gained by being no longer overflowed, why was the inundation at all times
ſo anxiouſly deſired ? " This is ſupplied by
" the banks." But the Delta muſt not be
compared to the marſhes of the Seine. The
water is only on a level with the land towards
the ſea ; every where elſe it is below the
level, and the ſhore riſes as we aſcend the
river. In ſhort, if I may give my teſtimony,
I muſt declare that, when I went from Cairo
to Roſetta, by the canal of Menouf, I obſerved,
on the 26th, 27th, and 28th of September,
1783, that, notwithſtanding the waters had de-
creaſed upwards of a fortnight, the country was
ſtill partly under water, and ſtill diſcovered, in
the places left dry, the traces of the inundation.
What M. Savary obſerved can, therefore, only
be attributed to an indifferent inundation ;
nor ought we to imagine, either that the
riſing has changed the ſtate of the Delta *(y)*,
or that the Egyptians can have no water but

(y) The bed of the river itſelf has riſen, like the reſt of
the country.

what

what is procured by artificial means, as expenfive as infufficient (z).

It now remains for us to explain the difficulty of the eight cubits in the time of Mœris ; and I cannot help thinking this arifes
from caufes of the fame nature. It appears
that, fubfequent to this Prince, an alteration
took place in the meafures of the country,
and one cubit was made into two. This
conjecture is the more probable fince, in the
time of Mœris, Egypt was not united into
one kingdom ; there were at leaft three between Afouan and the fea. Sefoftris, who
was pofterior to Mœris, conquered and united
them. But, after this Prince, they were again
divided, and this divifion fubfifted till the
reign of Pfammeticus. Such a change in the
meafures of Egypt accords perfectly with the
character of Sefoftris, who effected a general
revolution in the government, eftablifhed new
laws, and a new adminiftration, raifed mounds

(z) In the lower Delta, the country is watered by the
means of fingle wheels, becaufe the water is on a level
with the land; but in the upper Delta, it is neceffary to
apply chain-buckets to the wheels, or raife the water by
moveable pumps. There is a great number on the road
from Rofetta to Cairo, and it is fufficiently evident this
laborious method produces no great effect.

and

and caufeways, on which to build villages and towns, and dug fo great a number of canals, according to Herodotus *(a)*, that the Egyptians laid afide ufing wheel-carriages, which they had till then employed.

It will be proper likewife to obferve. that the degrees of inundation are not the fame through all Egypt. On the contrary, a gradual diminution obtains as the river approaches the fea. At Afouan (Syene), the overflow is more confiderable, by one fixth, than at Grand Cairo; and, when the depth of water, at this latter city, is twenty-feven feet, it is fcarcely four at Rofetta and Damietta. The reafon of this is, that befides the quantity of water abforbed by the grounds, as it flows, the river, confined in one fingle bed, and within a narrow valley, rifes higher in the upper country; whereas, when it has paffed Cairo, being no longer obftructed by the mountains, and feparating into a thoufand

(a) Herodotus, lib. 2. This circumftance has greatly embarraffed our modern chronologifts, who place Sefoftris before Mofes, in whofe time chariots ftill fubfifted in Egypt; but it is not the fault of Herodotus if his fyftem of chronology, the beft of all antiquity, has not been underftood.

branches,

branches, it neceffarily lofes in depth what it
acquires in furface.

The reader will conclude, doubtlefs, from
what I have faid, that writers have flattered
themfelves too much in fuppofing they could
fix the precife limits of the enlargement and
rife of the Delta. But, though I would rejeɛt
all illufory circumftances, I am far from de-
nying the faɛt to be well founded; it is too
plain from reafon, and an examination of the
country. The rife of the ground appears to me
demonftrated by an obfervation on which little
ftrefs has been laid. In going from Rofetta
to Cairo, when the waters are low, as in the
month of March, we may remark, as we go
up the river, that the fhore rifes gradually
above the water; fo that, if it overflowed two
feet at Rofetta, it overflows from three to
four at Faoua, and upwards of twelve at Cairo *(k)*. Now, by reafoning from this faɛt,
we may deduce the proof of an increafe by
fediment ; for the layer of mud being in proportion to the thicknefs of the fheets of

---

(k) It would be curious to afcertain in what proportion it continues up to Afouan. Some Copts whom I
have interrogated on the fubjeɛt, affured me that it was
much higher through all the Said than at Cairo.

water by which it is depofited, muft be more
or lefs confiderable as thefe are of a greater
or lefs depth; and we have feen that the
like gradation is obfervable from Afouan to
the fea.

On the other hand, the increafe of the
Delta manifefts itfelf in a ftriking manner,
by the form of Egypt, along the Mediterranean. When we confider its figure on the
map, we perceive, that the country, which is
in the line of the river, and evidently formed
of foreign materials, has affumed a femi-cir-
cular fhape, and that the fhores of Arabia
and Africa, on each fide, have a direction
towards the bottom of the Delta, which
manifeftly difcovers this country was formerly a gulph, that, in time, has been filled
up.

This accumulation is common to all rivers,
and is to be accounted for in the fame manner
in all: the rain water, and the fnow, defcending
from the mountains into the vallies, hurry
inceffantly along with them the earth they
wafh away in their defcent. The heavier
parts, fuch as pebbles and fands, foon ftop,
unlefs forced along by a rapid current. But
when the waters meet only with a fine and
light

light earth, they carry away large quantities with the greateft facility. The Nile meeting with fuch a kind of earth, in Abyffinia, and the interior parts of Africa, its waters are loaded, and its bed filled with it; nay, it is frequently fo embarraffed with this fediment, as to be ftraightened in its courfe. But, when the inundation reftores to it its natural force, it drives the mud that has accumulated towards the fea, at the fame time that it brings down more for the enfuing feafon; and this, arrived at its mouth, heaps up, and forms fhoals, where the declivity does not allow fufficient action to the current, and where the fea produces an equilibrium of refiftance. The ftagnation, which follows, occafions the groffer particles, which till then had floated, to fink, and this takes place more particularly in thofe places where there is leaft motion, as toward the fhores, till the fides become gradually enriched by the fpoils of the upper country, and of the Delta itfelf; for, if the Nile takes from Abyffinia, to add to the Thebais, it likewife takes from the Thebais to give to the Delta, and from the Delta to carry to the fea. Wherever its waters have a current, it defpoils the fame

territory

territory it enriches. As we afcend toward Cairo, when the river is low, we may obferve on each fide the banks worn fteep, and crumbling in large flakes. The Nile, which undermines them, depriving their light earth of fupport, it falls into the bed of the river, for when the water is high, the earth imbibes it; and when the fun and drought return, cracks and moulders away in great flakes, which are hurried along by the Nile. Thus are feveral canals choaked up, and others enlarged, while the bed of the river continually rifes. This is the cafe with the moft frequented of thefe at prefent, I mean that which runs from Nadir to the branch of Damietta. This canal, at firft dug by the hand of man, is in feveral places become as wide as the Seine. It fupplies even the mother branch, which runs from Batn-el-Bakara to Nadir, and which is filling up fo faft, that if it be not fpeedily cleanfed, it will foon become firm ground : the reafon of this is, that the river tends perpetually to the right line, in which it has the greateft force; wherefore it has preferred the Bolbitine, which was at firft but an artificial canal, to the Canopic branch *(c)*.

_____

(c) Herodot. lib. II.

From this mechanifm of the river, it further refults that the principal encroachment
muft be formed in the line of the moft confiderable mouths, and of the ftrongeft current; and the afpect of the country is conformable with this theory. If we caft our
eye on the map, we fhall perceive that the
projection of the lands is chiefly in the direction of the branches of Rofetta and Damietta.
The lateral and intermediate country entirely confifts of lakes and moraffes between
the Continent and the fea, becaufe the fmall
canals, which terminate there, have only
been able to produce an imperfect accumulation; for this mud and fediment caufe a
very flow rife : nor would this indeed ever
fuffice to elevate them above the water, without the addition of a more powerful agent,
which is 'the fea, that perpetually raifes the
level of the low banks above its own waters.
For the waves, beating on the fhore, repel
the fand and mud which they meet; their
dafhing afterwards accumulates that flender
bank, and gives it an elevation which it never
would have attained in ftill waters. The
truth of this is manifeft to every perfon
who has ever obferved the fea, on a low and
changing fhore; but the fea muft have no

current

current on the beach : for if it lofes in thofe parts where it is in eddy, it gains in thofe where it is in motion. When the fhoals are at length formed on the level of the water, human induftry foon endeavours their improvement. But inftead of faying it raifes their level above the water, we ought to fay, it finks the level of the water, fince the canals which are excavated collect, in narrow channels, thofe waters which were fpread over a great extent of ground *(d)*.

There remain unqueftionably many obfervations to make, or to reconfider, in this country ; but, as I have already faid, they are attended with great difficulties, to overcome which, much time, expence, and addrefs are neceffary; and in many refpects, the acceffary obftacles are even more infuperable than the fundamental. Baron de Tott experienced the truth of this very lately, with refpect to the Nilometer. In vain did he endeavour to feduce the guardians; in vain did he give

(d) The great number of canals may be the caufe of variation in the degrees of the inundation; for if there be many, and thofe deep ones, the water will run off quicker, and rife lefs ; if there be few, and thofe fhallow, the contrary will happen.

'and

and promife fequins to the cryers, in order to
obtain the true heights of the Nile ;   their
contradictory reports proved either their deceit, or their univerfal ignorance.   It will be
obferved, perhaps, that meafuring columns
might be erected in private houfes ; but fuch
experiments, fimple in theory, are impoffible
in practice : they would expofe to too ferious
dangers.   Even the curiofity natural to the
Franks, every day renders the Turks more
jealous.   They are perfuaded we have formed
defigns on their country ; and the invafions
of the Ruffians, added to popular prejudice, ftrengthens their fufpicions.   It is generally believed, at this moment, throughout their empire, that the predicted hour is
arrived, when the power and religion of the
Muffulmen are about to be deftroyed, and
that the *Yellow King* is coming to eftablifh
a new empire, &c. &c.   But it is time to re-
fume our fubject.

I pafs flightly over the feafon *(e)* of the
inundation, which is fo well known;   its

(e) It is fixed precifely to the 19th of June, but it
would be difficult to determine the firft inftant of it fo
exactly as the Copts wifh to do.

infen-

infenfible increafe, fo unlike the fudden fwel-
ling of our rivers ; its diverfities, according
to which it is fometimes feeble, fometimes
ftrong, and fometimes even entirely fails ; a
very rare cafe, but of which two or three
inftances have happened : all thefe particulars
are too well known to be repeated. It is
known likewife that the caufes of this phenomenon, which were an enigma to the
ancients *(f)*, are no longer fo to the Europeans. Since travellers have informed
them that Abyffinia and the adjacent part
of Africa, are deluged with rain in May,
June, and July, they have, with reafon, concluded, that it muft be thefe rains, which,
by the fituation of the country, abounding
with a thoufand rivers, collect together in
the fame valley, direct their courfe to diftant fhores, and prefent the ftupendous fight
of a mafs of water, which employs three
months in draining off. We leave to Grecian
naturalifts their action of the northerly or,
Etefian winds, which, by a pretended preffure,
ftayed the courfe of the river ; it is aftonifhing

(f) Democritus, however, had conjectured the true
caufe. See Diodorus Siculus, lib. 11.

that

that even they fhould ever have admitted this
explication, for the wind, acting only on the
furface of the water, can never prevent the
inferior mafs from obeying the laws of gravity.   In vain have fome moderns alleged
the example of the Mediterranean, which,
from the continuance of eafterly winds, leaves
dry the coaft of Syria, a foot, or a foot and a
half, to gain as much on thofe of Spain and
Provence, on which wefterly winds have
a contrary effect; there is no comparifon to
be made between a fea without declivity, and
a river; between the vaft furface of the Mediterranean, and that of the Nile; between
twenty-fix feet and eighteen inches.

CHAP.

CHAP. IV.

Of the Winds and their Phænomena.

THE northerly winds, which blow at
ftated periods every year, anfwer a more certain and effectual purpofe; that of carrying
into Abyffinia a prodigious quantity of clouds.
From the month of April to July we fee
thefe inceffantly afcending towards the fouth,
and might be fometimes tempted to expect
rain from them ; but this parched country
requefts in vain from them a benefaction
which it is to receive under a different form.
Never does it rain in the Delta in fummer,
and but rarely, and in fmall quantities, during the whole courfe of the year. The year
1761, obferved by M. Niebuhr, was an extraordinary cafe, which is ftill frequently
mentioned. The accidents occafioned by the
rains in Lower Egypt, in which a number of
villages, built with earth, crumbled to pieces,
afford a fufficient proof that this abundance
of water is there looked upon as very rare.
It muft be obferved likewife, that it rains

E 4 ftill

ſtill leſs as you aſcend towards the Said, Thus, rain is more frequent at Alexandria and Roſetta than at Cairo, and at Cairo than at Miniah, and is almoſt a prodigy at Djirdja. As for us, the inhabitants of humid countries, we cannot conceive how it is poſſible for a country to ſubſiſt without rain *(g)* ; but in Egypt, beſides the quantity of water which the earth imbibes at the inundation, the dews which fall in the ſummer might ſuffice for vegetation. The water-melons afford a remarkable proof of this ; for though they have frequently no-thing under them but a dry duſt, yet their leaves are always freſh. Theſe dews, as well as the rains, are more copious towards the ſea, and leſs confiderable in proportion to their diſtance from it ; but differ from the latter by being more abundant in ſummer than in winter. At Alexandria, after ſunſet, in the month of April, the clothes expoſed to the air,

(g) When rain falls in Egypt and in Paleſtine, there is a general joy among the people : they aſſemble toge-ther in the ſtreets, they ſing, are all in motion, and ſhout, *ya allah! ya molerek!* that is to ſay, O God ! O Bleſſed ! &c.

and

and the terraces are foaked with them, as if it had rained. Like the rains, again, thefe dews are more or lefs plentiful, according to the prevailing wind. The foutherly and the foutheafterly produce none; the north wind a great deal, and the wefterly ftill more. Thefe varieties are eafily explained, by obferving that the two former proceed from the deferts of Africa and Arabia, which afford not a drop of water; while the northerly and wefterly winds, on the contrary, convey over Egypt the vapours from the Mediterranean, which the firft croffes, and the other traverfes lengthways. I find, even, on comparing my obfervations on this fubject in Provence, in Syria, and in Egypt, with thofe of M. Niebuhr in Arabia and at Bombay, that this relative pofition of the feas and continents is the caufe of the various qualities of one and the fame wind, which produces rain in one country, while it is invariably dry in another; a remark which deranges not a little the fyftems of both ancient and modern aftrologers refpecting the influence of the planets.

Another phenomenon, no lefs remarkable, is the periodical return of each wind, and its appropriation, if I may ufe the expreffion, to

certain

certain feafons of the year. Egypt and Syria prefent, in this refpect, a regularity worthy of attention.

In Egypt, when the fun approaches the tropic of Cancer, the winds, which before blew from the eaft, change to the north, and become conftant in that point. In June they always blow from the north and north-weft; this therefore is the proper feafon for going up the Levant, and a veffel may expect to anchor in Cyprus, or at Alexandria, the fourteenth, nay, fometimes the eleventh day, after her departure from Marfeilles. The winds continue northerly in July, but vary fometimes toward the weft, and fometimes toward the eaft. About the end of July, during all the month of Auguft, and half of September, they remain conftantly in the north, and are moderate; brifker in the day, however, and weaker at night. At this period an univerfal calm reigns on the Mediterranean, fo that fhips would be feventy or eighty days in returning to France.

Towards the end of September, when the fun repaffes the line, the winds return to the eaft; and, though not fixed, blow more regularly from that than any other point,

except

except the north. Veffels avail themfelves
of this feafon, which lafts all October and
part of November, to return to Europe; and
the run to Marfeilles is from thirty to five-
and-thirty days. As the fun approaches the
other tropic, the winds become more variable
and more tempeftuous; they moft ufually
blow from the north, the north-weft, and
weft, in which points they continue during
the months of December, January, and February, which is the winter feafon in Egypt,
as well as with us. The vapours of the
Mediterranean, condenfed by the coldnefs of
the atmofphere, defcend in mifts and rains.
About the end of February and in March,
when the fun returns towards the equator,
the winds are more frequently foutherly than
at any other feafon. During this laft month,
and that of April, the fouth-eafterly, fouth,
and fouth-wefterly winds prevail; and at
times the weft, north, and eaft; the latter of
which becomes the moft prevalent about the
end of April; and during May it divides with
the north the empire of the fea, and renders
the paffage to France ftill more expeditious
than at the other equinox.

Of

Of the hot Wind, or Kamsin.

The foutherly winds, of which I have been fpeaking, are known in Egypt by the general name of *winds of fifty (days) (b)*; not that they laft fifty days without intermif-fion, but becaufe they prevail more frequent-ly in the fifty days preceding and following the equinox. Travellers have mentioned them under the denomination of *poifonous winds (i)*; or, more correctly, *hot winds of the defert*. Such, in fact, is their quality; and their heat is fometimes fo exceffive, that it is difficult to form any idea of its violence without having experienced it; but it may be compared to the heat of a large oven at the moment of drawing out the bread. When thefe winds begin to blow, the atmofphere

(b) In Arabic, *kamfin*; but the *k* reprefents the Spanifh *jota*, or the German *ch*.

(i) The Arabs of the defert call them *femoum*, or poi-fon; and the Turks *fhamyela*, or wind of Syria, from which is formed the *Samiel* wind. (Baron de Tott tranf-lates this word the *wind of Damafcus*, which is the capital of Syria. See alfo Note *(c)* to Chapter I. of our author's account of Syria, where *el Sham* is faid to be the Arabic name of the city of Damafcus. T.)

assumes

affumes an alarming afpect. The fky, at other times fo clear, in this climate, becomes dark and heavy; the fun lofes his fplendour, and appears of a violet colour. The air is not cloudy, but grey and thick, and is, in fact, filled with an extremely fubtle duft, which penetrates every where. This wind, always light and rapid, is not at firft remarkably hot, but it increafes in heat in proportion as it continues. All animated bodies foon difcover it, by the change it produces in them. The lungs, which a too rarefied air no longer expands, are contracted, and become painful. Refpiration is fhort and difficult, the fkin parched and dry, and the body confumed by an internal heat. In vain is recourfe had to large draughts of water; nothing can reftore perfpiration. In vain is coolnefs fought for; all bodies in which it is ufual to find it, deceive the hand that touches them. Marble, iron, water, notwithftanding the fun no longer appears, are hot. The ftreets are deferted, and the dead filence of night reigns every where. The inhabitants of towns and villages fhut themfelves up in their houfes, and thofe of the defert in their tents, or in pits they dig in the earth, where

they

they wait the termination of this destructive heat. It usually lasts three days, but if it exceeds that time it becomes insupportable. Woe to the traveller whom this wind surprizes remote from shelter; he must suffer all its dreadful consequences, which sometimes are mortal. The danger is most imminent when it blows in squalls, for then the rapidity of the wind encreases, the heat to such a degree, as to cause sudden death. This death is a real suffocation; the lungs being empty, are convulsed, the circulation disordered, and the whole mass of blood driven by the heart towards the head and breast; whence that hæmorrhage at the nose and mouth which happens after death. This wind is especially fatal to persons of a plethoric habit, and those in whom fatigue has destroyed the tone of the muscles and the vessels. The corpse remains a long time warm, swells, turns blue, and is easily separated; all which are signs of that putrid fermentation which takes place in animal bodies when the humours become stagnant. These accidents are to be avoided, by stopping the nose and mouth with handkerchiefs; an efficacious method likewise is that practised by the camels, which bury their

nofes

noſes in the ſand, and keep them there till the ſquall is over.

Another quality of this wind is its extreme aridity; which is ſuch, that water ſprinkled on the floor evaporates in a few minutes. By this extreme dryneſs, it withers and ſtrips all the plants, and, by exhaling too ſuddenly the emanations from animal bodies, criſps the ſkin, cloſes the pores, and cauſes that feveriſh heat which is the invariable effect of ſup-preſſed perſpiration.

Theſe hot winds are not peculiar to Egypt; they blow likewiſe in Syria; more frequently, however, near the ſea, and in the deſert, than on the mountains. M. Niebuhr met with them in Arabia, at Bombay, and in the Diar-bekir: they are alſo known in Perſia, in the reſt of Africa, and even in Spain; every where their effects are ſimilar, but their di-rection varies according to the ſituation of the country. In Egypt, the moſt violent proceed from the ſouth-ſouth-weſt; at Mec-ca, from the eaſt; at Surat, from the north; at Baſſora, from the north-weſt; from the weſt at Bagdad; and in Syria from the ſouth-eaſt. Theſe varieties, which ſeem embarraſ-ſing at firſt ſight, on reflection, furniſh the

means

means of folving the enigma. We find, on
examination, that thefe winds always proceed
from defert continents; and, in fact, it is natural that the air which covers the immenfe
plains of Lybia and Arabia, meeting there neither with rivulets, nor lakes, nor forefts, but
fcorched by the rays of a burning fun, the
violence of which is ftill more increafed by
the reflection of the fand, fhould acquire a
prodigious degree of heat and aridity; and if
any caufe intervenes to fet it in motion, it
cannot but carry with it the deftructive qualities it has imbibed; it is fo true that thefe
qualities are owing to the action of the fun
upon the fands that thefe fame winds produce
not the fame effects at every feafon. In
Egypt, for example, I am affured, that the
foutherly winds in December and January
are as cold as thofe from the north; and
the reafon of this is, that the fun, having
reached the fouthern trophic, no longer burns
up the northern parts of Africa, and that
Abyffinia, which is extremely mountainous,
is covered with fnow. The fun muft approach the equator to produce thefe pheno-
mena. From a fimilar reafon, the fouth wind
has much lefs effect in Cyprus, where it arrives
cooled by the vapours of the Mediterranean.

That

That from the north poffeffes its characteriftic qualities in this ifland, where
the inhabitants complain that its heat is infupportable in fummer, while it is freezing
cold in winter; which evidently arifes from
the ftate of Afia Minor, which in fummer is
burnt up, and in winter covered with ice. In
fact, this fubject offers a multitude of problems, calculated to excite the curiofity of the
naturalift.—Would it not, for inftance, be
interefting to know,

1ft, Whence proceeds this connection of
the feafons, and the progrefs of the fun, with
the various winds, and the points from
whence they blow?

2dly, Why, throughout the Mediterranean, does the wind moft frequently blow
from the north, infomuch, that we may fay it
continues in that point nine months out of
twelve?

3dly, Why do the eafterly winds return
fo regularly after the equinoxes; and why
are the winds, in general, higher at this
period?

4thly, Why are the dews more abundant
in fummer than in winter; and why, fince
the clouds are caufed by the evaporation of

the fea, and that evaporation is more copious in fummer than in winter, why, notwith- ftanding, are there more clouds in winter than in fummer?

5thly, In fhort, why is rain fo rare in Egypt, and why do the clouds rather collect in Abyffinia?

But it is time to complete our obfervations on the phyfical ftate of this country.

CHAP.

CHAP. V.

Of the Climate and Air.

THE climate of Egypt is, with reafon, ef-teemed extremely hot, fince in July and Au-guft, Reaumur's thermometer ftands, in the moft temperate apartments, at 24 and 25 de-grees above the freezing point*. In the Said, it rifes ftill higher, though I can affert no-thing precife in that refpect. The height of the fun, which, in fummer, nearly approaches the zenith, is doubtlefs a primary caufe of this heat; but when we confider that, in other countries, under the fame latitude, the heat is lefs, we may conclude there exifts a fecon-dary caufe, equally powerful with the former, and this perhaps, is the country being fo lit-tle elevated above the level of the fea. On this account, two feafons only fhould be dif-tinguifhed in Egypt; the fpring and fum-mer, that is to fay, the cool feafon, and the hot. The latter continues from March to No-vember; and even from the end of February, the fun is not fupportable, for an European, at nine o'clock in the morning. During the

* 86° and 88° of Fahrenheit's fcale.

whole

whole of this feafon the air is inflamed, the fky fparkling, and the heat oppreffive to all unaccuftomed to it. The body fweats pro-fufely, even under the lighteft drefs, and in a ftate of the moft profound repofe; and this perfpiration becomes fo neceffary, that, the flighteft fuppreffion of it is a ferious malady; infomuch, that, the ordinary falute " How do " you do?" ought in Egypt to be: " How " do you fweat?" The departure of the fun tempers, in fome degree, thefe heats. The vapours from the earth foaked by the Nile, and thofe brought by the weft, and north-weft winds, abforbing the fire difperfed throughout the atmofphere, produce an agree-able frefhnefs, and even piercing cold, if we may credit the natives, and fome European merchants; but the Egyptians, almoft naked, and accuftomed to perfpire, fhiver at the leaft coolnefs. The thermometer, which, at the loweft, in the month of February, ftands at the eighth or ninth degree of Reaumur's fcale *, above the freezing point, enables us to deter-mine with certainty, and we may pronounce, that fnow, and hail, are phœnomena which no

* 50° or 52° of Fahrenheit's.

Egyptian

Egyptian has feen in fifty years. As for our merchants, their fenfibility is owing to their improper ufe of furs, which is carried fo far, that, in winter, they have frequently two or three coverings of foxes-fkin, and, even in fummer, retain the ermine or *petit gris*. In excufe for this, they plead the chillinefs they feel in the fhade, as an indifpenfable reafon ; and in fact, the northerly and wefterly currents of air, which almoft continually prevail, caufe a pretty confiderable coolnefs out of the fun ; but the fecret and real reafon is, that the peliffe is to be confidered as the lace of Turkey, the favourite object of luxury; it is the fign of opulence, and the etiquette of dignity ; for the inveftiture of important offices is always accompanied with the prefent of a peliffe, as if they were to fay of him to whom they give it, he is now arrived at fo great eminence, he need concern himfelf with nothing, but perfpire at his eafe.

It might naturally be imagined that Egypt, from thefe heats, and its wet and marfhy condition for three months, muft be an unhealthy country; this was my firft idea on my arrival there; and, when I beheld, at Cairo, the houfes of our merchants ranged along the Kalidj, where the water ftagnates till the month of April, I made no doubt that the exhalations thence arifing, muft caufe many maladies; but experience proves the fallacy of this theory; the vapours of the ftagnant waters, fo fatal in Cyprus, and Alexandretta, are not fo pernicious in Egypt. This appears to me to be owing to the natural drynefs of the air, to the proximity of Africa and Arabia, which inceffantly draw off the humidity, and the perpetual currents of wind, which meet with no obftacle. This aridity is fuch, that flefh meat expofed, even in fummer, to the north wind, does not putrefy, but dries up, and becomes hard as wood. In the deferts, dead carcafes are found dried in this manner, which are fo light, that a man may eafily lift with one hand the entire body of a camel. *(k)*

The air, befides poffeffing this drying quality, appears to be ftrongly impregnated with falts, the proofs of which are every where apparent. The ftones are corroded by natrum,

(k) It muft be remarked, however, that the air near the fea is infinitely lefs dry than higher up the country: Thu , at Alexandria, and Rofetta, iron cannot be expofed four-and-twenty hours to the air, without rufting.

                  and

and in moiſt places, long cryſtallizations of it are to be found, which might be taken for ſalt-petre. The wall of the Jeſuits garden, at Cairo, built with earth and bricks, is every where covered with a cruſt of this natrum, as thick as a crown-piece ; and when this garden has been overflowed by the waters of the Kalidj, the ground, after they have drained off, appears ſparkling on every ſide with white cryſtals, which certainly were not brought thither by the water, ſince it ſhows no ſign of ſalt, either to the taſte, or in diſtillation.

It is no doubt, this property of the air, and the earth, which, added to the heat, gives vegetation an activity almoſt incredible in our cold climates. Wherever plants have water, the rapidity of their growth is prodigious. Whoever has travelled to Cairo, or Roſetta, knows, that the ſpecies of gourd called *kara*, will, in twenty-four hours, ſend out ſhoots near four inches long ; but it is worthy obſervation, that this ſoil appears extremely unfavourable to all exotics. Foreign plants degenerate there rapidly : the truth of which remark is proved by daily experience. Our merchants are obliged every year to renew their ſeeds, and to ſend to Malta for their

F 4   cauli-

cauliflowers, beet-root, carrots, and falfify:
thefe, when fown, fucceed at firft very well;
but if they again fow the feed they produce,
the plants run up tall and weak. The fame
happens to apricots, pears, and peaches, when
tranfported to Rofetta. The vegetation of
this earth feems too violent for fpungy and
pulpy fruits, which fhould be gradually accuftomed, by the arts of culture, to the foil
and climate.

CHAP.

C H A P. VI.

Of the various Inhabitants of Egypt.

AMID thofe revolutions which all nations have experienced, there are few countries which have preferved their original and
primitive inhabitants pure and unmixed.
Throughout the world, the fame avarice and
ambition which prompt individuals to en-
croach on each other's property, have excited
nations one againft another ; and the confequence of this oppofition of interefts and
powers, has been to introduce into ftates
a foreign conqueror, who, now an infolent
ufurper, has defpoiled the vanquifhed nation of the domain granted them by nature ;
..nd now, a more timid or more civilized
invader, has contented himfelf with parti-
cipating in advantages refufed him by his
native foil. Here we fee various races of
inhabitants fettling themfelves in the fame
country, who, adopting the fame manners
and interefts, have fometimes united in the
moft intimate alliances ; but more frequently
we

we find them feparated · by political or religious prejudices, and remaining perpetually
diftinct. In the firft cafe, the different races,
lofing by the mixture their diftinguifhing
characters, have formed an homogeneous people, among whom it is impoffible to difcover
any traces of the revolution ; in the fecond,
living diftinct, their perpetuated differences
are become a monument which has out-
lived ages, and which in fome cafes may fupply the filence of hiftory.

Such is the cafe with Egypt: deprived,
three-and-twenty centuries ago, of her natural
proprietors, fhe has feen her fertile fields
fuceffively a prey to the Perfians, the Macedonians, the Romans, the Greeks, the
Arabs, the Georgians, and, at length, the race
of Tartars, diftinguifhed by the name of
Ottoman Turks. Among fo many nations,
feveral of them have left veftiges of their
tranfient poffeffion ; but as they have been
blended in fucceffion, they have been fo confounded as to render it very difficult to dif-
criminate their refpective characters. We
may, however, ftill diftinguifh the inhabitants
of Egypt into four principal races, of different origin.

The

The firft, and moft generally difperfed, is that of the Arabs, which may be divided into three claffes. Firft, the pofterity of thofe who, on the conqueft of Egypt by Amrou, in the year 640, haftened from the Hedjaz, and every part of Arabia, to fettle in this country, fo juftly celebrated for its fertility. Every one was anxious to poffefs lands in it, and the Delta was prefently filled with foreigners, to the prejudice of the vanquifhed Greeks. This firft race is preferved in the prefent clafs of fellahs, or huibandmen, and artizans, who ftill retain the characteriftic features of their anceftors, but are tailer and ftronger made, the natural effect of a more plentiful nourifhment than that of the deferts. In general, the Egyptian peafants reach the height of five feet four inches, and many among them attain to five feet fix or feven*. They are mufcular, without being flefhy and corpulent, as men will be who are hardened to fatigue. Their fkin, tanned by the fun, is almoft black, but their countenances have nothing difagreeable. The greateft part of them have heads of a fine oval, large

* *Near five feet eight, and five feet ten or eleven inches, Englifh meafure; the French foot (meant through this work,) being to the Englifh as 144 to 135.*

and

and projecting foreheads, and, under a dark eyebrow, a black, funken, but brilliant eye, the nose large, but not aquiline, well-shaped mouths, and, without exception, fine teeth. The inhabitants of the great towns, more motley, have a less uniform and marked phyfiognomy. Those of the villages, on the contrary, forming no alliances but in their own families, have more general and more conftant characteriftics, and fomething of ferocity in their air, which originates in the paffions of a mind continually foured by the perpetual war and tyranny which furround them.

A fecond clafs of Arabs is that of the Africans, or Occidentals *(l)*, who have arrived at different periods, and under different chiefs, and united themfelves to the former; like them, they are defcended from the Muffulmen conquerors, who expelled the Greeks from Mauritania; like them, they exercife agriculture and trades; but they are more efpecially numerous in the Said, where they have villages, and even diftinct fovereigns of their own.

The third clafs is that of the *Bedouins*, or inhabitants of the deferts *(m)*, known to

(l) In Arabic *magarbe*, the plural of *magrebi*, weftern.

(m) In Arabic *bedaoui*, formed of *bid*, defert, country without habitations.

2   the

the ancients by the name of *Scenites*, that is,
dwellers in tents. Some of thefe, difperfed
in families, inhabit the rocks, caverns, ruins,
and fequeftered places where there is water;
others, united in tribes, encamp under low
and fmoaky tents, and pafs their lives in perpetual journeyings, fometimes in the defert,
fometimes on the banks of the river; having no other attachment to the foil than
what arifes from their own fafety, or the fubfiftence of their flocks. There are tribes of
them who arrive every year after the inundation, from the heart of Africa, to profit by
the fertility of the country, and who in the
fpring retire into the depths of the defert;
others are ftationary in Egypt, where they
farm lands, which they fow, and annually
change. All of them obferve among themfelves ftated limits, which they never pafs, on
pain of war. They all lead nearly the fame
kind of life, and have the fame manners and
cuftoms. Ignorant and poor, the Bedouins
preferve an original character diftinct from
furrounding nations. Pacific in their camp,
they are every where elfe in an habitual ftate
of war. The hufbandmen, whom they pillage, hate them; the travellers, whom they
despoil,

defpoil, fpeak ill of them; and the Turks who dread them, endeavour to divide and corrupt them. It is calculated that the different tribes of them in Egypt might form a body of thirty thoufand horfemen; but thefe are fo difperfed and difunited, that they are only confidered as robbers and vagabonds.

A fecond race of inhabitants are the Copts, called in Arabic *el Kobt*. Several families of them are to be found in the Delta; but the greateft part inhabit the Said, where they in fome places occupy whole villages. Both hiftory and tradition atteft their defcent from the people who were conquered by the Arabs, that is, from that mixture of Egyptians, Perfians, and, above all, Greeks, who, under the Ptolemies and Conftantines, were fo long in poffeffion of Egypt. They differ from the Arabs by their religion, which is Chriftianity; but they are again diftinct from other Chriftians by their fect, being Eutychians. Their adherence to the theological diftinctions of this herefy, has drawn perfecutions on them on the part of the other Greeks, which has rendered them irreconcileable enemies. When the Arabs conquered the country, they took advantage of thefe animofities, to enfeeble them

them both. The Copts have at length expelled their rivals, and, as they have been always intimately acquainted with the interior of the country, they are become the depofitaries of the regifters of the lands and tribes. Under the name of *writers*, they are at Cairo the intendants, fecretaries, and collectors of government. Thefe writers, defpifed by the Turks, whom they ferve, and hated by the peafants, whom they opprefs, form a kind of feparate clafs, the head of which is the writer to the principal Bey. He difpofes of all employments in that department, which, according to the fpirit of the Turkifh government, he beftows on the beft bidder.

It is pretended that the name of *Copts*, is derived from the city of *Coptos*, whither it has been affirmed they retired from the tyranny of the Greeks; but I am inclined to think it has a more natural and more ancient origin. The Arabic term *Kobti*, a Copt, feems to me an evident abbreviation of the Greek word *Ai-goupti-os*, an Egyptian; for the *y* was pronounced *ou*, among the ancient Greeks, and the Arabs having neither *p* nor *g* before *a, o, u,* always fubftitute for thefe letters *k* and *b*; the Copts then are properly the remains

of

of the ancient Egyptians *(n)*. This will be rendered still more probable, if we confider the diftinguifhing features of this race of people; we fhall find them all characterized by a fort of yellowifh dufky complexion, which is neither Grecian nor Arabian; they have all a puffed vifage, fwoln eyes, flat nofes, and thick lips, in fhort the exact countenance of a Mulatto. I was at firft tempted to attribute this to the climate *(o)*, but when I vifited the fphynx, I could not help thinking the figure of that monfter furnifhed the true folution of

(n) This is the more probable, fince we find them in the Said before the time of Dioclefian, and it is certain the Greeks were lefs numerous in the Said than the Delta.

(o) In fact, we may obferve the countenance of the negroes reprefents precifely that ftate of contraction which our faces affume when ftrongly affected by heat. The eyebrows are knit, the cheeks rife, the eye-lids are contracted, and the mouth diftorted. This ftate of contraction, to which the features are perpetually expofed in the hot climates of the negroes, is become the peculiar characteriftic of their countenance. Exceffive cold, wind and fnow produce the fame effect, and thus we difcover the fame faces among the Tartars; while, in the temperate zones, where thefe extremes are unknown, the features are lengthened, the eyes lefs prominent, and the whole countenance more expanded.

the

the enigma: when I faw its features precifely thofe of a negro, I recollected the remarkable paffage of Herodotus, in which he
fays, " For my part, I believe the Colchi to be
" a colony of Egyptians, becaufe, like them,
" they have black fkins and frizzled hair *(p)*:"
that is, that the ancient Egyptians were real
negroes, of the fame fpecies with all the natives of Africa; and though, as might be expected, after mixing for fo many ages with the
Greeks and Romans, they have loft the in-
tenfity of their firft colour, yet they ftill retain ftrong marks of their original confor-
mation.

This obfervation may be ftill farther extended, and it may be laid down as a general
principle, that the features are a kind of
monument capable, in many cafes, of elucidat-
ing and afcertaining the teftimony of hiftory,
concerning the origin of nations. Among
us, a lapfe of nine hundred years has not been
able to efface thofe difcriminating marks
which diftinguifhed the inhabitants of Gaul
from thofe northern invaders, who, under
Charles the Grofs, fettled themfelves in our

(p) Μελαγχροες εισι κ} ελοτριχες, Lib. II. p. 150.

richeft

richeſt provinces.   Travellers who go from
Normandy to Denmark, obſerve, with aſto-
niſhment, the extreme reſemblance of the inhabitants of thoſe two countries, which ſtill
ſubſiſts, notwithſtanding the diſtance of times
and places.   The ſame remark may be made
with reſpect to Franconia and Burgundy;
and throughout England, France, and every
other country, the ſame proofs of emigration
are found in the features of the inhabitants.
Do not the Jews, in whatever part of the
world they reſide, carry with them diſtinguiſhing marks never to be effaced?   In thoſe
ſtates where the nobility have deſcended from
a foreign people, introduced by conqueſt, if
thoſe nobles contract no alliance with the
natives, they will always remain diſtinct in
their features and perſons.   The Calmuc
race is, on this account, extremely diſtinguiſh-
able in India; and were we attentively to
examine the various nations of Europe, and
the North of Aſia, we might poſſibly diſcover many reſemblances which have been
long ſince forgotten.

But to return to Egypt : this hiſtorical fact
affords to philoſophy an intereſting ſubject of
reflection.   How are we aſtoniſhed when we
                                                          behold

behold the prefent barbarifm and ignorance of
the Copts, defcended from the profound genius of the Egyptians, and the brilliant imagination of the Greeks; when we reflect that
to the race of negroes, at prefent our flaves,
and the objects of our extreme contempt,
we owe our arts, fciences, and even the
very ufe of fpeech; and when we recollect
that, in the midft of thofe nations who call
themfelves the friends of liberty and humanity, the moft barbarous of flaveries is juftified; and that it is even a problem whether
the underftanding of negroes be of the fame
fpecies with that of white men!

Language may be confidered as another
monument whofe indications are neither lefs
juft nor lefs inftructive. That formerly
fpoken by the Copts well confirms this obfervation. On one hand, the form of their
letters, and the greater part of their words,
demonftrate that the Greek nation, during
the thoufand years it continued in Egypt, has
left deep marks of its power and influence;
but, on the other, the Coptic alphabet has
five letters, and the language a number of
words, which may be confidered as the remains
of the ancient Egyptian. Thefe words, criti-

cally

cally examined, have a fenfible analogy with
the dialects of the ancient neighbouring nations, fuch as the Arabs, Ethiopians, Syrians,
and even thofe who lived on the banks of the
Euphrates; nor can it be doubted but all
thefe languages are derived from one common ftock. For upwards of three centuries,
that of the Copts has fallen into difufe. The
Arabs, difdaining the language of the nations
they fubdued, impofed on them, together
with their yoke, the neceffity of learning that
of their conquerors. This obligation became
even a law, when, about the end of the firft
century of the Hejira, the Caliph Waled I.
prohibited the Greek tongue throughout his
whole empire. From that time the Arabic became univerfal; and the other languages, confined to books, fubfifted only for the learned,
who neglected them. Such has been the fate of
the Coptic; the priefts and monks no longer
underftand it, in their fcriptures and books of
devotion, in which alone it exifts; and in
Egypt, as in Syria, every one, whether Mahometan or Chriftian, fpeaks Arabic, nor is any
other language underftood.

Some obfervations, important to geography
and hiftory, here prefent themfelves. Travellers,

vellers, in treating of the countries they have feen, are accuftomed, and frequently find it abfolutely neceffary, to employ fome words of the language; as in giving the proper names of nations, men, cities, rivers, and natural productions peculiar to the country; but hence has arifen this inconvenience, that by conveying the words of one language in the characters of another, they have fo diffigured them, as to render them difficult to be known. This has happened particularly with refpect to the countries of which I treat; and, in books of hiftory and geography, the confequence has been an incredible and inexplicable confufion. Any Arab, who fhould learn French, would not recognize in our maps ten words of his own language, and, when we ourfelves have learnt Arabic, we experience the fame inconvenience. The caufes of this are various.

Firft, the ignorance of travellers, in general, of the Arabic language, and efpecially of the pronunciation; which ignorance occafions their ear, unaccuftomed to foreign founds, to make a vicious comparifon of them with thofe of their own language *(g)*.

(g) This is true even of the learned Pococke, who, notwithftanding his great knowledge of oriental books,

Secondly, the nature of feveral founds, which have nothing analogous to them in the language in which they attempt to convey them. This the French experience every day in the *th* of the Englifh, and in the *jota* of the Spaniards. Without hearing, it is impoffible for any man to form an idea of thefe; but this difficulty is ftill greater in the Arabic, in which language there are three vowels, and feven or eight confonants, to which Europeans are utter ftrangers. How then is it poffible to reprefent them, fo as to retain their true found, and not confound them with others totally different?

A third caufe of confufion has arifen from writers who have compiled books and maps. In collecting their information from all the Europeans who have travelled in the Eaft, they have adopted the orthography of proper names, fuch as they found it in the author they confulted, without confidering that the different

could never difpenfe with an interpreter; and very lately Vonhaven, Profeffor of Arabic in Denmark, was unable even to underftand the *falam alai kom* (good-morrow) when he arrived in Egypt; and his young companion Forfkal, at the end of a year, had made a much greater progrefs than he had.

nations

nations of Europe, though they equally ufe the Roman characters, found them differently.— For example, the *u* of the Italians is not the *u* of the French, but *ou*. Their *gh* is founded like *gu*, and their *c, tch:* hence an apparent diverfity of names, which are, in fact, the fame. Thus it is, that what fhould be written in French *chaik*, or *chék*, is varioufly expreffed by *(r) fchek, fhekh, fchech, fcick*, according as the word has been copied from Englifh, German, or Italian writers, with whom *fh, fch, fc*, are refpectively founded like our *ché*. The Poles would write *fzech*, and the Spaniards *chcj*. This difference of the final *j, ch,* and *kh,* arifes from the Arabic letter being the Spanifh *jota*, or German *ch (s)*, the found of which is unknown to the Englifh French, or Italians. Hence it is that the Englifh write *Rooda*, for the name of the ifland, which the Italians write *Ruda*, and which we, like the Arabs, fhould pronounce *Rouda*; that Pococke writes *harammee* for *harami*, a robber; and Niebuhr *dsjebel* for *djebel*, a mountain; that Danville, who has

(*r*) To make thefe differences fenfible in reading, the letters muft be pronounced one by one.

(*s*) Not in all cafes, but after *o* and *u*, as in *buch*, a book.

G 4   made

made great ufe of Englifh memoirs, writes *Shâm* for *Châm*, Syria; *wadi* for *ouadi*, a valley; and a thoufand other examples.

This, as I have faid, has introduced a great confufion in orthography; and, if it be not remedied, we fhall find the fame uncertainty in modern writers we fo juftly complain of in the ancients, who, by their ignorance of the barbarous languages, and by their rage for accommodating the founds of them to the tafte of the Greeks and Romans, have deftroyed all traces of the original names, and deprived us of an invaluable mean of difcovering the ancient ftate of things in that now fubfifting. Our language is fubject to the fame delicacy; it disfigures every thing, and our ear rejects, as barbarous, whatever it is not accuftomed to. It is ufelefs, no doubt, to introduce new characters; but it might not be amifs to approach, as near as poffible, the found of thofe we would exprefs, and reprefent them by thofe of our letters which are beft adapted, adding to them fome certain marks *(t)*. Were this done by every nation, there

(t) When the French travellers, who are making the tour of the world, return, we fhall, no doubt, fee no fmal con—

there would be but one nomenclature, and this would be a firſt ſtep towards an invention, which every day becomes more wanted, and more eaſy to effect, a *general alphabet*, adapted to all languages, or at leaſt to thoſe of Europe. In the courſe of this work I ſhall make as little uſe as poſſible of Arabic words; but when I ſhall be under that neceſſity, let not the reader be ſurpriſed, if I frequently depart from the orthography of the generality of travellers. To judge from what they have written, we ſhould be induced to think, that not one of them has known the true pronunciation of the Arabic alphabet, or underſtood how to convey the ſounds of that language in our characters. But I return to my ſubject.

A third race of inhabitants in Egypt are the Turks, who are the maſters of the country, or at leaſt poſſeſs that title. The name of

confuſion produced in their narratives, by the variations of the Engliſh and French orthography. (This confuſion is already ſufficiently exemplified in the different accounts of the ſame voyages, publiſhed reſpectively by Hawkeſworth, Parkinſon, Cook, Forſter, &c. and by the different modes of writing the ſame words, by the officers, and others, in the different ſhips. T.)

Turk

Turk, originally, was not peculiar to the nation to which it is now applied: it denoted, in general, all the hordes difperfed to the eaft, and even to the north, of the Cafpian Sea, as far as beyond Lake Aral, over thofe vaft countries which have taken from them the denomination of *Tourk-eftan (u)*. Thefe are the fame people, who were known to the ancient Greeks by the names of Parthians, Maffagetæ and even of Scythians, for which we have fubftituted that of Tartars. A nation of fhepherds, continually wandering, like the Bedouin Arabs; they have fhewn themfelves, in every age, brave and formidable warriors. Neither Cyrus nor Alexander were able to fubdue them. But the Arabs were more fortunate. About eighty years after Mahomet, they invaded, by order of the Caliph Waled I. the country of the Turks, and, by force of arms, impofed on them their religion: they even obliged them to pay tribute. But the empire falling into confufion, the rebel governors had recourfe to their aid to refift the power of

(u) *Eftan* is a Perfian word, fignifying *country*, and is ufed as a termination to proper names; as in *Arab-eftan*, *Frank-eftan*, and we may add *Kourd-eftan*, and *Indo-ftan*, &c.

the

the Caliphs, and they took part in every con-
test; nor were they long in acquiring the af-
cendant this might be expected to give them:
for, continually encamped, and with arms in
their hands, they became a warlike people,
and initiated in every military manœuvre.
Like the Bedouins, they were divided into
tribes, or camps, called, in their language,
ordou, of which we have made *horde*; and
these tribes, allied or at variance, according
to their several interests, were perpetually engaged in wars. Hence we fee, in their hiftory, several nations, all equally called Turks,
alternately attacking, deftroying, and expel-
ling each other. To avoid this confufion, I
shall confine the name of *Turks* to thofe of
Conftantinople, and shall give that of *Turkmans* to their predeceffors.

Some hordes of Turkmans, then, having
been introduced into the Arabian empire,
proceeded in a short time to give law to thofe
who had called them in, either as mercena-
ries or allies. This the Caliphs themfelves experienced in a remarkable inftance. Motaz-
zam *(x)*, brother and fucceffor of Almamoun,

(x) in 834.

having

having taken a body of Turkmans for his guards, faw himfelf compelled to quit Bagdad on account of their diforders; and, after his time, their power and infolence increafed to fuch a degree, that they became the difpofers of the throne and life of their Princes, and murdered three of them in lefs than thirty years. The Caliphs, when freed from this firft bondage, did not profit by their experience; for, about the year 935, Radi B'ellah (y) having again refigned his authority to a Turkman, his fucceffors were entangled in their former chains, and guarded by the Emirs-el-omara; poffeffed only the fhadow of power. Amid the diforders of this anarchy, a multitude of Turkman hordes penetrated into the empire, and founded different independent ftates, in the Kerman, and the Korafan; at Iconium, Aleppo, Damafcus, and in Egypt.

'Till then, the prefent Turks, diftinguifhed by the name of *Ogouzians*, had remained to the eaft of the Cafpian, and toward the Djihoun; but, about the beginning of the thirteenth century, Djenkiz-kan having unit-

(y) *Who delights in God.*

ed

ed all the tribes of Upper Tartary againſt the Princes of Balk and Samarcand, the Ogouzians did not think proper to wait for the Mogols, but began their march under their Chief Soliman, and, driving their herds before them, encamped (in 1214) in the Aderbedjân, to the number of fifty thouſand horſemen. The Moguls followed them, and puſhed them ſtill farther to the weſt, into Armenia. Soliman being drowned (in 1220), in endeavouring to paſs the Euphrates on horſeback, Ertogrul, his ſon, took the command of the hordes, and advanced into the plains of Aſia Minor, to which he was allured by the abundant paſturage they afforded for his cattle. The good conduct of this chief procured him, in theſe countries, a power and reſpect which made his alliance ſought after by other Princes. Among theſe was the Turkman Ala-el-din, Sultan of Iconium. Ala-el-din, finding himſelf old, and haraſſed by the Tartars of Djenkiz-kan, granted lands to the Turks under Ertogrul, and even made their Chief general of all his troops. Ertogrul proved himſelf deſerving the confidence of the Sultan, vanquiſhed the Mogols, acquired ſtill greater power and reputation, and tranſmitted

his

his honours to his fon Ofman, who received
from Ala-el-din, fucceffor of the former of
that name, the Kofetan, drum, and horfe-tails,
which are fymbols of command among all
the Tartars. This Ofman, to diftinguifh the
Turks, his followers, from the others, gave
them the name of *Ofmanles*, from which we
have made *Ottomans (z)*; which new name
foon became formidable to the Greeks of Conftantinople, from whom Ofman conquered a
fufficient extent of territory to found a powerful kingdom. He foon beftowed on it that title,
by affuming, in 1300, the dignity of *Sultan*,
which fignifies abfolute fovereign.

No one is ignorant in what manner his
fucceffors, the heirs of his ambition and activity, continued to aggrandize themfelves at
the expence of the Greeks; till, continually
depriving them of whole provinces in Europe
and Afia, they at length fhut them up within the walls of Conftantinople; and Mahomet II. fon of Amurath, having taken that
city in 1453, annihilated this branch of the

(z) This change of the *s* to the *t*, arifes from the
original letter being the Englifh *th*, which foreigners
exprefs fometimes by *t*, fometimes by *s*.

Roman

Roman empire. The Turks, now finding themfelves difengaged from the affairs of Europe, turned their ambitious arms againft the fouthern provinces. Bagdad, fubjugated by the Tartars, had been without Caliphs for two hundred years *(a)*, but a new power, eftablifhed in Perfia, had fucceeded to a part of their domains; and another, formed in Egypt, fo early as the tenth century, and fubfifting, at that time, under the name of Mamlouks, had feized on Syria.

The Turks determined to defpoil thefe two rivals. Bayazid, the fon of Mahomet, executed a part of this plan, by taking Armenia from the Sofi of Perfia, and Selim his fon completed it, by the conqueft of the Mamlouks. This Sultan having drawn them near to Aleppo, in 1517, under pretext of defiring their affiftance in the war with Perfia, fuddenly turned his arms againft them, and took from them fucceffively Syria and Egypt, whither he purfued them. From that time the Turks eftablifhed themfelves in that coun-

---

(a) In 1239, Holagoukan, a defcendant of Djenkiz, put an end to the Caliphat in the perfon of Moftazem.

try ;

try; but they are not settled much among the villages. We rarely meet with any individuals of that nation, except at Cairo; there they exercise the arts, and occupy the religious and military employments. Formerly they also were advanced to posts under government, but, within the last thirty years, a tacit revolution has taken place, which, without taking from them the title, has deprived them of the reality of power.

This revolution has been effected by a fourth and last race, of which it now remains for us to speak. The individuals of it, all born at the foot of Mount Caucasus, are distinguished from the other inhabitants by the flaxen colour of their hair, which is entirely different from that of the natives of Egypt. These were found there by the Crusaders in the thirteenth century, and called by them Mamelus, or, more correctly, Mamlouks. After remaining almost annihilated for two hundred and thirty years, under the government of the Ottomans, they have found means to regain their consequence. The history of this class of soldiers, the events which first brought them into Egypt, the

manner

manner in which they have continued, and re-eſtabliſhed themſelves in that country, and the nature of their government, are political phænomena of ſo very ſingular a nature, that they well deſerve we ſhould beſtow a few pages in giving a diſtinct account of them.

CHAP. VII.

A summary of the history of the Mamlouks.

THE Greeks of Conftantinople, debafed by
a defpotic and bigoted government, had feen,
in the courfe of the feventh century, the fineft
provinces of their empire fall a prey to a new
people. The Arabs, inflamed by the fana-
ticifm of their religion, and ftill more by
the enjoyment of luxuries to which they had
hitherto been ftrangers, conquered, within
eighty years, the whole north of Africa, as far
as the Canaries, and all the fouth of Afia, quite
to the river Indus, and the Tartarian deferts.
But the book of the Prophet, which prefcribed
them their ablutions, fafts, and prayers, did
not teach them either the fcience of legifla-
tion, or thofe principles of natural morality
which are the folid foundations of empires
and focieties. The Arabs knew how to con-
quer, but by no means to govern : wherefore,
the misfhapen edifice of their power foon
mouldered into ruins. The vaft empire of
the Caliphs, paffing from defpotifm to anarchy,

chy, was difmembered on every fide; and the temporal governors, undeceived refpecting the fanctity of their fpiritual chief, every where erected themfelves into fovereigns, and formed independent ftates.

Egypt was not the laft to follow this example; but it was not till 969, *(b)* that a regular power was eftablifhed, in that country, in the perfon of princes, who, affuming the name of Fatmite Caliphs, difputed, even the title of their dignity, with thofe of Bagdad. The latter, at this period, ftripped of their authority, by the Turkmen foldiers, were no longer capable of oppofing their pretenfions. Thus did the Egyptian Caliphs peaceably obtain poffeffion of that rich country, of which they might have formed a powerful ftate. But the whole hiftory of the Arabs uniformly tends to prove that this nation never knew the fcience of government. The fovereigns of Egypt, no lefs defpotic than thofe of Bagdad, proceeded, by like fteps, to the fame deftruction. They took part in the quarrels of religious fects; they even fet up new ones, and endeavoured to make profelytes by perfecution. One of them,

(b) Or, 972, according to D'Herbelot.

named *Hakem b'amr ellah, (c)* was fo abfurdly
extravagant as to declare himfelf an incarnate
God, and barbarous enough to fet fire to
Cairo, for his amufement.   Others diffipated
the public treafure in a capricious luxury.
The people, whom they oppreffed, held them
in abhorrence, and their own courtiers, em-
boldened by their weaknefs, were eager to
fhare their fpoils.   Thus it happened to Ad-
had-el-din, the laft of that race.   After having been invaded by the crufaders, who had
impofed on him a tribute, one of his generals,
whom he had difmiffed his fervice, threatened
to deprive him of a power of which he fhewed
himfelf fo unworthy.   Knowing, that he was
incapable of refifting by himfelf, and unable
to confide in a nation he had alienated from
him, he had recourfe to foreigners.   In vain
did reafon and experience dictate to him that
thefe, once employed as his defenders, would
foon become the mafters of his perfon; one
falfe ftep neceffarily led to a fecond.   He
called in that tribe of Turkmans who had en-

(c) *Governor by the command of God.* This is the apoftle
of the *Drufes.* See the curious account of that fingular
people, publifhed in 1786, from the manufcript of M.
Venture de Paradis, and printed for Robinfons.

flaved

flaved the Bagdad caliphs, and implored the aid of Nour-el-din, the fovereign of Aleppo, who, already ravaging Egypt, haftened to fend an army into that country. Thefe troops effectually delivered Adhad from the tribute of the Franks, and the menaces of his general. But the Caliph foon found he had only changed his enemies; they left him nothing but the fhadow of power; and Se-lah-el-din, who took the command of the army in 1171, concluded by ftrangling him. Thus, the Egyptian Arabs were fubjected to ftrangers, whofe princes commenced a new dynafty in the perfon of Selah-el-din.

During thefe tranfactions in Egypt, and while the crufaders were, by their ill-conduct, laying the foundation for their expulfion from Syria, other revolutions were preparing in upper Afia. Djenkiz-Kan, become the fole chief of almoft all the Tartar hordes, was only waiting for a favourable opportunity to invade the neighbouring ftates : an infult committed on fome merchants, under his protection, determined him to turn his arms againft the Sultan of Balk, and the eaftern part of Perfia; which countries, about the year 1218, became the theatre of one of the moft bloody

H 3   devaftations

devaſtations recorded in hiſtory. The Mogols, ſword in hand, pillaging, burning, and murdering, without diſtinction, either of age or ſex, reduced the whole country of Sihoun, quite to the Tigris, to a heap of aſhes ; and paſſing to the north of the Caſpian ſea, extended their ravages even into Ruſſia and the Cuban. This expedition, which took place in 1227, eventually introduced the Mamlouks into Egypt. The Tartars, weary of maſſacring, had brought back with them a prodigious quantity of young ſlaves, of both ſexes ; their camps, and the markets of Aſia, were full of them. The ſucceſſors of Selah-el-din, who, as Turkmans, correſponded with the coaſts of the Caſpian ſea, perceived they had now an opportunity of forming, at a cheap rate, a body of ſoldiers of tried courage, and remarkable beauty ; and about the year 1230, one of them purchaſed to the number of twelve thouſand of theſe young men, who were Tcherkaſſes, (Circaſſians), Mingrelians and Abazans. He had them trained up to military exerciſes, and ſoon obtained a body of the handſomeſt, and beſt ſoldiers in Aſia, though at the ſame time, the moſt mutinous, as he very ſoon experienced.

rienced. This foldiery, like the Pretorian bands, prefently gave laws to their mafter. They became ftill more infolent under his fucceffor, whom they depofed, in 1250, and, fhortly after the difafter of Saint Louis, flew the laft Turkman prince, and fubftituted one of their own chiefs, with the title of Sultan *(d)*, retaining themfelves that of Mamlouks, which fignifies military flaves. *(e)*

Such is this militia of flaves, converted into defpots, who, for many centuries, have continued to give law to Egypt. From their firft eftablifhment, the effects correfponded with the means. Without any other bond of union than the intereft of the moment, or any public right to authority, but that of conqueft, the Mamlouks had no other rule of conduct and government, than the violence of a licentious and infolent foldiery. The firft

(d) The old French writers made Soldan and Soudan of this word, by the frequent change of *ol* into *ou*; as in *fol fou, mol, mou,* &c.

(e) *Mamlouk,* the participle paffive of *malak,* to poffefs, fignifies one *poffeffed* by, or the property of, another; which gives the fenfe of *flave*. But thefe are to be diftinguifhed from domeftic flaves, or blacks, who are called *Abd.*

H 4

leader

leader whom they elected, having found employment for their turbulent spirit in the conquest of Syria, reigned seventeen years; but since him not one of them has governed so long. The sword, the bow-string, or poison, public murder, or private assassination, have been the fate of a series of tyrants, forty-seven of whom are enumerated in the space of two hundred and fifty-seven years. At length, in 1517, Selim, Sultan of the Ottomans, having taken and hanged Toumam Bey, their last chief, put a period to that dynasty.

Agreeable to the principles of Turkish policy, Selim should have exterminated the whole body of Mamlouks; but more refined views induced him, in this instance, to depart from that sanguinary custom. He was sensible that if he established a Pacha in Egypt, with the same authority as the Pachas in the other provinces, the distance from the capital would be a strong temptation to revolt. To prevent this inconvenience, he projected such a form of government that the power, being distributed among the different members of the state, should preserve such an equilibrium as should keep them all dependent on himself. The remnant of the Mamlouks, who had escaped

escaped his first massacre, appeared proper for this purpose; and he next established a Divan, or Council of Regency, composed of the Pacha and the chiefs of the seven military corps. The office of the Pacha was to notify to this council the orders of the Porte, to expedite the tribute to Constantinople, to watch over the safety of the country against foreign enemies, and to counteract the ambitious views of the different parties; on the other hand, the Members of the Council possessed the right of rejecting the orders of the Pacha, on assigning their reasons, nay, even of deposing him; they also must ratify all civil or political ordinances. As for the Mamlouks, it was agreed that from them should be chosen the twenty-four governors, or Beys (*), of the provinces: to them was intrusted the care of restraining the Arabs, superintending the collection of the tributes, and the whole civil government of the country; but their authority was purely passive, and they were only to be considered as the instruments of the determinations of the council. One of

(*) This word the author always writes *Bek*, but we have retained the most customary spelling, though the other is probably nearest the true pronunciation.

them,

them, refiding at Cairo, was to bear the title
of *Shaik-el-beled (f)*, which fhould be rendered *Governor of the city*, in a fenfe merely
civil, that is to fay, unaccompanied with any
idea of military power.

The Sultan likewife .eftablifhed tributes,
one part of which was deftined to pay twenty
thoufand infantry, and a corps of twelve
thoufand cavalry, refident in the country.;
the other, to procure for Mecca and Medina,
the fupplies of corn neceffary for them ; and
the third, to fwell the Kafna, or treafury of
Conftantinople, and to fupport the luxury of
the feraglio. In other refpects, the people,
who were to provide for thefe expences, have
. been confidered, as M. Savary very well obferves, only as mere paffive agents, and remain in fubjection, as heretofore, to all the
rigours of a military defpotifm.

This form of government has not ill correfponded with the views of Selim, fince it
has fubfifted about two centuries ; but within
the laft fifty years, the Porte having relaxed

(f) *Shaik* properly fignifies an old man, *fenior populi*;
it has the fame acceptation in the Eaft as among us, and
means a lord or chief.

from its vigilance, innovations have taken place ; the Mamlouks have increafed, become mafters of all the riches and ftrength of the country, and, in fhort, gained fuch an afcendency over the Turks, that the power of the latter is reduced almoft to nothing. To conceive the nature of this revolution, we muft confider the manner in which the Mamlouks are continued and multiplied in Egypt.

On feeing them fubfifting in this country for feveral centuries, we fhould be led to imagine their race is preferved by the ordinary means ; but if their firft eftablifhment was a fingular event, their continuation is not lefs extraordinary. During five hundred and fifty years that there have been Mamlouks in Egypt, not one of them has left fubfifting iffue ; there does not exift one fingle family of them in the fecond generation ; all their children perifh in the firft or fecond defcent. Almoft the fame thing happens to the Turks ; and it is obferved that they can only fecure the continuance of their families, by marrying women who are natives, which the Mamlouks have always

dif-

difdained *(g)*. Let the naturalift explain why men, well formed, and married to healthy women, are unable to naturalize on the banks of the Nile, a race born at the foot of Mount Caucafus! and let it be remembered, at the fame time, that the

(g) The wives of the Mamlouks, are, like them, flaves brought from Georgia, Mingrelia, &c. Their beauty is a conftant topic among us, and we muft be-lieve it on the credit of fame. But an European, who has only been in Turkey, has no right to give his teftimony on the fubject. Thefe women are more invifible there than the others, and to this no doubt the reputation they have for beauty is greatly owing. I had an opportunity of learning fome particulars concerning them from the wife of one of our merchants at Cairo, who, by dealing in the laces and ftuffs of Lyons, had accefs to all the Harems. This lady, who has more than one claim to form a cor-rect judgment of them, affured me that, among a thoufand, or twelve hundred, chofen women fhe had feen, fhe had not found ten real beauties. But the Turks are not difficult: provided a woman be fair, fhe is handfome; and if fhe be fat, fhe his enchanting: " her countenance " is like the full moon; her haunches are like cufhions," fay they, to exprefs the fuperlative of beauty. They may be faid to meafure them by the quintal. They have befides a proverb worthy the notice of naturalifts: " Take a " fair female for thy eyes, but for pleafure an Egyp- " tian." Experience has proved to them, that the Northern women are colder than thofe of the South.

plants

plants of Europe, in that country, are equally unable to continue their species! Some may refuse to believe this extraordinary fact, but it is not on that account less certain; nor does it appear to be new. The ancients have made observations of the same nature: thus, when Hippocrates *(h)* asserts, that among the Scythians and Egyptians, all the individuals resemble each other, though they are like no other nations; when he adds, that in the countries inhabited by these two races of men, the climate, seasons, elements, and soil possess an uniformity no where else to be found, does he not recognize that kind of exclusion of which I speak? When such countries impress so peculiar a character on every thing native, is it not a reason why they should reject whatever is foreign? It seems, then, that the only means of naturalizing animals, and plants would be to contract an affinity with the climate, by alliance with the native species; and this, as I have before said, the Mamlouks have constantly refused.

The means therefore by which they are perpetuated and multiplied, are the same by

(*h*) Hippocrates, lib. de Acre, Locis et Aquis.

4

which

which they were firſt eſtabliſhed ; that is to
ſay, when they die, they are replaced by
ſlaves brought from their original country.
From the time of the Mogols, this commerce
has been continued on the confines of the
Cuban and the Phaſis *(i)*, in the ſame manner as it is carried on in Africa, by the wars
among the numerous tribes, and by the miſery
of the inhabitants, who ſell their own children for a ſubſiſtence.

Theſe ſlaves, of both ſexes, carried firſt
to Conſtantinople, are afterwards diſperſed
throughout the empire, and purchaſed by the
wealthy. The Turks, when they ſubdued
Egypt, ſhould undoubtedly have prohibited
this dangerous traffic : their omitting this has
been the cauſe of that reverſe of fortune
which ſeems about to diſpoſſeſs them of
their conqueſt, and which many political
errors have been long preparing.

For a conſiderable time the Porte had neglected the affairs of this province; and, in

(i) This country has been at all times a nurſery for
ſlaves ; it furniſhed the Greeks, Romans, and ancient
Aſia with them. But is it not extraordinary to read in
Herodotus, that formerly Colchis (now called Georgia),
received black inhabitants from Egypt, and to ſee the
ſame country, at this day, make ſo different a return ?

order

order to reftrain the Pachas, had fuffered the Divan to extend its power, till the chiefs of the Janifaries and Azabs were left without controul. The foldiers themfelves, become citizens, by the marriages they had contracted, were no longer the creatures of Conftantinople; and a change introduced into their difcipline ftill more increafed thefe diforders.

At firft, the feven military corps had one common treafury, and, though the fociety was rich, individuals, not having any thing at their own difpofal, could effect nothing. The chiefs, finding their power diminifhed by this regulation, had intereft enough to get it abolifhed, and obtained permiffion to poffefs diftinct property, lands, and villages. And, as thefe lands and villages depended on the Mamlouk governors, it was neceffary to conciliate them, to prevent their oppreffions. From that moment, the Beys acquired an afcendancy over the foldiers, who, till then, had treated them with difdain; and this could not but continually increafe, fince their governments procured them confiderable riches. Thefe they employed in creating themfelves friends and creatures. They multiplied their flaves, and, after emancipating them, employed

ployed all their intereſt to advance them in the army, and promote them to various employments. Theſe upſtarts, retaining for their reſpective patrons the ſubmiſſive reverence uſual in the Eaſt, formed factions implicitly devoted to their pleaſure.

By ſuch means Ibrahim, one of the Kiayas, (k) or veteran colonels of the Janiſaries, about the year 1746, rendered himſelf, in reality, maſter of Egypt; he had ſo multiplied and advanced his freed men that, of the twenty-four Beys, which ſhould be their number, no leſs than eight were of his houſehold. His influence too was the more certain, as the Pacha always left vacancies in the number, in order to receive the emoluments. On the other hand, the largeſſes he beſtowed on the officers and ſoldiers of his corps, attached them to his intereſt, and Rodoan, the moſt powerful of the Azab colonels, uniting himſelf with him, completed his power.

The Pacha, incapable of oppoſing this faction, was now no more than a phantom,

(k) The military corps of the Janiſaries, Azabs, &c. were commanded by Kiayas, who, after the firſt year, laid down their employments, and became veterans, with a voice in the Divan.

and

and the orders of the Sultan vanifhed before
thofe of Ibrahim. At his death, which happened in 1757, his houfe, that is, his en-
franchifed flaves, divided among themfelves,
but united againft all others, continued to give
the law. Rodoan, who had fucceeded his col-
league, being expelled and flain by a party of
young Beys, feveral chiefs followed each other
in a very fhort interval. At length, about the
year 1766, Ali Bey, one of the principal ac-
tors in the troubles which attracted the attention of Europe for feveral years, gained a
decided afcendency over his rivals, and, under
the titles of Emir-Hadj, and Shaik-el-Beled,
rendered himfelf abfolute mafter of the country. The hiftory of the Mamlouks being
intimately connected with his, I fhall continue the former, by giving an abftract of the
latter.

C H A P. VIII.

Summary of the History of Ali Bey (1).

THE birth of Ali Bey is subject to the same uncertainty as that of the Mamlouks in general, who, sold by their parents, or carried off

by

(1) Since this chapter was written, M. Savary has published two more volumes on Egypt, in one of which is the life of this same Ali Bey. I expected to have found in it particulars proper to verify or correct my own narrative; but what was my astonishment to perceive, we have hardly a single circumstance in common? This disagreement was so much the more unpleasing to me, since, as I have already differed from him on several other subjects, it may seem, to many readers, as if I made a practice of contradicting that traveller. But, besides that I am not personally acquainted with M. Savary, I protest, that such partiality is no part of my character. How then does it happen that, having been upon the same spot, having necessarily drawn our materials from like sources, our accounts should be so different? I confess I cannot well discover the reason; all I can say is, that, during the six months I lived at Cairo, I carefully enquired of such of our merchants, as, from long residence in the country, and being persons of understanding, appeared to me likely to give the most authentic testimony.

I found

by their enemies, at a very early age, feldom remember much of their origin or their country; or if they do, conceal them. The opinion

I found them agreed on the principal facts, and I had the advantage of hearing the relations they gave me confirmed by a Venetian merchant (M. C. Rofetti) who was one of the confidential friends of Ali Bey, and the counfellor and promoter of his connections with the Ruffians, and his projects refpecting the commerce of India. In Syria I have met with great numbers who had been eye-witneffes of the principal events in the hiftory of Shaik-Daher and Ali Bey; and, from their teftimony, have been able to afcertain the degree of credit due to the information I received in Egypt. During eight months that I refided among the Druzes, I learnt from the Bifhop of Aleppo, formerly Bifhop of Acre, a thoufand anecdotes, the more indubitable, as Ibrahim Sabbar, the Minifter of Daher, was frequently in his houfe. In Paleftine I have lived with Chriftians and Muffulmen, who had been officers under Daher, were at the firft fiege of Yafa (Joppa) with Ali Bey, and defended that place in the fecond againft Mohammad Bey. I have been on the fpot, and examined all the neceffary witneffes. I have received hiftorical notes from the Venetian agent at Yafa, who had a confiderable fhare in all thefe troubles. Thefe are the materials from which I have compiled my narrative. Not but I have met with fome circumftances which are differently related; but from fuch what hiftory is free? Are there not ten different relations of the battle of Fontenoy? All we can hope is to collect what is

moft

opinion the moſt general reſpecting Ali is,
that he was born among the Abazans, a people inhabiting Mount Caucaſus, and which
furniſhes

moſt probable; for I cannot but confeſs I have myſelf
been frequently convinced, on this occaſion, how difficult it is to aſcertain the real truth in any hiſtorical
facts.

Not but I have heard before ſeveral of the ſtories related by M. Savary, who cannot be accuſed of having in-
vented them himſelf, for his account is taken, word for
word, from an Engliſh book, printed in 1783, and entitled
A Hiſtory of the Revolt of Ali Bey, though there are only
forty pages appropriated to that ſubject, the remainder
being common-place remarks on the manners and geography of the country. I was at Cairo when the public
papers gave an account of this work ; and I well recollect
that when our merchants heard of Maria, wife of Ali
Bey ; of the Greek Daoud, his father ; and his finding his
ſon, as Jacob found Joſeph, they were ſtrangely ſurpriſed,
and laughed heartily at the tales trumped up in Europe.
It is in vain, therefore, for the Engliſh Factor, who was in
Egypt in 1771, to appeal to the authority of the Kiaya of
Ali Bey, and a number of Beys, whom he conſulted,
without underſtanding Arabic ; he can never be looked upon
as well informed. I ſuſpect him the more ſince he ſets
out with an unpardonable error, in aſſerting that the
country of Abaza is the ſame as that of Amaſea ; for one
of theſe is a country of Caucaſus, ſtretching towards the
Cuban ; and the other a city of ancient Cappadocia, or
modern Natolia. To conclude, we may find at Paris
Memoirs

furnifhes the flaves in greateft requeft *(m)*.
The merchants, who carry on this traffic,
brought him to one of their annual fales, at
Cairo, were he was purchafed by the brothers
Ifaac and Youfef, Jews, employed in the cuftom-houfe, who made a prefent of him to
Ibrahim Kiaya. It is fuppofed he might
then be about twelve or fourteen years old;
but, in the Eaft, neither Mahometans nor
Chriftians keeping any regifters of births,
their precife age is never known.

Ali performed for his patron the ufual fer-
vices of the Mamlouks, which are nearly
fimilar to thofe of the pages to our Princes.
He received the cuftomary education, which
confifts in learning to manage a horfe well, fire
the carbine and piftol, throw the djerid, ufe the

Memoirs of Ali Bey, collected by a perfon of diftinction,
who has been in Egypt, as well as M. Savary and myfelf,
and thofe Memoirs will fatisfy all doubts which may remain on this fubject.

(m) The Turks hold the Tcherkaffes, or Circaffian
flaves, in the higheft eftimation; next to them the Abazans, next the Mingrelians, after them the Georgians,
after them the Ruffians and the Poles, next the Hunga-
rians and the Germans, then the Negroes, and, laft of
all, the Spaniards, Maltefe, and other Franks, whom
they defpife as drunkards, debauchees, idle, and mutinous.

fabre,

fabre, and even a little reading and writing. In all thefe exercifes he difplayed an activity and fire which obtained him the furname of *Djendali*, or madman. But the folicitude of ambition foon moderated this exceffive warmth. About the age of eighteen or twenty, his patron fuffered him to let his beard grow, that is to fay, gave him his freedom; for among the Turks, to want muftachios and beard, is thought fit only for flaves and women; and hence arifes the unfavourable impreffion they receive on the firft fight of an European. When he had made him free, Ibrahim gave him a wife and revenues, promoted him to the rank of Kachef, or Governor of a diftrict, and, at length, procured him to be elected one of the four and twenty Beys.

Thefe fucceffive promotions, and the power and riches he acquired, awakened the ambition of Ali Bey. The death of his patron, which happened in 1757, opened a free courfe for his projects. He engaged in every intrigue for raifing or difplacing the chiefs, and was the principal author of the ruin of Rodoan Kiaya. After Rodoan, various factions alternately advanced their leaders into

his

his ſtation. He who occupied it in 1762, was Abd-el-Rahman, of little conſequence himſelf, but ſupported by ſeveral confederate houſes. Ali was then Shaik-el-Beled, and ſeized the moment when Abd-el-Rahman was conducting the caravan of Mecca to get him exiled; but he himſelf had his turn, and was condemned to retire to Gaza. Gaza, dependent on a Turkiſh Pacha, was neither ſo agreeable nor ſo ſecure a reſidence as to tempt him to make it his abode; he therefore only made a feint of taking that route, and, on the third day, turned towards the Said, where he was joined by his partizans.

He reſided two years at Djirdja, where he matured his plans for obtaining and ſecuring that power to which he ſo ardently aſpired. The friends his money had gained him at Cairo having at length procured his recall, in 1766, he appeared ſuddenly in that city, and, in one night, ſlew four Beys who were his enemies, exiled four others, and became, from that time, the chief of the moſt numerous party. As he had now poſſeſſed himſelf of the whole authority, he reſolved to employ it ſtill further to promote his ambitious views. No longer contented with the trivial title of

I 4   Bey,

Bey, he could not submit to the supremacy of the Porte, and aimed at nothing less than the title of Sultan of Egypt. To this object all his measures tended; he expelled the Pacha, who possessed only the shadow of power; he refused the accustomed tribute : and, in 1768, even proceeded to coin money in his own name *(n)*.

The Porte did not see without indignation these attacks on her authority; but open war alone could repel them, and circumstances were not favourable. Daher, established in Acre, kept Syria in awe; and the Divan of Constantinople, occupied with the affairs of Poland, and the pretensions of Russia, bestowed its whole attention on the transactions in the North. The usual method of *capidjis* was had recourse to ; but poison, or the poniard, always anticipated the bow-string they bore. Ali Bey, availing himself of these circumstances, pushed forward his enterprizes with success. For several years a port of the

---

(n) After the ruin of his affairs, his piasters fell 20 per cent, because it was pretended they were too much debased with alloy; but a merchant sent ten thousand of them to Marseilles, and made a considerable profit by melting them down.

Said

Said had been occupied by Arab Shaiks under little fubjection. One of them, named Hammam, had formed there a power capable of giving difturbance. Ali began by delivering himfelf from this danger; and, under pretext that this Shaik concealed a treafure entrufted to him by Ibrahim Kiaya, and that he harboured rebels, fent a body of Mamlouks againft him, in 1769, commanded by his favourite Mohammad Bey, who deftroyed in one day both Hammam and his power.

The end of this year was productive of another expedition, which in its confequences muft have affected Europe. Ali Bey fitted out fome veffels at Suez, and, manning them with Mamlouks, ordered the Bey Haffan to fail with them to Djedda, (Gedda), the port of Mecca, which he was to feize on, while a body of cavalry, under the command of Mohammad Bey, marched by land to take poffeffion of Mecca itfelf, which was given up to plunder. His project was to render Djedda the emporium of the Indian commerce; and this plan, which was fuggefted by a young Venetian merchant, *(o)* who pof-

(o) M. C. Rofetti; his brother, Balthazar Rofetti, was to be made commiffioner of the cuftoms at Djedda.

feffed

feffed his confidence, was to make Europe abandon the paffage by the cape of Good Hope, by fubftituting the ancient route of the Mediterranean, and the Red Sea; but the event has proved that the attempt was too precipitate, and, that before gold is introduced into a country, laws fhould be eftablifhed.

Ali, the vanquifher of a petty prince of the Said, and conqueror of the huts of Mecca, from this time thought himfelf formed to command the whole world. His courtiers told him he was as powerful as the Sultan of Conftantinople, and he believed his courtiers. Had he exercifed his reafon, he would have perceived that Egypt, compared with the reft of the empire, conftituted only a very incon-fiderable ftate, and that the feven or eight thoufand cavalry he commanded were no-thing when oppofed to a hundred thoufand Janifaries, whom the Sultan has at his dif-pofal: but the Mamlouks know nothing of geography; and Ali, who viewed Egypt near, found it much larger than Turkey at a diftance. He determined therefore to com-mence his conquefts: Syria, which was in his neighbourhood, naturally prefented the firft object, and every thing was favourable to

his

his views. The war with the Ruffians, which broke out in 1769, occupied all the Turkifh forces in the north. Shaik Daher, in rebellion againft the Porte, was a powerful and faithful ally; and the extortions of the Pacha of Damafcus, by difpofing thofe he oppreffed to revolt, afforded the moft favourable opportunity of invading his government, and meriting the title of the deliverer of nations.

Ali faw perfectly well the advantage of this pofture of affairs, and made no delay in putting his forces in motion. All his meafures being at length taken, he detached, in 1770, under the command of five Beys, a corps of about five hundred Mamlouks, all cavalry, (for they never march on foot), and fent them to take poffeffion of Gaza, in order to fecure an entrance into Paleftine. Ofman, Pacha of Damafcus, no fooner heard of the invafion, than he flew to arms. The Mamlouks, terrified at his activity, and the number of his troops, held themfelves in readinefs to fly at the firft attack; but Daher, the moft indefatigable chief that Syria has feen for many centuries, haftened from Acre, and extricated them from their embarraffment. Ofman, who was encamped near Yafa, fled without even

offering

offering battle; and Daher, making himfelf mafter of Yafa, Ramla, and all Paleftine, opened a road for the grand army he expected.

This arrived about the end of February, 1771 : and the gazettes of that time, ftating it at fixty thoufand men, induced Europe to believe it was an army fimilar to thofe of Ruffia or Germany; but the Turks, and more efpecially thofe of Afia, differ ftill more from the Europeans in their military than their civil cuftoms. Sixty thoufand men with them are very far from being fynonimous with fixty thoufand foldiers, as in our armies. That of which we are now fpeaking affords a proof of this : it might amount in fact to forty thoufand men, which may be claffed as follows. Five thoufand Mamlouk cavalry, which was the whole effective army; about fifteen hundred Barbary Arabs on foot, and no other infantry, for the Turks are acquainted with none; with them, the cavalry is every thing. Befides thefe, each Mamlouk having in his fuite two footmen, armed with ftaves, thefe would form a body of ten thoufand valets; befides a number of fervants and ferradjis, or attendants on horfeback, for the

Beys

Beys and Kachefs, which may be eſtimated at two thouſand : all the reſt were ſutlers, and the uſual train of followers.

Such was this army, as deſcribed to me in Paleſtine by perſons who had ſeen and followed it. It was commanded by the friend of Ali, Mohammad Bey, ſurnamed *Aboudahab*, or father of gold, from the luxury of his tent and capariſons. As to order and diſcipline theſe muſt not be mentioned. The armies of the Turks and Mamlouks are nothing but a confuſed multitude of horſemen, without uniforms, on horſes of all ſizes and colours, riding without either keeping their ranks, or obſerving any regular order.

This rabble took the road to Acre, leaving, wherever they paſſed, ſufficient marks of their want of diſcipline and rapacity. At Acre, a junction was formed with the troops of Shaik Daher, which conſiſted of fifteen hundred Safadians *(p)*, on horſeback, and commanded by his ſon Ali ; twelve hundred Motualis cavalry, having for their leader the Shaik Naſif, and about one thouſand Mograbian in-

(p) Daher's ſubjects were called by his name, becauſe his ſeat of government was originally at Safad, a village of Galilee.

2   fantry.

fantry. . This union effected, and their plan concerted, they proceeded towards Damafcus fome time in the month of April. Ofman had employed this interval in preparations, and had, on his fide, collected an army equally numerous and ill-regulated. The Pachas of Said, *(q)* Tripoli, and Aleppo, had joined him with their forces, and were waiting for the enemy under the walls of Damafcus.

The reader muft not here figure to him-felf a number of complicated and artificial movements, fuch as thofe which within the laft century, have reduced war with us to a fcience of fyftem and calculation; the Afiatics are unacquainted with the firft elements of this conduct Their armies are mobs, their marches ravages, their campaigns mere inroads, and their battles, bloody frays; the ftrongeft or the moft ad-venturous party goes in fearch of the other, which not unfrequently flies without offering refiftance; if they ftand their ground, they engage pell-mell, difcharge their carbines, break their fpears, and hack each other with

---

(q) Pronounced Sêde, in French; in Englifh Said, as above; it is the ancient Sidon.

their

their fabres, for they rarely have any cannon; and when they have they are but of little fervice. A panic frequently diffufes itfelf without caufe; one party flies, the other purfues, and fhouts victory: the vanquifhed fubmit to the will of the conqueror, and the campaign often terminates without a battle.

Such, in a great meafure, were the military operations in Syria, in 1771. The combined army of Ali Bey and Daher marched to Damafcus. The Pachas waited for them; they approached, and, on the 6th of June, a decifive action took place; the Mamlouks and Safadians rufhed with fo much fury on the Turks, that, terrified at the carnage, they immediately took to flight, and the Pachas were not the laft in endeavouring to make their efcape. The allies became mafters of the country, and took poffeffion of the city without oppofition, there being neither walls nor foldiers to defend it. The caftle alone refifted. Its ruined fortifications had not a fingle cannon, much lefs gunners; but it was furrounded by a muddy ditch, and behind the ruins were pofted a few mufqueteers, and thefe alone were fufficient to check this army of cavalry. As the befieged, however, were

already

already conquered by their fears, they capitulated the third day, and the place was to be
furrendered the next morning, when at day-
break a moft extraordinary revolution took
place.

At the moment that the fignal of furrender
was expected, Mohammad fuddenly commanded a retreat, and all his cavalry turned
towards Egypt. In vain did the aftonifhed
Ali-Daher and Nafif fly to demand the caufe
of fo ftrange a meafure: the Mamlouk made
no other reply to their reiterated queftions,
than a haughty menace; and the whole army
decamped in confufion. Nor was this merely
a retreat, but a pofitive flight; they feemed
as if hotly purfued by a victorious enemy;
the road from Damafcus to Cairo was
covered with men on foot, fcattered horfemen, and ftores and baggage they had abandoned. This fingular occurrence was attributed, at the time, to a pretended report
of the death of Ali Bey; but the real folution
of the enigma was a fecret conference which
paffed at night in the tent of Mohammad
Bey. Ofman, finding himfelf too weak to
oppofe thefe combined forces, had recourfe
to artifice. He contrived to introduce to the
Egyptian

Egyptian general a crafty agent, who, under pretence of propofing terms of peace, endeavoured to diffeminate difcord and revolt. He infinuated to Mohammad that the part he was acting was equally ill befitting his honour, and contrary to his intereft; that he was deceived in imagining the Sultan would leave unpunifhed the offences of Ali Bey; that it was a facrilege to violate fo holy a city as Damafcus, one of the two gates of the Caaba *(r)*; that he was aftonifhed that Mohammad fhould prefer the favour of a flave of the Sultan, to that of the Sultan himfelf, and that he fhould fet up a fecond mafter between him and his fovereign; befides, that it was evident this mafter, by daily expofing him to new dangers, was facrificing him both to his own perfonal ambition, and to the jealoufy of his Kiaya, the Copt Rezk.

Thefe reafons, and efpecially the two latter, which were founded on indifputable facts, made a ftrong impreffion on Mohammad and his Beys: they immediately held a

(r) The two great caravans which make the pilgrimage to Mecca, fet out from Cairo and Damafcus.

council, and fwore folemnly, by the fabre
and the Koran, to return without delay to
Cairo. In confequence of this determination,
they decamped fo fuddenly, and abandoned
their conquefts with fuch precipitation, that
the report of their coming preceded their
arrival at Cairo only by fix hours. Ali Bey
was ftruck with terror, and wifhed to have
punifhed his general upon the fpot; but Mohammad appeared fo well fupported, that it
was impracticable to attempt any thing
againft his perfon; it was neceffary to dif-
femble, and Ali Bey fubmitted to this with
the lefs difficulty, as he owed his fortune
to his diffimulation much more than to his
courage.

Though thus deprived, at one ftroke, of
the fruits of fo expenfive a war, Ali Bey did
not renounce his projects. He continued to
fend fuccours to his ally, Daher, and prepared a fecond army for the campaign of
1772; but fortune, weary of effecting more
for him than his own abilities could have
accomplifhed, ceafed to favour him.

The firft reverfe he experienced was in
the lofs of feveral cayaffes, or boats, loaded
with rice, for Shaik Daher, which were taken
by

by a Ruffian privateer, within fight of Damietta; but another, and ftill more ferious
accident, was the efcape of Mohammad
Bey. Ali Bey could not eafily forget the
affair of Damafcus; neverthelefs, from the
remains of that affection we retain for thofe
whom we have ferved, he could ,net bring
himfelf to refolve on having recourfe to
violence, when an expreffion made ufe of by
the Venetian merchant who enjoyed his
confidence fixed his wavering refolution.

" Have the Sultans of the Franks," faid
Ali Bey, one day, to that European *(s)*,
" children as rich as my fon Mohammad ?"
" No, Seignior," replied the courtier, "they
" are careful of that; for they think that
" when children become too great, they are
" often in hafte to enjoy their inheritance."
This infinuation went to the heart of Ali
Bey. From that moment he beheld in Mohammad a dangerous rival, and refolved his
ruin. To effect this, without rifk, he firft
fent directions to all the gates of Cairo, that
no Mamlouk fhould be fuffered to pafs in
the evening, or at night; he then ordered

_____

(s) This anecdote I received from that merchant.

Mohammad

Mohammad into immediate exile in the Said. By thefe oppofite orders he imagined Mohammad would be ftopped at the gates, and that, the keepers taking him into cuftody, he fhould eafily free himfelf from his fears; but chance difconcerted thefe vague and timid meafures. Mohammad, by fome miftake, was fuppofed to be charged with private orders from Ali. He and his retinue were allowed to pafs, and from this moment all was loft. Ali Bey, informed of his flight, gave orders to purfue him; but Mohammad appeared fo well prepared and determined that none dared attack him. He retired into the Said, foaming with rage, and thirfting for vengeance. Even after his arrival there, he had another narrow efcape. Ayoub Bey, an officer of Ali's, feigning great deteftation of the injuftice of his mafter, received Mohammad with tranfport, and fwore upon his fabre and the Koran, to fhare his fortune; but, a few days after, letters were intercepted from this fame Ayoub, to Ali, in which he promifed him, without delay, the head of his enemy. Mohammad, having difcovered the plot, feized the traitor; and, after cutting off his hands

hands and tongue, fent him to Cairo to receive the recompenfe of his patron.

The Mamlouks, however, wearied with the infolence of Ali Bey, repaired in crowds to his rival; and, in about fix weeks, Mohammad faw himfelf fufficiently ftrong to leave the Said, and march towards Cairo. Ali Bey, on his fide, fent his troops againft him; but many of them likewife deferted to the enemy: at length, in the month of April 1772, the armies had a rencounter in the plain of El-Mafateb, at the gates of Cairo, the iffue of which was, that Mohammad and his party entered the city, fabre in hand. Ali Bey, having barely time to make his efcape with eight hundred of his Mamlouks, repaired to Gaza, for the firft time in his life, and endeavoured to get to Acre, to join his ally, Daher; but the inhabitants of Nablous and Yafa cut off his retreat; and Daher himfelf was obliged to open him a paffage. The Arab received him with that fimplicity and franknefs which in all ages have characterized that people, and conducted him to Acre. It was neceffary to fuccour Said (Sidon), then befieged by the troops of Ofman, in conjunction with the Druzes. He

accord-

accordingly marched thither, accompanied
by Ali. Their combined troops formed a
body of about feven thoufand cavalry, and,
at their approach, the Turks raifed the
fiege, and retired to a place a league to the
northward of the city, on the river Aoula.
There, in July 1772, the moft confiderable and
moft methodical engagement of the whole war
took place. The Turkifh army, three times
more numerous than that of the two allies,
was entirely defeated. The feven Pachas
who commanded it took to flight, and
Said remained in the poffeffion of Daher, and
his governor Degnizla.

Ali Bey and Daher, on their return to
Acre, proceeded to chaftife the inhabitants of
Yafa, who had revolted that they might
convert to their ufe the ammunition and
clothing left there by one of Ali's fleets,
before he was expelled from Cairo. The
city, which was held by a Shaik of Nablous,
fhut its gates, and refolved to ftand the fiege.
This commenced in July, and lafted eight
months, though Yafa had no other rampart
than a mere garden-wall, without a ditch;
but in Syria and Egypt they know ftill lefs
of carrying on a fiege than of engagements
in

in the field; at length, however, the befieged capitulated in February 1773.

Ali, now feeling himfelf difengaged, thought of nothing but his return to Cairo. Daher offered to furnifh him with fuccours; and the Ruffians, with whom Ali had contracted an alliance, while treating of the affair of the privateer, promifed to fecond him: time however was neceffary for collecting thefe fcattered aids, and Ali became impatient. The promifes of Rezk, his Kiaya and his oracle, rendered him ftill more defirous to be gone. This Copt never ceafed affuring him that the hour of his return was come; that the afpects of the ftars were moft propitious; and that the downfall of Mohammad was now moft certain. Ali, who like all the Turks, believed firmly in aftrology, and who put the greater faith in Rezk, becaufe he believed his predictions had been often verified, could no longer endure delay; and the news he received from Cairo completed his impatience.

In the beginning of April, letters were fent him by his friends, in which they informed him that the people were tired of his ungrateful flave, and that nothing but his prefence was wanting to expel him. He

K 4   determined,

determined, therefore, to set out immediately, and, without giving the Ruffians time to arrive, departed with his Mamlouks, and fifteen hundred Safadians, commanded by Ofman, the fon of Daher; but he was ignorant that the letters from Cairo were a ftratagem of Mohammad's, and that this Bey had extorted them by force, in order to deceive and lead him into the fnare he was preparing. In fact, no fooner had Ali advanced into the defert which feparates Gaza from Egypt, than he fell in, near Salakia, with a chofen body of a thoufand Mamlouks, who were lying in ambufh, waiting his arrival. This corps was commanded by the young Bey, Mourad, who, being enamoured of the wife of Ali Bey, had obtained a promife of her from Mohammad, in cafe he fhould bring him the head of that illuftrious unfortunate. Scarcely did Mourad perceive the duft which announced the approach of his enemies before he rufhed upon them with his Mamlouks, and threw them into confufion. To crown his good fortune, he met with Ali in the crowd, attacked, and wounded him in the forehead with a fabre, made him prifoner, and conducted him to Mohammad. The latter, who was encamped two leagues in

the

the rear, received his former mafter with all that exaggerated repeᴄt which is fo cuftomary with the Turks, and that fenfibility which perfidy knows fo well how to feign. He provided a magnificent tent for him, ordered him to be taken the greateft care of, ftiled himfelf a thoufand times, " his flave, who " licked the duft of his feet ;" but the third day, this parade of politenefs terminated by the death of Ali Bey, who died, according to fome, of his wounds ; or, as others report, by poifon : the probability of both thefe accounts is fo equal, that it is impoffible to decide between them.

Thus terminated the enterprizes of this celebrated man, who for fome time engaged the attention of Europe, and afforded many politicians hopes of a great revolution. That he was an extraordinary charaᴄter, cannot be denied ; but it is exaggeration to place him in the clafs of great men. The accounts given of him by witneffes highly worthy credit, prove that though he poffeffed the feeds of great qualities, the want of culture prevented them from coming to maturity. Let us pafs over his credulity in aftrology, which more frequently influenced his con-

duᴄt

duct than more substantial motives; let us
not mention his treacheries, his perjuries,
the murders even of his benefactors *(t)*, by
which he acquired, or maintained his power,
the morality of a rude society is doubtless
less rigid than that of a well-regulated state;
but, judging ambitious men on their own
principles, we shall find that Ali Bey either
ill understood, or erroneously pursued his
plan of greatness; and that it was he himself
who paved the way for his own ruin. We
are certainly justified in charging him with
three errors: First, that imprudent thirst
after conquest, which fruitlessly exhausted
his revenue, and his forces, and made him
neglect the interior administration of his
own country. Secondly, the premature indolence to which he resigned himself, exe-
cuting nothing, but by his lieutenants,
which diminished the respect entertained for
his person by the Mamlouks, and encouraged
the spirit of revolt. Thirdly, the excessive
riches he showered on his favourite, which
procured him the influence he abused. Sup-
posing Mohammad virtuous, ought not Ali

(t) Such as Saleh Bey.

to have dreaded the feduction of flatterers, who, in all countries, are the conftant attendants on opulence? In Ali Bey, however, we muft admire one quality, which diftinguifhes him from the multitude of tyrants who have governed Egypt : if a vicious education prevented him from knowing what true glory is, it is certain, at leaft, he was animated with the defire of obtaining it ; and this was never the portion of vulgar minds. He wanted nothing but to be advifed by thofe who knew the true road to it ; and among thofe who are born to command, how few are there who merit this eulogium !

I cannot proceed without a few remarks on an obfervation I remember to have frequently heard made at Cairo. Thofe among our merchants who had witneffed the reign of Ali, and his downfall, after extolling his good government, his zeal for juftice, and his beneficence to the Franks, never failed to exprefs their aftonifhment at his not being regretted by the people ; and thence took occafion to repeat thofe charges of inconftancy and ingratitude with which the orientals are ufually reproached ; but, on maturely examining
every

every circumftance, this does not appear to me fo extraordinary as it may at firft feem.

In Egypt, as in every other country, the judgment of the people is guided by the penury or plenty in which they live; their love or hatred, their cenfure or applaufe, are meafured by the eafe or difficulty with which they can procure the means of fubfiftence, in confequence of the adminiftration of their rulers; nor can this be efteemed an improper criterion. In vain may we tell them that the honour of the empire, the glory of the nation, the encouragement of commerce, and the improvement of the fine arts, require fuch and fuch meafures; every thing is fuper-feded by the neceffaries of life; and when the multitude want bread, they have at leaft a right to withhold their praife and ad-miration. Of what confequence was it to the people of Egypt, that Ali Bey had con-quered the Said, Mecca, and Syria, if thefe conquefts only augmented, inftead of relieving their burthens? The expences incurred by thefe wars, increafed the contributions they were obliged to raife. The expedition againft Mecca alone coft twenty-fix millions of French livres (above one million eighty-three

thoufand

thoufand pounds), and the exportation of
corn for the ufe of the armies, added to the
monopoly of fome merchants in favour, caufed
a famine, which defolated the country during
the whole of the years 1770 and 1771.
When, therefore, the inhabitants of Cairo,
and the peafants in the villages, were dying
with hunger, what wonder if they murmured
againft Ali Bey? Who can blame them for
difapproving of the commerce with India, if
all its advantages were to center in a few
hands? When Ali Bey expended two hundred and twenty-five thoufand livres (above
nine thoufand pounds), in the ufelefs handle
of a *kandjar (u)*, though jewellers might
applaud his magnificence, had not the people reafon to deteft his luxury? This libe-
rality, which his courtiers called virtue, the
people, at whofe expence it was exercifed,
were juftly entitled to ftigmatize as vice.
Had this man any merit in lavifhing what
coft him nothing? Was it an act of juftice to
gratify his favourite at the expence of the
people, or repay with their money his private
obligations, as in the cafe of his purveyor-

(*u*) A poniard carried in the belt.

general?

general *(x)* ? It muſt be confeſſed, that the greateſt part of the actions of Ali Bey were founded much leſs on general principles of juſtice and humanity, than perſonal motives of vanity and ambition. Egypt, in his eyes, was his private property, and the people a vile herd of worthleſs animals, of whom he might difpofe at his pleaſure. Ought we then to be aſtoniſhed, if thoſe whom he treated like an imperious maſter have vilified his fame like mercenary malecontents ?

(x) Ali Bey, fetting out to go into exile, for he was exiled no leſs than three times, was encamped near Cairo, being allowed a delay of twenty-four hours, to pay his debts: a Janifary, named Haſſan, to whom he owed five hundred fequins (one hundred and fifty-fix pounds), came to find him. Ali, thinking he wanted his money, began to make excufes. But Haſſan, producing five hundred more fequins, faid to him, " Thou " art in misfortune, take theſe alfo." Ali, confounded with this generofity, fwore, by the head of the Prophet, that, if ever he returned, he would beſtow on this man unexampled wealth ; and, on his return, created him Purveyor-general : and though he was informed of the fcandalous extortions of Haſſan, never even reprimanded him.

CHAP.

CHAP. IX.

Summary of occurences from the death of Ali Bey to the year 1785.

SINCE the death of Ali Bey, the fate of the Egyptians has not been bettered; his fuccef-fors have not even imitated what was laudable in his conduct. Mohammad Bey, who fuc-ceeded him in April 1773, during a reign of two years, difplayed nothing but the ferocity of a robber, and the bafenefs of a traitor. To colour his ingratitude towards his patron, he at firft pretended to be only the defender of the rights of the Sultan, and the minifter of his will; he therefore remitted to Conftanti-nople the tribute which had been interrupted for the laft fix years, and took the cuftomary oath of unlimited obedience. He renewed his fubmiffion at the death of Ali Bey; and, under pretext of proving his loyalty to the Sultan, demanded permiffion to make war on the Arab Daher. The Porte, who would gladly have folicited this, was happy to per-mit it as a favour: Mohammad was invefted

3 with

with the title of Pacha of Cairo, and every
thing immediately prepared for this expedition.   It may be afked what intereft an Egyptian Governor could have in deftroying the
Arab Daher, in rebellion in Syria? But refined
views of policy had no more fhare in this
than in other meafures. It originated merely
in private refentment. Mohammad Bey could
not forget a reproachful letter written to
him by Daher, at the time of the revolution of Damafcus, nor the part the Shaik had
taken againft him in his quarrel with Ali
Bey.   To hatred was added the profpect of
plunder.   Ibrahim Sabbar *(y)*, Daher's Minifter, was reputed to poffefs prodigious
wealth; and the Egyptian, could he deftroy
Daher, hoped equally to gratify his avarice
and revenge.

He did not hefitate, therefore, to undertake this war, and made his preparations with
all the activity which hatred infpires. He provided himfelf with an extraordinary train of
artillery, procured foreign gunners, and gave
the command of them to an Englifhman,

(y) Sabbâr, with the *r* pronounced thick, which fignifies *dyer*; with the ordinary *r*, it fignifies *plumber.*

named

named Robinfon; he brought from Suez a cannon fixteen feet in length, which had long remained ufelefs; and, at length, in the month of February, 1776, appeared in Paleftine, with an army equal to that he had formerly headed againft Damafcus. On his approach, Daher's forces, which occupied Gaza, defpairing of being able to defend it, retired; he took poffeffion of it, and, without ftopping, marched againft Yafa. This town, which had a garrifon, and whofe inhabitants were all inured to war, fhewed more refolution than Gaza, and determined to ftand the fiege. The hiftory of this fiege would well exemplify the ignorance of thefe countries in the art of war, as a few of the principal particulars will fufficiently evince.

Yafa, the ancient Joppa, is fituated on a part of the coaft the general level of which is very little above the fea. The city is built on an eminence, in the form of a fugar-loaf, in height about one hundred and thirty feet perpendicular. The houfes, diftributed on the declivity, appear rifing above each other, like the fteps of an amphitheatre. On the fummit is a fmall citadel, which commands the town; the bottom of the hill is fur-

VOL. I. L rounded

rounded by a wall without a rampart, of
twelve or fourteen feet high, and two or three
in thicknefs. The battlements at the top are
the only difference by which it is diftinguifhable from a common garden wall. This wall,
which has no ditch, is environed by gardens,
where lemons, oranges, and citrons, in this
light foil, grow to a moft prodigious fize. Such
was the city Mohammad undertook to be-
fiege. It was defended by five or fix hundred
Safadians, and as many inhabitants, who, at
fight of the enemy, armed themfelves with
their fabres and mufkets; they had likewife a few brafs cannon, twenty-four pounders, without carriages; thefe they mounted,
as well as they could, on timbers prepared in
a hurry; and, fupplying the place of experience and addrefs by hatred and courage, replied to the fummons of the enemy by menaces and mufket-fhot.

Mohammad, finding he muft have recourfe
to force, formed his camp before the town;
but was fo little acquainted with the bufinefs
in which he was engaged that he advanced
within half cannon fhot. The bullets, which
fhowered upon the tents, apprized him of his
error; he retreated, and, by making a frefh
                                    experiment,

experiment, was convinced he was ftill too near; at length he difcovered the proper diftance, and fet up his tent, in which the moft extravagant luxury was difplayed. Around it, without any order, were pitched thofe of the Mamlouks, while the Barbary Arabs formed huts with the trunks and branches of the orange and lemon trees, and the followers of the army arranged themfelves as they could: a few guards were diftributed here and there, and, without making a fingle entrenchment, they called themfelves encamped.

Batteries were now to be erected; and a fpot of rifing ground was made choice of, to the fouth-eaftward of the town, where, behind fome garden-walls, eight pieces of cannon were pointed, at two hundred paces from the town, and the firing began, notwithftanding the mufquetry of the enemy, who, from the tops of the terraces, killed feveral of the gunners. This conduct will appear fo fingular in Europe, that the truth of it may be, perhaps, called in queftion; but thefe things paffed only eleven years ago; I have been on the fpot, have feen many who were eye-witneffes, and I efteem it a duty, neither to alter for the better or the worfe, facts, by which the

character

character of a nation may fo well be eftimated.

It is evident, that a wall, only three feet
thick, and without a rampart, muft foon have a
large breach made in it ; and the queftion was,
not how to mount, but how to get through
it. The Mamlouks were for doing it on
horfeback ; but they were made to comprehend that this was impoffible ; and they con-
fented, for the firft time, to march on foot.
It muft have been a curious fight to fee them,
with their huge breeches of thick Venetian cloth, embarraffed with their tucked-up
benifhes, their crooked fabres in hand, and piftols hanging to their fides, advancing, and
tumbling among the ruins of the wall. They
imagined they had conquered every difficulty
when they had furmounted this obftacle ;
but the befieged, who formed a better judgment, waited till they arrived at the empty
fpace between the city and the wall ; there
they affailed them from the terraces, and the
windows, of the houfes, with fuch a fhower
of bullets, that the Mamlouks did not fo
much as think of fetting them on fire, but
retired, under a perfuafion that the breach
was utterly impracticable, fince it was impoffible

fible to enter it on horfeback. Morad Bey brought them feveral times back to the charge, but in vain.

Six weeks paffed in this manner, and Mohammad was diftracted with rage, anxiety, and defpair. The befieged, however, whofe numbers were diminifhed by the repeated attacks; and who did not fee that any fuccours were to be expected from Acre, became weary of defending alone the caufe of Daher. The Muffulmen, efpecially, complained, that the Chriftians, regarding nothing but their prayers, were more in their churches than the field of battle. Some perfons began to treat with the enemy, and it was propofed to abandon the place, on the Egyptians giving hoftages. Conditions were agreed on, and the treaty might be confidered as concluded, when, in the midft of the fecurity occafioned by that belief, fome Mamlouks entered the city; numbers followed them, and attempted to plunder; the inhabitants defended themfelves, and the attack recommenced: the whole army then rufhed into the town, which fuffered all the horrors of war: women and children, young and old, all were cut to pieces; and Mohammad, equally mean and

barbarous,

barbarous, caufed a pyramid, formed of the heads of thefe unfortunate fufferers, to be raifed as a monument of his victory. *(z)* It is faid the number of thefe exceeded twelve hundred. This cataftrophe, which happened the 19th of May, 1776, fpread terror through the country. Shaik Daher himfelf fled from Acre, the government of which he left to his fon Ali, whofe intrepidity is ftill celebrated in Syria, but whofe glory is tarnifhed by his frequent rebellions againft his father. Ali imagined, that Mohammad would pay refpect to the treaty he had made with him; but the Mamlouk, being arrived at the gates of Acre, declared, the price of his friendfhip muft be the head of Daher himfelf. Ali, finding himfelf deceived, refufed to commit this parricide, and abandoned the town to the Egyptians, who gave it up to be plundered. The French merchants, with difficulty, procured an exemption, and foon faw themfelves in moft imminent danger. Mohammad, informed that the wealth of Ibrahim, Kiaya of Daher, had been depo-

---

(z) See Memoirs of Baron de Tott, Part IV.

fited

fited with them, declared that, unlefs it was inftantly delivered up, they fhould all be put to death. The enfuing Sunday was the day appointed for this terrible refearch, when fortune happily freed them and Syria from the impending danger, for Mohammad was feized with a malignant fever, and died, after two days illnefs, in the prime of his age *(a)*.

The Chriftians of Syria are perfuaded his death was a punifhment of the prophet Elias, whofe church, on Mount Carmel, he had violated. They even affirm the prophet appeared to him feveral times in the form of an old man, and that Mohammad was afterwards continually exclaiming—" Take from " me that old man, who diftreffes and terrifies " me." But they who faw this General in his laft moments, have reported at Cairo, to perfons worthy of credit, that this vifion, the effect of a delirium, originated from the reproaches of his confcience on account of fome private murders : indeed, the death of Mohammad may eafily be accounted for from natural caufes, and is to be attributed to the known unhealthinefs of the climate, exceffive heat, immo-

(a) In the month of June, 1776.

L 4   derate

derate fatigue, and the anxiety occafioned by the fiege of Yafa. It may not be improper to remark, in this place, that were we to write the memoirs of modern times, as dictated by the Chriftians of Syria and Egypt, they would no lefs abound in prodigies and apparations, than the hiftories of antiquity.

The death of Mohammad was no fooner known than this whole army made a precipitate retreat, fimilar to that of Damafcus, and tumultuoufly took the road to Egypt. Morad Bey, who had acquired great credit by the favour of Mohammad, haftened to regain Cairo, that he might be enabled to difpute the fupreme command with Ibrahim Bey. The latter, alfo a freed-man and favourite of the deceafed, no fooner learnt the ftate of affairs, than he took meafures to fecure an authority with which he had been entrufted in the abfence of his patron. Every appearance threatened open war; but the two rivals, when each came to confider the power and refources of the other, found themfelves fo equal, as to make them dread the iffue of a combat. They determined therefore on peace, and entered into an agreement, by which the authority was to be divided, on condition that Ibrahim fhould re-

2   tain

tain the title of Shaik-el-Beled : this arrange-
ment was dictated by their common interest.
Since the death of Ali Bey, the Beys and
Cachefs, who owed their promotion to his
houfe *(b)*, had repined in fecret at feeing all
the authority paffed into the hands of a new
faction : the power poffeffed by Mohammad,
formerly their equal, had hurt their pride, and
that of his flaves appeared to them ftill more
infupportable : they refolved, therefore, to
fhake off this yoke, and entered into intrigues
and cabals, which terminated in a union of
the parties under the title of the Houfe of
Ali Bey. The chiefs were Haffan Bey, formerly Governor of Djedda, and furnamed, on
that account, El-djed-daoui ; and Ifmael,
the only remaining Bey of thofe created by
Ibrahim Kiaya. Thefe confederates conducted their plot fo well that Morad and
Ibrahim were obliged to abandon Cairo,
and retire into the Said, where they were
exiled ; but, being foon reinforced by the
refugees, who joined them, they returned,
and routed their enemies, who were three

(b) That is to fay, of whom he had been the patron :
among the Mamlouks, the freed-man is called the child
of the *houfe*.

times

times their number. Ifmael and Haffan, expelled in their turn, fled into the Said, where
they ftill remain. Morad and Ibrahim, jealous of this party, have made feveral efforts
to deftroy it, without fuccefs. They at laft
granted to the rebels a diftrict above Djirdja;
but the Mamlouks, who continually long for
the luxuries of Cairo, having made fome
movements in 1783, Morad Bey thought it
neceffary to make a frefh attempt to extermi-
nate them, and I arrived at the time when he
was making his preparations. His adherents,
difperfed alcng the Nile, ftopped all the boats
they met, and, ftaff-in-hand, forced the
wretched proprietors to follow them to Cairo.
Every body fled from a fervice which was to
produce them no profit. In the city a contribution of five hundred thoufand dollars (c)
was impofed upon commerce; the bakers and
different tradefmen were compelled to furnifh their commodities below prime coft, and
all thefe extortions, fo odious in Europe, were
deemed mere matters of courfe in Egypt.

Every thing was ready in the beginning of

(c) Two million, fix hundred and twenty-five thoufand livres, (109,375 l.)

April,

April, and Morad fet out for the Said.   The
advices from Conftantinople, and the gazettes
of Europe, which re-echoed them, reprefented
this expedition, at the time, as an important
war, and the force of Morad as a powerful
army, and it was fo relatively to the forces he
could raife, and the fituation of Egypt; but
it is no lefs true that it did not exceed two
thoufand horfemen.   To obferve the conftant falfification of news at Conftantinople,
one would believe, either that the Turks of
the capital are wholly ignorant of the affairs
of Egypt and Syria, or that they wifh to impofe on the Europeans.   The little communication there is between them and thefe remote provinces of the empire renders the
former fuppofition more probable than the
latter. On the other hand, it fhould feem as if
our merchants, who refide in the different factories, might procure us authentic information; but they, fhut up in their kans, as in
prifons, concern themfelves but little with
what is foreign to their commerce, and content themfelves with laughing at the newfpapers they receive from Europe.   Sometimes they have attempted to rectify thefe
errors; but their information was fo ill-em-
ployed,

ployed, that they have abandoned fo trouble-
fome and unprofitable an undertaking.

Morad, leaving Cairo, led his cavalry, by
forced marches, along the river ; his baggage
and ftores followed him in boats ; and the
north-wind, which is always moft prevalent,
was favourable to his defigns. The exiles, to
the number of five hundred, were pofted
above Djirdja. They no fooner were apprized of the enemy's approach than they
became a prey to diffenfion ; fome were for
fighting, and others advifed to capitulate ; feveral of them even adopted the latter meafure,
and furrendered to Morad Bey : but Haffan
and Ifmael, continuing inflexible, removed
up the river towards Afouan, followed by
about two hundred and fifty horfe. Morad
purfued them almoft to the Cataract, where
they took poft fo advantageoufly, on rocky precipices, that the Mamlouks, utterly ignorant
how to conduct a war of pofts, held it impoffible to force them. Befides, Morad, dread-
ing left too long an abfence from Cairo
might give encouragement to new projects,
haftened to return thither ; and the exiles, delivered from their embarraffment, returned
likewife to their former ftation in the Said.

In

In a fociety where the paffions of individuals are not directed to one general end,
where each man, attentive only to himfelf,
confiders the uncertainty of the next day,
merely as a motive to improve the advantage of
the moment; where the chiefs, impreffing no
fentiment of refpect, are unable to maintain
fubordination; in fuch a fociety, a fixed and
regular ftate of affairs is impoffible; and the
inceffant jarring of the incoherent parts muft
give a perpetual vibration to the whole ma-
chine. This is what continually happens
among the body of the Mamlouks at Cairo.
Scarcely was Morad returned, when a new
combination of interefts excited new troubles.
Befides his faction, and thofe of Ibrahim, and
the houfe of Ali Bey, there were, at Cairo,
other Beys allied to other houfes. Thefe
Beys, who from their individual weaknefs were
neglected by the ruling Beys, thought proper,
in the month of July, 1783, to unite their
hitherto detached forces, and form a party,
which alfo had its pretenfions to fovereign
power. This league, however, was difcovered
too foon, and the leaders, to the number of
five, found themfelves unexpectedly exiled to
the Delta. To this order they feigned fubmiffion;

miffion; but they had fcarcely left the city, before they took the route of the Said, the ufual and convenient afylum of all the male-contents : they were purfued to no purpofe for a day, through the defert of the Pyra-mids; but they efcaped both the Mamlouks and Arabs, and arrived fafe at Miniah, where they took up their refidence.

This village, fituated forty leagues above Cairo, on the banks of the Nile, which it commands, was well calculated to promote their defigns. Mafters of the river, they could ftop every thing which came from the Said; and they availed themfelves of this advantage : the corn, annually fent from that province, at this feafon, was a favourable circumftance; this they feized; and Cairo, deprived of provifions, was in danger of a famine; while the Beys, and others whofe lands lay in, or beyond, the province of Fayoum, no longer received their revenues, as the exiles had laid them under contri-bution. To remove thefe evils, a new ex-pedition was neceffary. Morad Bey, fa-tigued with the former, refufed to undertake a fecond; and Ibrahim Bey took it on him-felf. In the month of Auguft, notwith-standing ftanding the Ramadan, the preparations were begun; all the boats, and their owners, were feized on, as before. Contributions were levied, and the dealers compelled to fupply the troops.

At length, in the beginning of October, Ibrahim fet out with an army which was thought formidable, fince it confifted of about three thoufand cavalry. It was re-folved to go down the Nile, the waters of the inundation having not yet left the whole coun-try, and the ground continuing to be marfhy. In a few days the armies came in fight of each other; but Ibrahim, who had not the fame fondnefs for war with Morad, did not attack the confederates; he entered into a negociation, and concluded a verbal treaty, the conditions of which were the return of the Beys, and their re-eftablifhment. Mo-rad, who fufpected fome plot againft him-felf, was much diffatisfied with this con-vention; diftruft took place more than ever between him and his rival; and the arrogance difplayed by the exiles, in a general Divan, ftill more increafed his fears. He thought himfelf betrayed, and, to fecure himfelf from treachery, fet out from Cairo with his ad-

4   herents,

herents, and retired into the Said. Open war was expected to be the consequence, but Ibrahim temporized, and, at the end of four months, Morad advanced to Djiza, as if to decide the quarrel by a battle.

For five-and-twenty days the two parties, separated by the river, remained opposite each other, without attempting any thing. A treaty was proposed, but Morad, dissatisfied with the conditions, and too weak to dictate others, returned into the Said, whither he was followed by deputies, who, after four months negociation, at length succeeded in bringing him back to Cairo: the conditions stipulated were, that he should continue to share the authority with Ibrahim, and that the five Beys should be deprived of their possessions. These Beys, perceiving they were given up by Ibrahim, took to flight; Morad pursued them, and the Arabs of the desert having taken them, he brought them back to Cairo, that they might be under his eye. Peace now seemed re-established; but what had passed between the two chiefs had too clearly manifested their respective views to suffer them to continue friends; and each, well convinced that his rival was only watch-
ing

ing an opportunity to deftroy him, kept conftantly on his guard, either to avoid or endeavour a furprize.

Thefe fecret machinations obliged Morad
Bey again to quit Cairo, in 1784; but, forming his camp clofe to the gates, he appeared
fo determined, that Ibrahim, terrified in his
turn, fled with his partifans into the Said,
where he remained till March 1785, when,
in confequence of a new treaty, he returned
to Cairo, where he now fhares, as formerly,
the fupreme authority with his rival, until
fome frefh intrigue fhall afford him an opportunity of taking his revenge.

Such is the fummary of the revolutions
which have taken place in Egypt for fome
years paft. I have not circumftantially related
the various incidents of thefe events, becaufe,
not to mention their uncertainty, they can
neither intereft nor convey information. The
whole is a tiffue of cabals, intrigues, treachery,
and murthers, which could only weary the
reader in the repetition ; it is fufficient if he is
acquainted with the leading facts, and is enabled from them to form juft ideas of the
manners and political ftate of the country,
which fubject I fhall now proceed to difcufs
more amply.

VOL. I.   M   CHAP.

C H A P. X.

Prefent State of Egypt.

SINCE the revolution of Ibrahim Kiaya, and efpecially fince the revolt of Ali Bey, the Ottoman power has become more precarious in Egypt than in any other province. It is true the Porte ftill retains there a Pacha; but this Pacha, confined and watched in the caftle of Cairo, is rather the prifoner of the Mamlouks, than the reprefentative of the Sultan. He is depofed, exiled, or expelled at pleafure; and, on the mere fummons of a herald, clothed in black *(d)*, muft defcend *(e)* from his high ftation. Some Pachas, chofen exprefsly for that purpofe by the Porte, have endeavoured, by fecret intrigues, to recover the power formerly annexed to their title ; but the Beys have rendered all fuch attempts fo dangerous, that they now fubmit quietly to their three years captivity, and confine themfelves to the peaceable enjoyment of their falary and emoluments.

(d) This officer is named *Caracoulouk.*

(e) The formulary of depofition confifts in the word *enzel,* that is, *defcend* from the caftle.

The

The Beys, however, apprehenſive of driving the Porte to adopt ſome violent meaſure,
dare not declare their independence. Every
thing continues to be tranſacted in the name
of the Sultan ; his orders are received, as they
expreſs it, *on the head and on the eyes*; that is
with the greateſt reſpect ; but this ridiculous
appearance of reverence is never followed by
obedience. The tribute is frequently inter-
mitted, and always undergoes great deductions. Various expences are carried to account, ſuch as the maintenance of the canals,
the carriage of the rubbiſh of Cairo to the ſea,
the pay of the troops, the repair of the moſques,
&c. &c. which are all ſo many falſe and
fraudulent charges. Deceit is practiſed reſpecting the degree of inundation ; and nothing ſhort of the dread inſpired by the
Turkiſh Caravelles, which come annually to
Damietta and Alexandria, could procure the
contribution of rice and grain : even in this
too, means are found to diminiſh the effective
ſupplies, by a colluſion with thoſe appointed
to receive them. On the other hand, the
Porte, abiding by her uſual policy, is blind to
all theſe abuſes, well knowing, that to correct
them, will require expenſive efforts, and poſ-

ſibly

fibly an open war, in which the dignity of the empire might fuffer confiderably. Other, and more urgent affairs, have, befides, for fome years paft, made it abfolutely neceffary for the Turks to collect all their forces towards the North. Obliged to beftow all their atten-tion on their immediate fafety in Conftanti-nople, they leave the reftoration of their autho-rity in the diftant provinces to time, and the courfe of events. They take care, however, to foment divifions among the rival parties, that none of them may acquire an eftablifhed power; and this method has been found equally beneficial to the ftate, and advantageous to the great officers, who derive large profits from the rebels, by felling them their influence and protection. The prefent Admiral, Hafan Pacha, has more than once availed himfelf of this practice, fo as to obtain confiderable fums from Ibrahim and Morad.

C H A P. XI.

Military Conſtitution of the Mamlouks.

THE Mamlouks, on obtaining the government of Egypt, adopted meaſures which
ſeem to ſecure to them the poſſeſſion of
the country. The moſt efficacious is the
precaution they have taken to degrade the
military corps of the Azabs and Janiſſaries:
Theſe two bodies, which were formerly
the terror of the Pacha, are now as inſignifi-
cant as himſelf. Of this the corrupt and
wretched government of the Turks has alone
been the cauſe; for, previous to the inſurrec-
tion of Ibrahim Kiaya, the number of Turkiſh
troops, which ſhould conſiſt of forty thouſand
men, infantry and cavalry, had been reduced
to leſs than half that number, by the avarice
of their officers, who diverted the pay to their
own uſe. After Ibrahim, Ali Bey completely
deſtroyed their conſequence. He firſt diſ-
placed all the officers who gave him um-
brage; left unfilled the places that became

vacant;

vacant; deprived the commanders of all influence; and fo degraded all the Turkifh troops,
that at this day the Janiffaries, the Azabs,
and the five other corps, are only a rabble of
artizans and vagabonds, who guard the gates
of thofe who pay them, and tremble in the
prefence of the Mamlouks, as much as the
populace of Cairo. The whole military
force of Egypt really confifts in the Mamlouks. Some hundreds of thefe are difperfed
throughout the country, and in the villages,
to maintain the authority of their corps,
collect the tributes, and improve every opportunity of extortion; but the main body
continually remains at Cairo. From the
computation of well-informed perfons, it appears, their number cannot exceed eight
thoufand five hundred men, reckoning Beys
and Cachefs, common freed-men, and Mamlouks who are ftill flaves. In this number
there are a multitude of youth under twenty
and twenty-two years of age.

The moft powerful houfe is that of Ibrahim Bey, who has about fix hundred Mamlouks. Next to him is Mourad, who has
not above four hundred, but who, by his
audacity and prodigality, forms a counter-

3   poife

poife to the infatiable avarice of his rival:
the reft of the Beys, to the number of eighteen or twenty, have each of them from fifty
to two hundred. Befides thefe, there is a
great number of Mamlouks who may be
called *individual,* who, being fprung from
houfes which are extinct, attach themfelves
fometimes to one, and fometimes to another,
as they find it their intereft, and are always
ready to enter into the fervice of the beft
bidder. We muft reckon likewife fome
Serradjes, a fort of domeftics on horfeback,
who carry the orders of the Beys; but the
whole together does not exceed ten thoufand
horfe. No mention is here made of infantry, which is neither known nor efteemed
in Turkey, efpecially in the Afiatic provinces.
The prejudices of the ancient Perfians, and of
the Tartars, ftill prevail in thofe countries,
where war, confifting only in flight and pur-
fuit, the horfeman, who is beft qualified for
both thefe, is reputed the only foldier; and
as, among Barbarians, the warrior is alone
the man of diftinction; to walk on foot is
held to be degrading, and is, for that reafon
referved for the common people. The Mamlouks, therefore, permit the inhabitants of

Egypt

Egypt to be carried only by mules or affes *(f)*, referving to themfelves the exclufive privilege of riding on horfeback; and of this they make fufficient ufe; for whether they are in town or the country, or if they only make a vifit to the next door, they are never feen but on horfeback. Their drefs, as well as the fupport of their dignity, obliges them to this. This drefs, which does not differ from that of every other perfon in eafy circumftances in Turkey, deferves to be defcribed.

S e c t. I.

Drefs of the Mamlouks.

Firft, they have a wide fhirt of thin cotton, of a yellowifh colour, over which they wear a fort of gown of Indian linen, or the

---

(f) The Franks of all nations are fubjected to the fame humiliating reftriction, but, by proper management, and liberal prefents, this may be got over by ftrangers of confequence, who come only to vifit the country. *Lord Algernon Percy*, now *Lord Louvaine*, and the *Earl of Charlemont*, obtained permiffion to ride on horfeback in 1776.——See Colonel Capper's excellent little work, p. 31. T.

light

light ſtuffs of Damaſcus and Aleppo. This
robe, called *antari*, deſcends from the neck
to the ankles, and folds over the fore-part
of the body, towards the hips, where it is
faſtened by two ſtrings. Over this firſt
covering is a ſecond, of the ſame form
and width, the ample ſleeves of which de-
ſcend likewiſe to the finger ends. This is
called a *coſtan*, and is uſually made of ſilk
ſtuff, richer than the former. Both theſe are
faſtened at the waiſt by a long belt, which
divides the whole dreſs into two bundles.
Above them is a third, which is called
djouba, which is of cloth without lining,
and is made nearly in the ſame manner, only
the ſleeves are cut at the elbow. In winter,
nay frequently even in ſummer, this djouba
is lined with fur, and is converted into a
peliſſe. Laſtly, over theſe three wrappers,
they put on an outer garment, called the *beniſhe*. This is the cloke or robe of ceremony,
and completely covers the whole body, even
the ends of the fingers, which it would be
deemed highly indecent to ſuffer to appear
before the great. The whole habit, when
the beniſhe is on, has the appearance of a
long ſack, from out of which is thruſt a

bare

bare neck, and a bald head, covered with a turban. The turban of the Mamlouks, called a *Kaouk*, is of a cylindrical fhape, yellow, and turned up on the outfide with a roll of muflin artificially folded. On their feet, they wear a fock of yellow leather, which reaches up to the heels, and flippers without quarters, always liable to be left on the road. But the moft fingular part of this drefs is a fort of pantaloon, or trowfers, fo long as to reach up to the chin, and fo wide, that each of the legs is large enough to contain the whole body, and made of that kind of Venetian cloth which the French call *faille*, which, although as pliant as the *d'Elbœuf* cloth, is thicker than the *burre* of Rouen; and that they may walk more at their eafe, they faften, with a running fafh, all the loofe parts of the drefs I have been defcribing. Thus fwaddled, we may imagine the Mamlouks are not very active walkers; and thofe who are not acquainted by experience with the prejudices of different countries, will find it fcarcely poffible to believe, what however is the fact, that they look on this drefs as exceedingly commodious. In vain may we object that it hinders them from walking,

and

and encumbers them, unneceffarily, on horfeback, and that in battle a horfeman, once
difmounted, is a loft man ; they reply, *It is
the cuftom,* and every objection is anfwered.

S e c t. II.

Horfe accoutrements of the Mamlouks.

Let us now examine, whether their horfe
accoutrements are more rational. Since the
Europeans have had the good fenfe to examine
the principles of every art, they have found
that the horfe, in order to move freely
under his rider, fhould be as little harneffed
as the folidity neceffary would permit. This
improvement, which has taken place among
us in the eighteenth century, is ftill very
far from being adopted by the Mamlouks,
who have fcarcely arrived at the knowledge
of the ninth. Continually the flaves of
cuftom, the horfe's faddle among them is a
clumfy frame, loaded with wood, leather,
and iron, on which a truffequin rifes behind,
eight inches in height above the hips of
the horfeman. A pummel before projects four or five inches, fo as to endanger
his

his breaft, fhould he ftoop. Under the faddle, inftead of a ftuffed frame, they fpread three thick woollen coverings, and the whole is faftened by a furcingle, which, inftead of a buckle, is tied with leather thongs, in very complicated knots, and liable to flip. They ufe no crupper, but have a large martingale, which throws them on the fhoulders of the horfe. Each ftirrup is a plate of copper longer and wider than the foot, with circular edges, an inch high in the middle and gradually de-clining toward each end; the edges are fharp, and are ufed inftead of fpurs, to make long wounds in the horfe's fides. The common weight of a pair of thefe ftir-rups is between nine and ten pounds, and frequently exceeds twelve or thirteen. The faddle and faddle-cloths do not weigh lefs than five-and-twenty; thus the horfe's fur-niture weighs above fix-and-thirty pounds, which is fo much the more ridiculous, as the Egyptian horfes are very fmall.

The bridle is equally ill contrived; it is a kind of fnaffle, but without a joint, and with a curb, which, being only an iron ring, binds the jaw fo as to lacerate the fkin, fo that the bars are injured, and the horfe ab-

felutely

folutely has no mouth. This necessarily refults from the practice of the Mamlouks, who, inftead of managing the mouth, like us, deftroy it by violent and fudden checks, which they employ particularly in a manœuvre peculiar to them. This confifts in putting the horfe on a full gallop, and fuddenly ftopping him, when at his higheft fpeed. Checked thus by the bit, the horfe bends in his hind legs, ftiffens the fore, and flides along like a horfe of wood. How much this manœuvre muft injure the legs and mouth may eafily be conceived; but the Mamlouks think it graceful, and it is adapted to their mode of fighting. Notwithftanding however their fhort ftirrups, and the perpetual motion of their bodies, it cannot be denied that they are firm and vigorous horfemen, and that they have a warlike appearance, which pleafes the eye even of a ftranger; it muft alfo be allowed, they have fhewn more judgment in the choice of their arms.

SECT

S E C T.   III.

Arms of the Mamlouks.

Their principal weapon is an Englifh carbine, about thirty inches long, and of fo large a bore as to difcharge ten or twelve balls at a time, which, even without fkill, cannot fail of great execution. They befides carry at their belt two large piftols, which are faftened to fome part of their garments by a filk ftring. At the bow of the faddle fometimes hangs a heavy mace, to knock down their enemy, and on the left thigh is fufpended, by a fhoulder-belt, a crooked fabre, of a kind little known in Europe; the length of the blade, in a right line, from the hilt to the point, is not more than twenty-four inches, but meafured in the curve is at leaft thirty. This form, which appears whimfical to us, has not been adopted without motives ; experience teaches us, that the effect of a ftrait blade is limited to the place and moment of its fall, as it acts merely from preffure : a crooked blade, on the contrary, prefenting its edge in re-
tiring,

tiring, flides by the effort of the arm, and continues its action longer. The Barbarians, who generally apply themfelves moft to the deftructive arts, have not fuffered this obfer-vation to efcape them; and hence the ufe of fcymetars, fo general and fo ancient in the Eaftern world. The Mamlouks commonly procure theirs from Conftantinople, and from Europe; but the Beys rival each other in Perfian blades, and in fabres of the ancient fteel of Damafcus (g), for which they frequently pay as high as forty or fifty pounds fterling. The qualities they efteem in them are lightnefs, the equality and ring of the temper, the waving of the iron, and, above all, the keennefs of the edge, which it muft be allowed is exquifite; but thefe blades have the defect of being as brittle as glafs.

S E C T. IV.

Education and Exercifes of the Mamlouks.

The art of ufing thefe arms conftitutes the education of the Mamlouks, and the whole occupation of their lives. Every day, early

(g) I fay ancient, for fteel is now no longer made there.

in

in the morning, the greater part of them refort to a plain, without Cairo, and there,
riding full fpeed, exercife themfelves in drawing out their carbine expeditioufly from the
bandaleer, difcharging it with good aim, and
then throwing it under their thigh, to feize a
piftol, which they fire and throw over their
fhoulder; immediately firing a fecond, and
throwing it in the fame manner, trufting to
the ftring by which they are faftened, without
lofing time to return them to their place.
The Beys who are prefent encourage them;
and whoever breaks the earthen veffel which
ferves by way of butt, receives great com-
mendations and money, as a recompenfe.
They practife alfo the management of the
fabre, and efpecially the *coup de revers* which
cuts upwards, and is the moft difficult to
parry. Their blades are fo keen, and they
handle them fo well, that many of them can
cut a clew of wet cotton, like a piece of butter. They likewife fhoot with bows and
arrows, though they no longer ufe them in
battle. But their favourite exercife is throwing the *djerid:* this word, which properly
means a reed, is generally ufed to fignify any
ftaff thrown by the hand, after the manner of

the

the Roman pilum. Inſtead of a ſtaff, the Mamlouks make uſe of branches of the palm-tree, freſh ſtripped. Theſe branches, which have the form of the ſtalk of an artichoke, are four feet long, and weigh five or ſix pounds. Armed with theſe, the Cavaliers enter the liſts, and, riding full ſpeed, throw them at each other from a conſiderable diſtance. The aſſailant, as ſoon as he has thrown, turns his horſe, and his antagoniſt purſues, and throws his in his turn. The horſes, accuſtomed to this exerciſe, ſecond their maſters ſo well, that they ſeem alſo to ſhare in the pleaſure. But this pleaſure is attended with danger; for ſome can dart this weapon with ſo much force, as frequently to wound, and ſometimes mortally. Ill-fated was the man who could not eſcape the djerid of Ali Bey! Theſe ſports which to us ſeem barbarous, are intimately connected with the political ſtate of nations. Not three centuries ago they exiſted among ourſelves, and their being laid aſide is leſs owing to the accident of Henry the Second, or to a ſpirit of philoſophy, than to the ſtate of internal peace which has rendered them uſeleſs. Among

N the

the Turks and Mamlouks, on the contrary, they are retained, becaufe the anarchy in which they live continues to render whatever relates to the art of war abfolutely neceffary. Let us now confider whether their progrefs in this art be proportionate to their practice.

SECT. V.

Military Skill of the Mamlouks.

In Europe, when we hear of troops, and of war, we immediately figure to ourfelves a number of men diftributed into companies, battalions, and fquadrons ; with uniforms well fitted, and of different colours, ranks and lines formed, combinations of particular manœu-vres, or general evolutions; and, in a word, a complete fyftem of operations founded on eftablifhed principles. Thefe ideas are juft, relative to ourfelves, but, when applied to the countries of which we are treating, are erroneous indeed. The Mamlouks know nothing of our military arts; they have nei-ther uniforms, nor order, nor difcipline, nor even fubordination. Their troops are a mob,

their

their march a riot, their battles duels, and their war a scene of robbery and plunder, which ordinarily begins even in the very city of Cairo; and, at the moment when there is the least reason to expect it. A cabal gathers together, the Beys mount on horseback, the alarm spreads, and their adversaries appear: they charge each other in the street, sabre in hand: a few murthers decide the quarrel, and the weakest or most timid is exiled. The people are mere cyphers in these affrays. Of what importance is it to them that their tyrants cut each others throats? But it must not be imagined that they stand by indifferent spectators, that would be too dangerous in the midst of bullets and scymetars; every one makes his escape from the scene of action till tranquillity is restored. Sometimes the populace pillage the houses of the exiled, which the conquerors never attempt to prevent. And it will not be improper here to observe, that the phrases employed in the European Gazettes, such as " *The Beys have* " *raised recruits, the Beys have excited the* " *people to revolt, the Beys have favoured this* " *or that party,*" are ill calculated to furnish accurate ideas. In the differences of the Beys, the people are never any thing more than merely paſſive inſtruments.

Sometimes the war is transferred to the country, but the art and conduct of the combatants is not more conſpicuous. The ſtrongeſt, or moſt daring party purſues the other. If they are equal in courage, they wait for each other, or appoint a rendezvous, where, without regarding the advantages of ſituation, the reſpective troops aſſemble in platoons, the boldeſt marching at their head. They advance towards their enemies, mutual defiances paſs, the attack begins, and every one chooſes his man : they fire, if they can, and preſently fall on with the ſabre : it is then the manageableneſs of the horſe and dexterity of the cavalier are diſplayed. If the former falls, the deſtruction of the latter is inevitable. In defeats, the valets, who are always preſent, remount their maſters ; and if there are no witneſſes near, frequently knock them on the head to get the ſequins they happen to have about them. The battle is often decided by the death of two or three of the combatants. Of late years, eſpecially, the Mamlouks ſeem convinced, that as their patrons are the perſons principally intereſted, they

they ought to encounter the greateſt dangers, and therefore preſently leave them the enjoyment of that honour. If they gain the advantage, ſo much the better for all concerned; if they are overcome, they capitulate with the conqueror, who frequently makes his conditions before hand. There is nothing to be gained but by remaining quiet; they are ſure of finding a maſter who pays, and they return to Cairo to live at his expence until ſome new revolution takes place.

S E C T. VI.

Diſcipline of the Mamlouks.

The intereſted and inconſtant character of this militia, is a neceſſary conſequence of its origin and conſtitution. The young peaſant, ſold in Mingrelia or Georgia, no ſooner arrives in Egypt, than his ideas undergo a total alteration. A new and extraordinary ſcene opens before him, where every thing conduces to awaken his audacity and ambition; though now a ſlave, he ſeems deſtined to become a maſter, and already aſſumes the

N 3 ſpirit

spirit of his future condition. He calculates how far he is neceſſary to his patron, and obliges him to purchaſe his ſervices and his zeal; theſe he meaſures by the ſalary he receives, or that which he expects; and as in ſuch ſtates money is the only motive, the chief attention of the maſter is to ſatisfy the avidity of his ſervants, in order to ſecure their attachment. Hence, that prodigality of the Beys, ſo ruinous to Egypt, which they pillage; that want of ſubordination in the Mamlouks, ſo fatal to the chiefs whom they deſpoil; and thoſe intrigues, which never ceaſe to agitate the whole nation. No ſooner is a ſlave enfranchiſed than he aſpires to the principal employments; and, who is to oppoſe his pretenſions? In thoſe who command, he diſcovers no ſuperiority of talents which can impreſs him with reſpect; in them he only ſees ſoldiers like himſelf, arrived at power by *the decrees of fate*; and if it pleaſe fate to favour him, he will attain it alſo, nor will he be leſs able in the art of governing, which conſiſts only in taking money, and giving blows with the ſabre.

From this ſyſtem alſo has ariſen an unbridled luxury, which, indulging the gratifi-

cation

cation of every imaginary want, has opened
an unlimited field to the rapacity of the great.
This luxury is so exceffive, that there is not
a Mamlouk, whofe maintenance cofts lefs
than twenty-five hundred livres (a hundred
and four pounds) annually, and many of
them coft double that fum. At every return
of the Ramadan, they muft have a new fuit,
French and Venetian cloths, and Damafcus
and India ftuffs. They muft often likewife
be provided with new horfes and harnefs.
They muft have piftols and fabres from Damafcus, gilt ftirrups, and faddles and bridles
plated with filver. The chiefs, to diftinguifh
them from the vulgar, muft have trinkets,
precious ftones, Arabian horfes of two or three
hundred pounds value, fhawls of Cafhmire
worth from five-and-twenty to fifty pounds
each, and a variety of peliffes, the cheapeft of
which cofts above twenty pounds *(h)*. The women have rejected the ancient cuftom of wear-
ing fequins on the head and breaft, as not fufficiently fplendid and coftly, and in their ftead

(h) The European merchants, who have adopted this
luxury, do not think they have a decent wardrobe, unlefs its value exceeds twelve or fifteen thoufand livres
(five or fix hundred pounds.)

N 4 have

have fubftituted diamonds, emeralds, rubies, and the fineft pearls; and to their fondnefs of fhawls and furs, have added a paffion for Lyons ftuffs and laces. When fuch luxuries are become the neceffaries of thofe whofe authority is without controul, and who neither refpect the rights of property, nor the life of their inferiors, it is eafy to conceive what muft be the condition of their fubjects who are obliged to furnifh them with whatever their caprice may require.

S E C T. VII.

Manners of the Mamlouks.

The manners of the Mamlouks are fuch, that though I fhall ftrictly adhere to truth, I am almoft afraid I fhall be fufpected of prejudice and exaggeration. Born for the moft part in the rites of the Greek church, and circumcifed the moment they are bought, they are confidered by the Turks themfelves as Renegadoes, void of faith and of religion. Strangers to each other, they are not bound by thofe natural ties which unite the reft of mankind.

mankind. Without parents, without children, the paft has done nothing for them, and they do nothing for the future. Ignorant and fuper-ftitious from education, they become fero-cious from the murders they commit, perfi-dious from frequent cabals, feditious from tumults, and bafe, deceitful, and corrupted by every fpecies of debauchery. They are, above all, addicted to that abominable wick-ednefs which was at all times the vice of the Greeks and of the Tartars, and is the firft leffon they receive from their mafters. It is difficult to account for this tafte, when we confider that they all have women, unlefs we fuppofe they feek in one fex, that poig-nancy of refufal which they do not permit the other. It is however very certain, that there is not a fingle Mamlouk but is polluted by this depravity; and the contagion has fpread among the inhabitants of Cairo, and even the Chriftians of Syria who refide in that city.

CHAP.

C H A P. XII.

Government of the Mamlouks.

SUCH are the men who at prefent govern
and decide the fate of Egypt: a few lucky
ftrokes of the fabre, a greater portion of cun-
ning, or audacity, have conferred on them
this pre-eminence; but it is not to be imagined that in changing fortune thefe upftarts
change their character; they have ftill the
meannefs of flaves, though advanced to the
rank of monarchs.   Sovereignty with them
is not the difficult art of directing to one
common object the various paffions of a numerous fociety, but only the means of poffeffing more women, more toys, horfes, and
flaves, and fatisfying all their caprices.   The
whole adminiftration, internal and external,
is conducted on this principle.   It confifts in
managing the court of Conftantinople, fo as
to elude the tribute, or the menaces of the
Sultan; and in purchafing a number of
flaves, multiplying partifans, countermining
plots, and deftroying their fecret enemies by
the dagger, or by poifon.   Ever tortured by
the

the anxiety of fufpicion, the chiefs live like the ancient tyrants of Syracufe. Morad and Ibrahim fleep continually in the midft of carbines and fabres, nor have they any idea of police or a well-regulated government *(i)*. Their only employment is to procure money; and the method confidered as the moft fimple, is to feize it wherever it is to be found, to wreft it by violence from its poffeffor, and to impofe arbitrary contributions every moment on the villages, and on the cuftom-houfe, which, in its turn, levies them again upon commerce.

Sect. I.

Condition of the People in Egypt.

We may eafily judge that in fuch a country, every thing is analogous to fo wretched

(i) When I was at Cairo, fome Mamlouks carried off the wife of a Jew, who was paffing the Nile with her hufband. The Jew having complained to Morad, that Bey replied in his rough tone of voice : *Well, let the young folks amufe themfelves!* In the evening, the Mamlouks acquainted the Jew that they would reftore him his wife if he would pay them one hundred piafters *for their trouble*; and to this he was obliged to fubmit. This inftance is the more in point, fince in this country women are held more facred than life itfelf.

a government.

a government. Wherever the cultivator enjoys not the fruit of his labour, he works
only by conftraint, and agriculture lan-
guifhes: Wherever there is no fecurity in
property, there can be no induftry to procure
it, and the arts muft remain in their infancy.
Wherever knowledge has no object, men
will do nothing to acquire it, and their
minds will continue in a ftate of barbarifm.
Such is the condition of Egypt. The greater
part of the lands are in the hands of the
Beys, the Mamlouks, and the profeffors of
the law; the number of the other proprietors is extremely fmall, and their property
liable to a thoufand impofitions. Every
moment fome contribution is to be paid, or
fome damage repaired; there is no right of
fucceffion or inheritance for real property;
every thing returns to government, from
which every thing muft be re-purchafed.
The peafants are hired labourers, to whom no
more is left than barely fuffices to fuftain life.
The rice and corn they gather are carried to
the table of their mafters, and nothing is referved for them but dourra or Indian millet,
of which they make a bread without leaven,
which is taftelefs when cold. This bread,
baked

baked by a fire kindled with the dried dung of buffaloes and cows *(k)*, is, with water and raw onions, their only food throughout the year ; and they efteem themfelves happy if they can fometimes procure a little honey, cheefe, four milk, and dates. Flefh meat, and fat, which they are paffionately fond of, make their appearance only on the great feftivals, and among thofe who are in the beft circumftances.

Their whole clothing confifts in a fhirt of coarfe blue linen, and in a clumfy black cloak. Their head-drefs is a fort of cloth bonnet, over which they roll a long hand-kerchief of red woollen. Their arms, legs, and breafts are naked, and the greateft part of them do not even wear drawers. Their habitations are mud-walled huts, in which they are fuffocated with heat and fmoke, and frequently attacked by maladies arifing from uncleannefs, humidity, and unwholefome food ; and, to fill the meafure of their wretchednefs, to thefe phyfical evils are added continual alarms, the dread of the robberies of

(k) The reader will recollect that Egypt is a naked country, which affords no fire-wood.

the

the Arabs, and the extortions of the Mamlouks, family feuds, and all the calamities of
a perpetual civil war.

This is a juft picture of all the villages,
and equally refembles the towns. At Cairo itfelf, the ftranger, on his arrival, is ftruck with
the univerfal appearance of wretchednefs and
mifery. The crowds which throng the
ftreets, prefent to his fight nothing but
filthy rags, and difgufting nudities. It is
true, he often meets with horfemen richly
clad; but this difplay of luxury only renders
the contraft of indigence the more fhocking.
Every thing he fees or hears, reminds him
he is in the country of flavery and tyranny.
Nothing is talked of but inteftine diffenfions,
the public mifery, pecuniary extortions, baf-
tinadoes and murders. There is no fecurity
for life or property. The blood of men is
fhed like that of the vileft animals. Juftice
herfelf puts to death without formality. The
officer of the night in his rounds, and the
officer of the day in his circuit, judge, con-
demn, and execute in the twinkling of an eye,
without appeal. Executioners attend them,
and, on the firft fignal, the head of the un-
happy victim falls into the leathern bag, in
which

which it is received for fear of foiling the place. Were even the appearance of criminality neceſſary to expoſe to the danger of puniſhment, this would be more tolerable; but, frequently, without any other reaſon than the avarice of a powerful chief, or the information of an enemy, a man is ſummoned before ſome Bey, on ſuſpicion of having money. A ſum is demanded from him, and if he denies that he poſſeſſes it, he is thrown on his back, and receives two or three hundred blows on the ſoles of his feet, nay, ſometimes is put to death. Unfortunate is he who is ſuſpected of being in eaſy circumſtances! A hundred ſpies are every moment ready to accuſe him; and it is only by aſſuming the appearance of poverty, that he can hope to eſcape the rapaciouſneſs of power.

SECT. II.

The Miſery and Famine of late Years.

During the laſt three years, the capital of Egypt, and all the country, has preſented a
ſpectacle

fpectacle of the moft deplorable mifery. To the conftant evils of an uncontrouled tyranny, and the confequences of the troubles of the preceding years, were added natural calamities ftill more deftructive. The plague, brought from Conftantinople in the month of November, 1783, made its accuftomed ravages during the whole winter. Not lefs than fifteen hundred dead bodies were eftimated to be carried out of the gates of Cairo in a day *(l)*. The fummer, as is ufual, affwaged its fury; but to this fcourge another equally terrible, foon fucceeded. The inundation of 1783 was not fufficient, great part of the lands therefore could not be fown for want of being watered, and another part was in the fame predicament for want of feed. In 1784, the Nile again did not rife to the favourable height, and the dearth immediately became exceffive. Soon after the end of November, the famine carried off, at Cairo, nearly as

(l) In Turkey, the tombs, according to the cuftom of the ancients, are always without the towns; and as each tomb has ufually a large ftone, and fome mafonry, they conftitute what may almoft be called a fecond town, which may be named, as formerly at Alexandria, *Necropolis*, or the city of the dead.

many

many as the plague; the ftreets, which before were full of beggars, now afforded not a fingle one: all had perifhed, or deferted the city. Nor were its ravages lefs dreadful in the villages; an infinite number of wretches, who attempted to efcape death, were fcattered over the adjacent countries. I faw Syria full of them. In January 1785, the ftreets of Saide and Acre, and every town in Paleftine, were crowded with Egyptians, eafily diftinguifhable by their tawny fkin; and fome of them had wandered even as far as Aleppo and the Diarbekar. The depopulation of thefe two years cannot be precifely eftimated, as the Turks keep no regifters of births, deaths, or the number of the people *(m)*; but it was the received opinion, that the country had loft one-fixth part of its inhabitants.

In thefe circumftances were renewed all thofe dreadful fcenes at the bare relation of which human nature fhudders, and the fight of which impreffes a melancholy horror never to be effaced. For, as was the cafe, during the famine, fome years ago in Bengal, the

(m) They have fuperftitious prejudices againft this practice.

ſtreets and public places ſwarmed with meagre and dying ſkeletons ; whoſe faultering voices implored, in vain, the pity of paſ-ſengers, the common danger having hardened every heart. Theſe wretches expired before the doors of the Beys, who, they knew had large hoards of rice and corn ; and, not unfre-quently, the Mamlouks, importuned by their cries, chaſed them away with blows. Every diſguſting means of appeaſing the rage of hunger was tried, every thing the moſt filthy devoured ; nor, ſhall I ever forget that, when I was returning from Syria to France, in March 1785, I ſaw, under the walls of ancient Alex-andria, two wretches ſitting on the dead carcaſe of a camel, and diſputing its putrid fragments with the dogs.

We have among us, minds of noble and exalted ſentiments, who, though they pay the tribute of compaſſion due to ſuch diſmal cala-mities, find their indignation rouſed, and im-pute it as a crime to the men who will ſub-mit to ſuffer them. They deem thoſe well-deſerving death, who have not the courage to defend themſelves from it, or at leaſt, to ſeek the conſolation of exemplary vengeance. They even go ſo far as to adduce theſe facts

in

in proof of a moral paradox, perhaps rafhly advanced, and endeavour to demonftrate from them the pretended axiom—" that the inha-
" bitants of hot countries, debafed by climate
" and temperament, are deftined, by nature,
" to be the flaves of defpotifm."

But have they maturely examined whether the fame abject fubmiffion is never obfervable in climates they are pleafed to honour with the exclufive privilege of liberty? Have they carefully confidered whether the general facts on which they build be not accompanied with circumftances and acceffaries which make an effential difference in the confequences? In politics, as in medicine, detached phænomena continually lead us into error refpecting the real caufes of the malady. Men are too anxious to erect particular cafes into general rules; and yet thofe univerfal principles, which are fo flattering to the mind, have almoft invariably the defect of being vague. So rarely are the facts on which we reafon exact, and fo liable to miftake is the moft careful obferver, that we ought to be extremely cautious, or we fhall be continually raifing fyftems on imaginary foundations.

In

In the cafe of which we are treating, if we attentively examine the caufes of the debafe-ment of the Egyptians, we fhall find that this people, depreffed by cruel circumftances, are more deferving of pity than contempt, for the political fituation of this country is very unlike that of Europe. Among us, the traces of ancient revolutions are becoming fainter every day; the foreign conquerors have affimilated with the conquered natives; and from this mixture has been formed one national body, all the members of which have the fame intereft. In Egypt, on the contrary, and throughout almoft all Afia, the original inhabitants, enflaved by revolutions, the effects of which are ftill apparent, are become a prey to foreign conquerors, who, mixing with the natives, have formed diftinct parties, whofe interefts are directly oppofite. The ftate is properly divided into two fac-tions; one, that of the conquering nation, who are in poffeffion of all the civil and military employments; and the other, that of the vanquifhed, who conftitute the fubal-tern claffes of fociety. The ruling party affuming, by right of conqueft, an ex-

clufive

clufive title to all property, treat the governed faction as merely the paffive inftrument
of their pleafures, while the latter, in their
turn, deftitute of all perfonal intereft, contribute as little as poffible to the fervice of
the other. Their ftate is that of a flave,
to whom the opulence of his mafter is a
burthen, and who would willingly free himfelf
from his fervitude, were it in his power.

This feeblenefs is another characteriftic
which diftinguifhes the conftitution of thefe
nations from thofe of Europe. In the European ftates, the governments, deriving
from each refpective nation the means of
governing it, find it neither an eafy matter,
nor their intereft to abufe their power. And
even fuppofing they formed diftinct interefts,
they would ftill be unable to obtain unlimited powers. The reafon is, that befides
the multitude called *people*, which, though
powerful from its number, is always feeble
from its difunion, there exifts a middle order,
which, partaking of the qualities of the
governors and the governed, maintains, in
fome meafure, an equilibrium between the
one and the other. This is the clafs of the
opulent and independent citizens, who, dif-

perfed

perfed through the different occupations of
fociety, have a common intereft in feeing
thofe rights of property and fecurity which
they enjoy refpected. In Egypt, on the
contrary, there is no middle ftate; none of
our numerous claffes of nobility; no clergy,
merchants, or landholders, which, in fome
degree, conftitute an intermediate body between the common people and the government.
There, every man is a foldier, or profeffor
of the law, that is to fay, a creature of government; or he is a labourer, an artizan, or
fhopkeeper, that is to fay, one of the people,
and the people above all are deficient in the
firft requifite to combat oppreffion, the art of
combining and directing their force. To
deftroy or to reform the Mamlouks, a general
league of the peafantry is neceffary; and this
it is impoffible to form. The fyftem of oppreffion is methodical. One would imagine
thefe tyrants were every where endued with
an intuitive knowledge of its principles.
Each province, each diftrict, has its governor, and each village its lieutenant *(n)*, who

---

(n) In Arabic *kaiem makam*, literally *locum tenens*, from
which is formed *caimacan*, lieutenant.

watches

watches the motions of the multitude. Single againſt ſuch numbers, he may appear feeble; but the power he repreſents renders him formidable. Beſides, experience proves that wherever a man has the courage to make himſelf maſter he finds enough whoſe meanneſs will ſecond his pretenſions. This lieutenant transfers a portion of his authority to ſome individuals of the ſociety he oppreſſes, and theſe become his ſupporters: jealous of each other, they ſtrive who ſhall beſt merit his favour, and he employs them alternately to effeƈt their mutual deſtruction.

The ſame jealouſies and inveterate hatreds pervade alſo and diſunite the villages. But even ſuppoſing an union which is ſo difficult to take place, what could a crowd of bare-footed and almoſt naked peaſants, with only ſticks, or even with muſkets, effeƈt againſt a body of diſciplined and well-armed cavalry? I am, above all, led to believe Egypt can never ſhake off this yoke, when I conſider the nature of the country, which is but too advantageous for cavalry. If the beſt regulated infantry among us dread to en-

counter

counter the horfe in a plain, how formidable muft they be to a people who are wholly ignorant of the very firft elements of tactics, and who can never poffibly acquire a knowledge which can only be the refult of an experience their fituation denies them. Mountainous countries, alone, afford to liberty its great refources. It is there that fkill and addrefs, favoured by fituation, fupply the deficiency of numbers. The revolters, unanimous, becaufe they are at firft not numerous, acquire every day new ftrength, from the habit of exercifing it, while the oppreffor, lefs active, becaufe he is already powerful, delays his attack, till at length thefe bands of peafants, or plunderers, whom he defpifed, become foldiers inured to war, and difpute with him, even in the plains, the fuperiority in military fkill, and the palm of victory. In flat countries, on the contrary, the firft tumult is fuppreffed, and the ignorant peafant, who does not even know how to throw up an entrenchment, has no other refource but in the clemency of his mafter, and a quiet fubmiffion to his flavery. We fhall therefore find, that no general prin-.

ciple

ciple can be advanced more true than the
following : *That plains are the habitation of
indolence and of flavery, and mountains the
country of energy and freedom (o)*.

In the prefent fituation of the Egyptians,
it is poffible they might not difplay much
courage ; and yet it may not be true that
the feeds of it are wanting in them, or that
it is denied them by the climate. For that
continued effort of the mind, called courage,
is a quality more nearly allied to our moral,
than our phyfical conftitution. It is not the
greater or lefs degree of heat in the climate,
but rather the ardour of the paffions, and

(o) In fact, the ancient and modern nations in general, who have difplayed the greateft activity, were moun-
taineers. The Affyrians, who extended their conquefts
from the Indus to the Mediterranean, came from the
mountains of Atouria. The Chaldeans were originally
from the fame countries; the Perfians who conquered
under Cyrus, defcended from the mountains of the
Elymais, and the Macedonians from Mount Rhodope.
In modern times, the Swifs, the Scots, the Savoyards, the
Miquelets, the Afturians, the inhabitants of the Cevennes,
always free, or difficult to fubject, would feem to prove
this a general rule, did not the exception of the Arabs
and the Tartars indicate fome other moral caufe, common to the plains as well as to the mountains.

the

the confidence we have in our own powers, which enables us to brave danger. Where thefe two requifites do not exift, courage may remain inert ; though circumftances alone are wanting to call it into action. Befides, if any men are capable of this ardour, it fhould be thofe whofe minds and bodies, inured to fuffering by habit, have acquired a hardinefs which blunts the edge of pain, and fuch are the Egyptians. We deceive ourfelves when we reprefent them as enervated by heat, or effeminate from debauchery. The inhabitants of the cities, and men of opulence, may indeed be a prey to that effeminacy which is common to them in every climate ; but the poor defpifed peafants, denominated *fellahs*, fupport aftonifhing fatigues. I have feen them pafs whole days in drawing water from the Nile, expofed naked to a fun which would kill us. Thofe who are valets to the Mamlouks, continually follow their mafters. In town, or in the country, and amid all the dangers of war, hey accompany them every where, and always on foot ; they will run before or after their horfes for days together, and when they

are

2

are fatigued, tie themfelves to their tails rather than be left behind.

The character of their minds is every way correfpondent to the hardinefs of their bodies. The implacability difplayed by thefe peafants in their hatreds, and their revenges *(p)*; their obftinacy in the battles which frequently happen between different villages; their fenfe of honour in fuffering the baftinado, without difcovering a fecret, *(q)* and even the barbarity with which they punifh the flighteft deviation from chaftity in their wives and daughters *(r)*, all prove that their minds, when fwayed by certain

---

(p) When a man is flain by another, the family of the deceafed demand a retaliation from the family of the affaffin, and this vengeance is purfued from generation to generation, without ever being forgotten.

(q) When a perfon has undergone the torture, without difcovering his wealth, he is faid to be *a man*, and this eulogium indemnifies him for his fuffering.

(r) They frequently put them to death on mere fufpicion; and this is equally true in Syria. When I was at Ramla, a peafant came into the market for feveral days, with his cloak ftained with the blood of his daughter, whom he had thus killed: the action indeed was generally approved. Turkifh juftice never meddles with thefe affairs.

preju-

prejudices, are capable of great energy, and that that energy only wants a proper direction, to become a formidable courage. The cruelties and feditions which have fometimes been the confequence of their exhaufted patience, efpecially in the province of Sharkia, indicate a latent fire, which waits only for proper agents to put it in motion, and produce great and unexpected effects.

S e c t.   III.

State of the Arts.

But a powerful obftacle to every fortunate revolution in Egypt, is the profound ignorance of the nation, which equally prevents them from perceiving the caufes of their evils, or applying the neceffary remedies.

As I propofe treating this article, which, like feveral of the preceding ones, is common to all the Turkifh empire, more fully in another place, I fhall not at prefent dwell on particulars. It will be fufficient to obferve, that this ignorance, diffufed through every clafs, extends its effects to every fpecies of

moral

moral and phyfical knowledge, to the fciences, and the fine arts, and even to the mechanical profeffions. The moft fimple of thefe are ftill in a ftate of infancy. The work of their cabinet-makers, lockfmiths, and gunfmiths, is extremely clumfy. Their mercery, their hardware, their gun and piftol barrels, are all imported from foreign countries. With difficulty can you find one watchmaker at Cairo who knows how to repair a watch, and he too is an European. Jewellers are more common there than at Smyrna and Aleppo; but they know not how to mount properly the fimpleft rofe. Gunpowder is made there, but it is coarfe. Sugar is refined there, but it is full of melaffes, and the white is exceffively dear. The only manufacture in any degree of perfection is their filk ftuffs; and the workmanfhip of them is much lefs highly finifhed, and the price far greater than in Europe.

C H A P. XIII.

State of Commerce.

IN this ftate of univerfal barbarifm, it cannot but appear aftonifhing that commerce fhould ftill continue fo flourifhing as we find it at Cairo; but an attentive enquiry into the fources from whence it is derived will explain the reafon.

Two powerful caufes have contributed to render Cairo the feat of an extenfive commerce; the firft of which is, that all the commodities confumed in Egypt are collected within the walls of that city; and all the perfons of property, that is, the Mamlouks and lawyers, are affembled there, and draw thither their whole revenues, without making any return to the country from which they receive them.

The fecond is the fituation, which makes this city a centre of circulation, while by the Red Sea, it correfponds with Arabia and India; by the Nile, with Abyffinia and the interior parts of Africa; and by the Mediterranean, with Europe and the empire of Turkey.

Turkey. Every year a caravan from Abyffinia arrives at Cairo, and brings from a
thoufand to twelve hundred black flaves,
as alfo elephants teeth, gold duft, oftrich-
feathers, gums, parrots, and monkeys *(s)*,
while another, deftined for Mecca, leaves the
extremities of Morocco, and receiving pilgrims even from the river of Senegal *(t)*,
coafts along the Mediterranean, collecting
thofe of Algiers, Tripoli, and Tunis, and
arrives by the defert at Alexandria, confifting of not lefs than three or four thoufand
camels. From thence it proceeds to Cairo,
where it joins the caravan of Egypt. They
then jointly fet out for Mecca, whence they
return one hundred days after. But the pilgrims of Morocco, who have fix hundred
leagues more to travel, do not reach home

(s) This caravan comes by land along the Nile ; it
was with that Mr. *Bruce* returned in 1772, from Abyffinia, after having performed, the moft adventurous journey attempted in the prefent age. In traverfing the defert, the provifions of the caravan fell fhort, and the travellers lived feveral days on *gum* alone.

(t) I faw feveral negroes who came by this caravan,
from the country of the *Foulis*, to the north of Senegal,
and who faid they had feen Europeans in their country.

till after an abfence of more than a year.
The lading of thefe caravans confifts in India
ftuffs, fhawls, gums, pearls, perfumes, and
efpecially the coffee of Yemen.

The fame commodities arrive by another
route at Suez, to which port the foutherly
winds bring, in May, fix or eight and twenty
fail of veffels from Djedda. Cairo does not retain the whole quantity of this merchandize;
but, befides what is there confumed, confiderable profits arife from the duties, and the
fums expended by the pilgrims. On the other
hand, fmall caravans arrive from time to time
from Damafcus, with filk and cotton ftuffs,
oils, and dried fruits. During the favourable
feafon, there are always fome veffels in the
road of Damietta, unloading hogfheads of
tobacco from Latakia, the confumption of
which in Egypt is enormous. Thefe
veffels take rice in exchange, whilft others
arrive fucceffively at Alexandria, bringing
clothing, arms, furs, paffengers, and wrought
filk, from Conftantinople. Veffels come
likewife from Marfeilles, Leghorn, and Venice, with cloths, cochineal, Lyons ftuffs,
and laces, grocery, paper, iron, lead, Venetian fequins, and German dollars. All thefe
articles

articles conveyed by fea to Rofetta in barks called *djerm (u)*, are firft landed there, then re-imbarked on the Nile, and fent to Cairo. From this account, it is not furprizing that commerce fhould continue fo flourifhing in that capital, and we need not hefitate to admit the report of the commiffioner general of the cuftoms, who afferted, that in 1783, Cairo had traded to the amount of near a hundred and fifty millions of livres, (fix million two hundred and fifty thoufand pounds.) But if we examine the channels into which this wealth is poured, if we con-fider that a great part of the merchandize and coffee of India paffes into foreign coun-tries, the value of which is paid in goods from Europe and Turkey; that the confump-tion of the country almoft entirely confifts of articles of luxury completely finifhed, and that the produce given in return is princi-pally in raw materials, we fhall perceive that all this commerce is carried on without contributing greatly to the real riches of Egypt, or the benefit of the people.

(u) A fort of boat which carries an extremely large lateen fail, ftriped with blue and brown, like ticking.

VOL. I.　　　P　　　CHAP.

C H A P.   XIV.

Of the Isthmus of Suez, and the Possibility of effecting a Junction of the Red Sea with the Mediterranean.

I HAVE mentioned the commerce carried on at Cairo, with Arabia and India, by the way of Suez; and this subject naturally leads to a question frequently agitated in Europe; which is, whether it would be practicable to cut through the Isthmus which separates the Red Sea from the Mediterranean, that vessels might arrive at India by a shorter route than by the Cape of Good Hope. The narrowness of the Isthmus induces us to believe it might easily be effected; but, in a journey I made to Suez, the following reasons induced me to change my opinion.

First, It is certainly true, that the space which separates the two seas is not more than eighteen or nineteen ordinary leagues; it is true, also, that this interval is not intersected by mountains, and that, from the tops of the terraces at Suez, we cannot discover,

with

with any telefcopes, a fingle obftacle on the
naked and barren plain to the north-weft;
it is not therefore the difference of levels
which prevents the junction *(x)*; but, the
great difficulty arifes from the nature of the
correfponding coafts of the Mediterranean and
the Red Sea, which are of a low and fandy
foil, where the waters form lakes, fhoals,
and moraffes, fo that veffels cannot approach
within a confiderable diftance. It will therefore be found fcarcely poffible to dig a per-
manent canal amid thefe fhifting fands;
not to mention that the fhore is deftitute of
harbours, which muft be entirely the work
of art. The country befides has not a drop
of frefh water, and to fupply the inhabitants,
it muft be brought as far as from the Nile.

The beft and only method therefore of
effecting this junction, is that which has been

(x) The ancients were of opinion that the Red Sea
was higher than the Mediterranean; and, in fact, if we
obferve that, from the canal of Kolzoum to the fea, the
Nile has a declivity, for the fpace of thirty leagues, this
idea will not appear fo ridiculous; befides that, to me, it
appears probable the level will be found at the Cape of
Good Hope.

P 2 already

already fuccefsfully practifed at different times; which is, by making the river itfelf the medium of communication, for which the ground is perfectly well calculated; for Mount Mokattam fuddenly terminating in the latitude of Cairo, forms only a low and femicircular mound, round which is a continued plain from the banks of the Nile, as far as the point of the Red Sea. The ancients, who early underftood the advantage to be derived from this fituation, adopted the idea of joining the two feas by a canal connected with the river. Strabo (lib. 17.) obferves, that this firft was executed under Sefoftris, who reigned about the time of the Trojan war *(y)*; and this work was fo confiderable as to occafion it to be remarked; " that it was a hundred cubits (or a hundred " and feventy feet) wide, and deep enough " for large veffels." After the Greeks conquered the country, it was reftored by the Ptolemies, and again renewed by Trajan. In fhort, even the Arabs themfelves followed

(y) That is, according to certain calculations of mine, in the time of Solomon. See *Memoire fur la Chronologie Ancienne*, inferted in the *Journal des Sçavans*, of January 1782.

thefe

thefe examples. " In the time of Omar ebn-el-Kattab," fays the hiftorian El Makin, " the " cities of Mecca and Medina fuffering from " famine, the Caliph ordered Amrou, Go- " vernor of Egypt, to cut a canal from the Nile " to Kolzoum, that the contributions of corn " and barley, appointed for Arabia, might be " conveyed that way."

This canal is the fame which runs at prefent to Cairo, and lofes itfelf in the country to the north-eaft of *Berket-el-Hadj*, or the Lake of the Pilgrims. Kolzoum, the Clyfma of the Greeks, where it terminated, has been deftroyed for many ages; but the name and fituation ftill fubfift in a hillock of ' fand, bricks, and ftones, three hundred paces to the north of Suez, on the border of the fea, oppofite the ford which leads to the fpring of El-Naba. I have been on the fpot as well as M. Niebuhr, and the Arabs told me, as they did him, it was called *Kol-zoum*; Danville therefore is deceived, when, copying an error of Ptolemy's, he places Clyfma eight leagues more to the fouthward. I am of opinion that he is likewife miftaken, in fuppofing Suez the Arfinoe of the ancients.

This

This city having been fituated, according to the Greeks and Arabs, to the north of Clyf-ma, we fhould endeavour to trace it according to the words of Strabo *(c)*, " quite at " the bottom of the gulph, as we approach " Egypt," without proceeding however with M. Savary as far as Adjeroud, which is too far to the weftward. We ought to confine ourfelves to the low country, which extends about two leagues from the bottom of the prefent gulph, that fpace being all we can reafonably allow for the retreat of the fea in feventeen centuries.

Formerly thefe diftricts were covered with towns which have difappeared with the waters of the Nile; the canals which conveyed thefe are deftroyed, for in this fhifting foil they are prefently filled up, both by the fands driven by the winds, and by the cavalry of the Bedouin Arabs. At prefent the commerce of Cairo with Suez is only carried on by means of caravans, which wait the arrival, and fet out on the departure of the veffels, that is, towards the end of April,

(c) Strabo, lib. 17.

or

or the beginning of May, and in the courfe of the months of July and Auguft. That which I accompanied in 1783, confifted of about three thoufand camels, and five or fix thoufand men *(z)*. The merchandize con-fifted in wood, fails, and cordage for the fhips at Suez; in fome anchors, carried each of them by four camels, iron bars, carded wool, and lead; it likewife carried bales of cloth, and barrels of cochineal, corn, barley, and beans, Turkifh piaftres, Venetian fequins, and Imperial dollars. All thefe commodities were deftined for Djedda, Mec-ca, and Moka, where they were to be bar-tered for Indian goods, and the coffee of Arabia, which forms the principal article of the returns. There was befides a great num-ber of pilgrims, who preferred the voyage by fea to a land journey; and it alfo carried

---

(z) It remained upwards of forty days affembled, deferring its departure for various reafons; among others, on account of the *unlucky* days, in which refpect the Turks are as fuperftitious as the Romans formerly were. At length it fet out on the 27th of July, and arrived the 29th at Suez, having journeyed twenty-nine hours by the route of the Haouatat Arabs, a league farther to the fouth than the Lake of the Pilgrims.

the

the neceffary provifions, fuch as rice, meat, wood, and even water; for no place in the world is more deftitute of every neceffary than Suez. From the tops of the terraces, the eye, furveying the fandy plain to the north-weft, the white rocks of Arabia to the eaft, or the fea, and the Mountain Mo-kattam, to the fouth, cannot difcern even a fingle tree, or the fmalleft fpot of verdure. Suez prefents no profpect but extenfive yellow fands, or a lake of green water; the ruinous condition of the houfes heightens this melancholy fcenery. The only water which can be drunk is brought from *El-Naba*, or the *fpring*, fituated at the diftance of three hours journey on the Arabian fhore; but it is fo brackifh that without a mixture of rum, it is infupportable to Europeans. The fea might furnifh a quantity of fhell and other fifh; but the Arabs feldom attempt fifhing, at which they are far from expert; when the veffels are gone, therefore, no-body remains at Suez, but the governor, who is a Mamlouk, and twelve or fourteen perfons, who form his houfehold, and the garrifon.

The fortrefs is a defenceless heap of ruins, which

which the Arabs confider as a citadel, becaufe it contains fix brafs four pounders, and
two Greek gunners, who turn their heads
afide when they fire. The harbour is a
wretched quay, where the fmalleft boats are
unable to reach the fhore, except at the
higheft tides. There, however, the merchandize is embarked, to convey it over the
banks of fand, to the veffels which anchor in
the road. This road, fituated a league from
the town, is feparated from it by a fhore
which is left dry at low water; it has no
works for its defence, fo that the veffels
which I have feen there, to the number of
eight-and-twenty at a time, might be attacked without oppofition; for the fhips
themfelves are incapable of refiftance, none
having any other artillery than four rufty
fwivels. Their number diminifhes every
year, fince, by continually coafting along a
fhore full of fhoals, one out of nine, at leaft,
is fhipwrecked. In 1783, one of them, having anchored at *El-Tor*, to take in water,
was furprifed by the Arabs, while the crew
were fleeping on fhore. After plundering it
of fifteen hundred bags of coffee, they abandoned the veffel to the wind, which threw

it

it upon the coaſt. The dock at Suez is ill adapted to repair ſuch damages; ſcarcely do they build a *cayaſſe* in three years. Beſides that the ſea, which, from its flux and reflux, accumulates the ſand upon that coaſt, will at laſt choak up the entrance, and the ſame change will take place at Suez, which has already at Kolzoum and Arſinoe.

Were Egypt under the adminiſtration of a wiſe government, advantage might be then taken of that accident to build another town in the ſame road, which might be done on a cauſeway of only ſeven or eight feet in height, as the tide uſually riſes no more than three feet and a half; the canal of the Nile would be cleanſed and repaired, and the five hundred thouſand livres (near twenty-one thouſand pounds), paid annually to the eſcort of the Arabs of Haouatat and Ayaidi entirely ſaved: in ſhort, to avoid the very dangerous bar of the Bogaz of Roſetta, the canal of Alexandria would be rendered navigable, from whence the merchandize might be conveyed immediately to the Porte. But ſuch are not the cares of the preſent government. The ſmall degree of encouragement it grants to commerce is not even founded on rational motives;

motives; if it be tolerated, it is merely be-
eaufe it furnifhes a means of gratifying rapacity, and is a fource from whence tyranny
perpetually derives profit, without confidering
how foon it may be exhaufted.   The Turks
do not even know how to make advantage
of the eagernefs of the Europeans to com-
municate with India.   In vain have the Englifh and French attempted to concert with
them a plan for opening fuch a paffage; they
either inflexibly refufe, or difcourage every
application.   We fhould be wrong in flattering ourfelves with any durable fuccefs; for
even were treaties concluded, the revolutions
which, between evening and morning, fo
often alter the face of affairs at Cairo, would
render them of no effect, as was the cafe
with the treaty concluded in 1775, between
Mohammad Bey and the Governor of Bengal.
Such befides is the avarice and treachery of
the Mamlouks, that they would never want
pretexts to harafs the merchants, and would
augment, in fpite of every engagement, the
duties on commodities.

Thofe on coffee are at this moment enormous.   The *farde*, or bale of this commodity,
weighing

weighing from three hundred and feventy to three hundred and feventy-five pounds, and cofting at Moka, forty-five pattaques *(a)*, or two hundred and thirty-fix livres Tournois, (nine pounds fixteen and eight-pence), pays in *bahr*, or fea duties, one hundred and forty-feven livres (fix pounds two fhillings and fix-pence), befides an addition of fixty-fiine livres (two pounds feventeen fhillings and fix-pence) laid on in 1783 *(b)*. So that on adding the fix per cent. collected at Djedda, we

---

(a) This is the name given by the merchants of Provence to the dollar of the empire, after the Arabs, who call it *Rial aboutaka*, or *Father of the window*, on account of the arms on the reverfe, which, according to them, refemble a window. The dollar is worth five livres, five fols (four and four-pence halfpenny.)

(b) In May 1783, the fleet of Djedda, confifting of twenty-eight fail, four of which were veffels pierced for fixty guns, brought near thirty thoufand fardes of coffee, which, at the rate of 370 pounds the farde, amount to eleven millions one hundred thoufand pounds weight, or one hundred and one thoufand quintals; but it muft be obferved, that the demand of that year was more than a third greater than ufual. Accordingly, we muft only reckon, on an average, from fixty to feventy thoufand quintals annually. The farde, paying two hundred

we fhall find that the duties nearly equal the prime coft *(c)*.

hundred and fixteen livres (nine pounds), duty at Suez, the thirty thoufand fardes of 1783 produced to the cuftom-houfe fix millions four hundred and eighty thoufand livres Tournois (two hundred and feventy thoufand pounds.)

(c) At Moka – – –		16 livres.
At Suez – – –		147
Extra-duty – –		69
		——
Total of duties –		232
Prime coft – –		236
		——
Total – –		468

adding to which the freight, loffes, and wafte, it is not aftonifhing that the Moka coffee fhould fell at five-and forty, and fifty fols (one and ten-pence, and two and a a penny), the pound in Egypt, and for three livres, (half a crown) at Marfeilles.

C H A P. XV.

Of the Custom-houses and Imposts.

THE administration of the customs forms,
in Egypt, as in all Turkey, one of the principal offices of government. He who exer-
cises it is at once the comptroller and farmer-
general. All the duties on entry, exports,
and the circulation of commodities, depend on
him. He names all the subalterns who collect them. To this he adds the *paltes,* or
exclusive privileges of the natron of Terane,
the kali of Alexandria, the caffia of the Thebais, the senna of Nubia, and, in a word,
is the despot of commerce, which he regu-
lates at his pleasure. His office is never
held for longer than a year. The price
of his contract in 1783, was one thousand
purses, which, at the rate of five hundred
piasters the purse, and fifty sols the piaster,
make twelve hundred and fifty thousand livres, (above fifty-two thousand pounds.) It
is true we must include among the conditions of his farm eventual extortions, or casual
demands ;

demands ; that is, when Mourad Bey, or
Ibrahim, are in want of five hundred thoufand livres, they fend for the commiffioner of
the cuftoms, who cannot difpenfe with advancing them that fum ; but he receives a
warrant in return, which empowers him to
levy this extortion on commerce, for which
he taxes, in a friendly way, the different
corps or nations, fuch as the Franks, the
Barbary Arabs, and the Turks ; and this frequently turns out not a little to his advantage. In fome provinces of Turkey, he
has alfo the collecting of the *miri*, or tax levied
only on the lands. But in Egypt, this adminiftration is entrufted with the Copt writers, who exercife it under the direction of
the fecretary of the ruling Bey. Thefe
writers have regifters of each village, and are
employed in receiving the payments, and ac-
counting for them to the treafury ; they frequently profit by the ignorance of the peafants, in not carrying to account the partial
payments, and by obliging them to difcharge
the debt a fecond time : they often fell the
oxen, the buffaloes, and even the mat on
which thefe wretches lie ; and it may be
truly faid, that they are agents every way

3   worthy

worthy of their masters. The ordinary tax should amount to thirty-three piasters for each *feddan*; that is, to near eighty-three livres (three pounds nine and two-pence) for every yoke of oxen; but this is sometimes carried, by abuse, as far as two hundred livres, (four pounds six and sixpence.) It is calculated that the whole produce of the miri, collected as well in money as in corn, barley, beans, rice, &c. may amount to from forty-six to fifty millions of French money (about two millions sterling) when bread sells at one *fadda* the *rotle*, that is, at five liards (something more than a half-penny) the pound of fourteen ounces.

But to return to the custom-houses; they were managed formerly, according to ancient custom, by the Jews; but Ali Bey having completely ruined them in 1769, by an enormous extortion, they passed into the hands of the Christians of Syria, with whom they still remain. These Christians, who came from Damascus to Cairo, about fifty years ago, consisted at first of but about two or three families; their profits attracted others, and their number is now multiplied to near five hundred. Their original modesty and œconomy

nomy enabled them to gain poffeffion, firft of one branch of commerce, and then of another, fo that at length they were able to take the farm of the cuftom-houfe after the ruin of the Jews. From that time they have acquired great opulence, and taken advantages which may poffibly end by a fate fimilar to that of their predeceffors. Their hour was thought to be come when their chief, Anthony Faraoun, fled from Egypt, in 1784, and went to Leghorn, to enjoy in fafety a fortune of feveral millions; but this event, as it was without example *(d)*, fo it had no confequences.

S E C T. I.

Of the Commerce of the Franks at Cairo.

Next to thefe Chriftians of Syria, the moft confiderable body of merchants is that of the Europeans, known in the Levant under the name of *Franks*. From a very early period

(d) In general the orientals hold the manners of Europe in deteflation, which prevents every idea of emigration.

the Venetians have had eftablifhments at
Cairo, to which they fend fadlery, filk ftuffs,
looking glaffes, mercery, &c. The Englifh
alfo partook of this trade, and fent cloths,
arms, and hardware, which have to this day
preferved their fuperiority of reputation. But
the French, by furnifhing fimilar articles at a
much cheaper rate, have obtained the preference, to the exclufion of their rivals. The
pillage of the caravan which attempted to
pafs from Suez to Cairo, in 1779 *(e)*, has
given

(e) The newfpapers of the day fpoke much of this
pillage, on account of M. de St. Germain, of the ifle of
Bourbon, whofe misfortunes were greatly talked of in
France. The caravan was compofed of Englifh officers
and paffengers, who had landed from two veffels at Suez,
in their way to Europe, by Cairo. The Bedouin Arabs
of Tor, informed that thefe paffengers were richly laden,
refolved to plunder them, and attacked them five leagues
from Suez. The Europeans, ftripped ftark naked, and
difperfed by fear, feparated into two parties. Some of
them returned to Suez ; the remainder, to the number
of feven, thinking they could reach Cairo, pufhed forward into the Defert. Fatigue, thirft, hunger, and the
heat of the fun, deftroyed them one after the other. M. de
Saint Germain alone furvived all thefe horrors. During
three days and two nights, he wandered in this parched and
fandy defert, frozen at night by the north wind, (it was
in

given the laſt blow to the Engliſh; and ſince
that period there has not appeared in either
of

in the month of January) and burnt by the ſun during
the day, without any other ſhade but a ſingle buſh, into
which he thruſt his head among the thorns, or any
drink but his own urine. At length, on the third day,
perceiving the water of *Berket-el-Hadj*, he ſtrove to
make towards it; but he had already fallen three times
from weakneſs, and undoubtedly would have remained
where he laſt fell, but for a peaſant, mounted on a camel, who ſaw him at a great diſtance. This charitable
man conveyed him to his dwelling, and took care of him
for three days with the utmoſt humanity. At the expiration of that time, the merchants of Cairo, apprized of
his misfortune, procured him a conveyance to that city,
where he arrived in the moſt deplorable condition. His
body was one entire wound, his breath cadaverous, and
he had ſcarcely a ſpark of life remaining. By dint of
great care and attention, however, Mr. Charles Magal-
lon, who received him in his houſe, had the ſatisfaction
of ſaving him, and even of re-eſtabliſhing his health.
Much was ſaid at the time of the barbarity of the Arabs,
who notwithſtanding killed no one: at preſent we may
venture to blame the imprudence of the Europeans, who
conducted themſelves throughout the whole affair like
madmen. So great was the diſcord among them, and
they had carried their negligence ſo far, as not to have
a ſingle piſtol fit for uſe. All their arms were at the
bottom of their cheſts. Beſides, it appears that the Arabs
did not act merely from their uſual motives; well in-

Q 2   formed

of thefe towns, a fingle factor of that nation.

The principal article of the French trade
in Egypt confifts, as throughout the Levant,
in light cloths of Languedoc, called firft
Londrins, and fecond *Londrins*. They fell
annually, upon an average, between nine
hundred and a thoufand bales. The profit is
from thirty-five to forty per cent, but their
drawing and re-drawing caufing a lofs of
from twenty to twenty-five, the net produce is only fifteen per cent. The other
articles of importation are iron, lead, groceries,
cochineal, fome laces, and Lyons ftuffs,
various articles of mercery, and dollars and
fequins.

In exchange they take coffee of Arabia,
African gums, coarfe cottons, manufac-
tured at Manouf, and which are re-fhipped
to the French Weft-Indies, untanned hides,

formed perfons affert that the plan was concerted at Conftantinople, by *the Englifh Eaft-India Company's agents*,
who faw, with a jealous eye, individuals entering into
competition with them for the traffic of Bengal; and
what has tranfpired in the courfe of the enquiries into this
affair, has proved the truth of the affertion.

                                    fafranum,

fafranum, fal ammoniac, and rice *(f)*. Thefe articles rarely balance the exports, and the merchant is at a lofs for his returns, not however from a want of a variety of productions, as Egypt furnifhes corn, rice, doura, millet, fefamum, cotton, flax, fenna, caffia, fugarcanes, nitre, natrum, fal ammoniac, honey, and wax; filks alfo and wine might be produced: but induftry and exertion are wanting, becaufe the cultivator would not be permitted to enjoy the fruits of his labour.

The importation of the French is eftimated, *communibus annis*, at three millions of livres (a hundred and twenty-five thoufand pounds). France maintained a Conful at Cairo till 1777, when he was withdrawn on account of the expence. He was transferred to Alexandria, and the merchants, who fuffered him to go without demanding an indemnity, remained at Cairo at the peril of their lives and fortunes. Their fituation, which has not changed, is nearly fimilar to that of the

---

(f) The exportation of corn is prohibited, and Pococke remarked in 1737, that this meafure had been detrimental to agriculture.

Q 3 Dutch

Dutch at Nangazaki ; that is to fay, fhut up in a confined place, they live among themfelves, with fcarcely any external communication ; they even dread it, and go as little out as poffible, to avoid the infults of the common people, who hate the very name of the Franks, and the infolence of the Mamlouks, who force them to difmount from their affes in the middle of the ftreets. In this kind of habitual imprifonment, they tremble every inftant, left the plague fhould oblige them entirely to fhut themfelves up in their houfes, or fome revolt expofe their quarter to be plundered ; left the chief of fome party fhould make a pecuniary demand *(g),* or the Beys compel them to furnifh them with what they want, which is always attended with no little danger.

Nor do their mercantile affairs caufe them lefs uneafinefs. Obliged to fell on credit, they are rarely paid at the ftipulated time. There are no regulations even for bills of exchange, no recourfe can be had to juftice,

(g) They have obferved, that thefe extortions amount, annually, on an average, to fixty-three thoufand livres (two thoufand fix hundred and twenty-five pounds.)

becaufe

becaufe juftice there is always worfe than
bankruptcy. Every thing depends on confcience, and that confcience has been fenfibly
lofing its influence for fome time paft.
Payments are delayed for whole years; frequently they receive no payment at all, and
great deductions are almoft always made.
The Chriftians, who are their principal cor-
refpondents, are, in this refpect, more faith-
lefs even than the Turks; and it is remarkable that, throughout the empire, the character of the Chriftians is greatly inferior to that
of the Muffulmen; they are reduced, however, to the neceffity of letting every thing
pafs through fuch hands. Add to this, that it
is impoffible ever to realize their capital; and
to obtain an outftanding debt they are under a neceffity of giving ftill greater credit.
For all thefe reafons, Cairo is the moft
precarious and moft difagreeable factory of
the Levant. Fifteen years ago, there were
nine French mercantile houfes at Cairo; in
1785, they were reduced to three, and fhortly
perhaps there will not remain one. The
Chriftians of Syria, fettled fome time ago at
Leghorn, have given another fatal blow to

Q 4   the

the French factories at this place, by the immediate correspondence they carry on with their countrymen; and the Grand Duke of Tuscany, who treats them like his other subjects, contributes every thing in his power to the encouragement of their trade.

CHAP.

C H A P. XVI.

Of the City of Cairo.

G RAND Cairo, of which I have already
faid fo much, is fo celebrated a city that it
well deferves a ftill more particular defcription.   This capital does not, in the country,
bear the name of *El-Kahera*, given it by its
founder ; the Arabs know it only by that of
Mafr, which has no known fignification,
but which feems to have been the ancient
eaftern name of the Lower Egypt *(h)*.

This city ftands on the eaftern bank of
the Nile, at the diftance of a quarter of a
league from the river, which deprives it of
a great advantage ; for the lofs of which the
canal, which comes up to it, cannot com-
penfate, fince it contains no running water,
except in the time of the inundation.

(h) This name of *Mafr* has the fame confonants with
that of *Mefr*-aim, ufed by the Hebrews ; which, on account of its plural form, feems properly to denote the inhabitants of the Delta, while thofe of the Thebais are
called *Beni Kous*, or children of Kous.

When

When we hear of *Grand Cairo*, we are led to imagine that it muſt be a capital, at leaſt, like thoſe of Europe; but if we reflect that, even among ourſelves, towns have only begun to be rendered convenient and elegant within theſe hundred years, we ſhall eaſily believe that, in a country where nothing has been improved ſince the tenth century, they muſt partake of the common barbariſm; and, indeed, we ſhall find that Cairo contains none of thoſe public or private edifices, thoſe regular ſquares, or well-built ſtreets, in which the architect diſplays his genius. Its environs are full of heaps of dirt, formed by the rubbiſh which is accumulating every day *(i)*, while the multitude of tombs, and the ſtench of the common ſewers, are at once offenſive to the ſmell and the ſight. Within the walls, the ſtreets are winding and narrow; and as they are not paved, the crowds of men, camels, aſſes, and dogs, with which they are thronged, raiſe a very diſagreeable duſt; individuals often water their doors, and

---

E *(i)* Sultan Selim had appointed boats to carry it to the ſea; but this regulation has been laid aſide, to divert the money to other purpoſes.

to this duft fucceeds mud and peftiferous exhalations. Contrary to the general cuftom of the eaft, the houfes have two and three ftories, over which is a terrace of ftone or tiles; in general they are of earth and bricks badly burnt; the reft are of foft ftone, of a fine grain, procured from the neighbouring Mount Mokattam. All thefe houfes have the appearance of prifons, for they have no light from the ftreet; as it is extremely dangerous to have many windows in fuch a country: they even take the precaution to make the entering door very low. The rooms within are ill contrived. Among the great, however, are to be found a few ornaments and conveniencies, their vaft halls, efpecially, in which water fpouts up into marble bafons, are peculiarly well adapted to the climate. The paved floor, inlaid with marble and coloured earthern ware, is covered with mats and mattreffes, and over all is fpread a rich carpet, on which they fit crofs-legged. Around the wall is a fort of fofa, with cufhions, to fupport the back and elbows; and above, at the height of feven or eight feet, a range of fhelves, decked out with China and Japanefe porcelain. The walls, naked in other refpects,

are

are chequered with fentences extracted from the Koran, and painted foliage and flowers, with which alfo the porticos of the Beys are covered; the windows have neither glafs, nor moving fafhes, but only an open lattice work, which frequently cofts more than our glazing. The light enters from the inner courts, from whence the fycamores reflect a verdure pleaf-ing to the eye. An opening to the north, or at the top of the cieling, admits a refrefh-ing breeze, while, by a whimfical contra-diction, they wrap themfelves up in warm woollen cloths and furs. The rich pretend by this means to efcape difeafes; but the common people, with their blue fhirts and hard mats, are lefs liable to take cold, and enjoy better health.

S E C T. I.

Of the Population of Cairo and Egypt.

The population of Cairo has frequently been a fubject of difpute. If we may credit the head officer of the cuftoms, Anthony Faraoun, cited by Baron De Tott, it approaches feven hundred thoufand fouls, including Boulak, a port and fuburb detached from the city; but all calculations of the number of inhabitants in Turkey are arbitrary, as no regifters are kept of births, deaths, or marriages. The Mahometans have even fuperftitious prejudices againft numbering their people. The Chriftians may indeed be eftimated by means of their tickets of capitation *(k)*. All we know with certainty is, that, according to the plan of M. Niebuhr, taken in 1761, Cairo is three leagues in circumference, which is about the fame with Paris, by the line of the Boulevards. Within this fpace is comprifed a number of gardens, courts, vacant grounds and ruins. Now, if Paris, within the Boulevards, does not contain above feven hundred thoufand inhabitants, though the houfes are five ftories high, it is difficult to conceive that Cairo, where they are only two ftories, can contain more than two hundred and fifty thoufand. It is equally impracticable to form a juft eftimate of the population of all Egypt. Neverthelefs, as it is known that the number of towns and villages does not exceed two thoufand three hun-

(k) Called *karadj* ; *k* is here the Spanifh *jota.*

3

dred,

dred *(l)*, and the number of inhabitants in each of them, one with another, including Cairo itself, is not more than a thousand, the total cannot be more than two millions three hundred thousand. The cultivable lands, according to Danville, contain two thousand one hundred square leagues, whence there results, for each square league, one thousand one hundred and forty-two inhabitants. This number, which is greater than even that of France, may lead us to imagine that Egypt is not so depopulated as it has been represented; but if we observe that the lands never lie fallow, but are continually productive, it must be allowed that its population is very little in comparison of what it has been, and of what it is capable of becoming.

Among the singularities which appear most extraordinary to a stranger at Cairo, may be

(l) Danville had seen two lists of villages in Egypt; one, which is of the last century, gives two thousand six hundred and ninety-six towns and villages; the other, of the middle of the present century, two thousand four hundred and ninety-five, nine hundred and fifty-seven of which are in the Said, and one thousand four hundred and thirty-nine in the Delta: that I have given is of 1783.

mentioned

mentioned the great number of ugly dogs which roam about the ftreets, and the kites which fkim over the houfes, with frequent and doleful cries. The Muffulmen kill neither of thefe, though they are both held to be unclean *(m)*; on the contrary, they often throw them the fragments of their tables ; and devotees even endow charitable foundations of bread and water for the dogs. Thefe animals have befides the refource of the common fewers, which, however, does not prevent them from fuffering greatly by hunger and thirft ; but it is very aftonifhing that thefe extremities never occafion madnefs. Profper Alpinus has already made this remark in his treatife on the Phyfic of the Egyptians. Canine madnefs is equally unknown in Syria; the name of the malady, however, is to be found in the Arabic language, and is not borrowed from any foreign tongue.

(m) The turtle-doves, which are extremely numerous build their nefts in the houfes ; and even the children do not touch them.

CHAP,

C H A P. XVII.

Of the Diseases of Egypt.

S e c t. I.

Of Blindness.

THIS malady, of which so much as been said, is not the only remarkable one in E-gypt; there are several which equally deserve our notice.

Yet nothing can appear more extraordinary to a stranger than the prodigious number of persons whose sight is either lost or impaired, and which is so great, that out of a hundred persons I have met while walking the streets of Cairo, twenty have been quite blind, ten wanting an eye, and twenty others have had their eyes red, purulent, or blemished. Almost every one wears a fillet, a token of an approaching or convalescent ophthalmy; but nothing astonished me more than the indifference and apathy with which they support so dreadful a misfortune. *It was decreed,*

says

fays the Muffulman: *praife be to God! God has willed it,* fays the Chriftian, *bleffed be his name.* This refignation is undoubtedly the beft refource when the evil has happened; but, as it prevents an enquiry into the caufe of the diforder, it precludes the difcovery of its cure. Some phyficians among us have written on this diftemper, but from not being acquainted with all the circumftances, could not treat it with fufficient accuracy. I fhall therefore add a few obfervations, which may affift others in future enquiries.

1ft. Defluxions on the eyes are not peculiar to Egypt; they are alfo frequent in Syria, with this difference, that they are there lefs general; and it is remarkable that the inhabitants of the fea-coaft alone are fubject to them.

2d. In the city of Cairo, which is always full of filth, thefe diforders are more prevalent than in all the reft of Egypt *(n)*. The common people are more liable to them than perfons in eafy circumftances, and the natives more than foreigners. The Mamlouks

---

(n) It muft be obferved, however, that the blind people of the villages come and refide in the *mofque of flowers,* where they have a fort of hofpital.

are

are rarely attacked by them; and the peafants of the Delta, are more fubject to them than the Bedouin Arabs.

3d. Thefe defluxions happen at no certain feafon, notwithftanding what is faid by Prof-per Alpinus. They are an endemial difor-der, common to every month of the year, and to every age.

In reafoning from thefe facts, it feems to me that we cannot admit the foutherly winds as a principal caufe, fince, in that cafe, this complaint would be peculiar to the month of April, and the Bedouins be affected with it like the peafants; nor can we afcribe thefe maladies to any fubtile duft with which the air is filled, becaufe the peafants are more expofed to this than the inhabitants of towns; the cuftom of fleeping on the terraces feems a much more probable caufe (o); but it is nei-ther confined to this country, nor adequate to the effects afcribed to it; for in countries remote from the fea, as the valley of Balbec, the Diarbekar, the plains of Hauran, and the mountains, the inhabitants fleep alfo on their terraces, and yet their fight is not

(o) See De Tott's Memoirs, part IV. T.

injured.

injured. If, therefore, at Cairo, throughout the Delta, and on the coaft of Syria, it is
dangerous to fleep in the open air, this air
muft acquire fome noxious quality from the
vicinity of the fea : and this quality doubtlefs is moifture combined with heat, which
then becomes a firft principle of thefe diforders. The faline quality of the air, fo remarkable in the Delta, contributes ftill farther to this, by the irritation and itching it
occafions in the eyes, as I have myfelf experienced.

The ufual diet of the Egyptians appears
likewife to be a powerful caufe. The cheefe,
four milk, honey, confection of grapes, green
fruits, and raw vegetables, which are the ordinary food of the people, produce in the
ftomach a diforder, which phyficians have
obferved to affect the fight; the raw onions,
efpecially, which they devour in great quantities, have a peculiar heating quality, as the
Monks of Syria made me remark on myfelf.
Bodies thus nourifhed, abound in corrupted
humours, which are conftantly endeavouring
a difcharge. Diverted from the ordinary
channels, by habitual perfpiration, they fly to
the exterior parts, and fix themfelves where

R 2   they

they find the leaſt reſiſtance. They therefore naturally attack the head, becauſe the
Egyptians, by ſhaving it once a week, and
covering it with a prodigiouſly hot head-dreſs,
principally attract to that the perſpiration;
and if the head receives ever ſo ſlight an im-
preſſion of cold, on being uncovered, this
perſpiration is ſuppreſſed, and falls upon the
teeth, or ſtill more readily on the eyes, as
being the tendereſt part. On every freſh
cold this organ is weakened, and at length
entirely deſtroyed. A diſpoſition to this diſorder, tranſmitted by generation, becomes a
freſh cauſe of malady; and hence the natives
are more expoſed to it than ſtrangers. It
will appear more probable that the exceſſive
perſpiration of the head is a principal cauſe,
when we conſider that the ancient Egyptians,
who went bare headed, are not mentioned
by phyſicians as being ſo much afflicted with
ophthalmies *(p)*; and that the Arabs of the
deſert, who cover it very little, eſpecially
when young, are equally exempt from
them.

(*p*) Hiſtory, however, informs us that ſeveral of the
Pharaohs died blind.

S E C T.

S E C T. II.

Of the Small Pox.

Blindneſs in Egypt is in many inſtances occaſioned by the conſequences of the ſmall pox. This diſorder, which is very fatal in that country, is not treated after a good method. During the three firſt days, *debs*, or confection of grapes, honey, and ſugar, are adminiſtered to the ſick, and, after the ſeventh, they are allowed milk, meat, and ſalt-fiſh, as if they were in full health; at the period of ſuppuration, they are never purged, and they particularly avoid waſhing their eyes, though they are full of pus, and their eyelids cloſed by the glutinous matter; this operation they never perform till after forty days, and, in that time, the pus, by irritating the ball, has produced an inflammation which affects the whole eye. Inoculation is not unknown among them, but they make little uſe of it; nor is it more practiſed by the Syrians and the inhabitants of

Anadolia,

Anadolia, who have long been acquainted with it *(q)*.

This improper regimen is certainly far more pernicious than the climate, which is by no means unhealthy *(r)*. To unwhole-fome food, efpecially, muft we attribute both the deformity of the beggars, and the mifer-able appearance of the children at Cairo, which are no where to be met with fo mif-fhapen and wretched. Their hollow eyes, their pale and puffed faces, fwollen bellies, meagre extremities, and yellow fkins, make them always feem as if they had not long to live. Their ignorant mothers pretend that this is the effect of the *evil eye* of fome envious per-fon, which has bewitched them; and this ancient prejudice *(s)* is ftill general in Tur-key; but the real caufe is the badnefs of their food. In fpite of the *Talifmans*, there-

---

(q) They perform the operation by inferting a thread into the flefh, or by making the patient inhale, or fwal-low, the powder of dried puftules.

(r) The Mamlouks are a proof of this, who, from wholefome diet, and a proper regimen, enjoy the moft robuft ftate of health.

(s) Nefcio quis teneros cculus mihi fafcinat agnos. Virgil.

fore,

fore *(t)*, an incredible number of them perifh, nor is any city more fatal to the population of the neighbouring country than Grand Cairo.

Another very general diftemper at Cairo, is that which the vulgar there call the *blefled evil*, and which we alfo improperly term the *Neapolitan difeafe :* one half of Cairo is infeded with it. The greateft part of the inhabitants believe it proceeds from *fright,* from *witchcraft,* or from *uncleanlinefs.* Some of them fufped the real caufe; but as that is conneded with a fubjed on which they are remarkably referved, they chufe not to mention it. This *blefled evil* is very difficult to cure; mercury, under whatever form adminiftered, generally fails: fudorific vegetables fucceed better, without being however infallible; happily, the virus is not very adive, on account of the great natural and artificial perfpiration. We fee there, as in Spain, old men carrying this diforder about them to the

(t) We often fee, in Egypt, little pieces of red ftuff, or branches of coral, and coloured glafs, hanging on the faces of children, and even of grown perfons. Thefe are fuppofed, by their colour and motion, to fix the firft glance of the *envious,* for it is that, they fay, which *ftrikes.*

R 4

age

age of eighty. But its effects are fatal to children born with the infection, the danger also is imminent for such as carry it into a cold country; for it there never fails to make a rapid progress, and shews itself always more inveterate from this transplantation. In Syria, at Damascus, and in the mountains, it is the more dangerous, as the winter is very severe there: when neglected, it terminates in all its well-known symptoms, as I myself witnessed in two instances.

There is a troublesome complaint peculiar to the climate of Egypt, which is a cutaneous eruption that returns every year. Towards the end of June, or the beginning of July, the body is covered with red spots and pimples, the smarting of which is very troublesome. Several physicians, perceiving that this eruption regularly happened at the time of the new waters, have been of opinion, that it was occasioned by the salts with which they supposed these waters impregnated; but the existence of these salts is not proved, and a more simple reason may be assigned. I have already said, that the waters of the Nile become corrupted, towards the end of April, in the bed of the river, and,

and, when drunk, produce humours of a malignant quality. When the new water arrives, it occasions a sort of fermentation in the blood, which separates the vicious humours, and expels them towards the skin, whither they are invited by the perspiration. It is, in its effect, a real purgative depuration, and is always salutary.

Another disease, but too common at Cairo, is a swelling of the testicles, which frequently turns to an enormous hydrocele. It is observed to attack, principally, the Greeks and Copts, and hence arises the suspicion that it is occasioned by the great quantity of oil which they make use of two-thirds of the year. It is conjectured, also, that the hot-baths contribute to it, the immoderate use of which produces other effects not less injurious to health *(u)*. I shall remark

on

(u) The Egyptians, and the Turks in general, have a fondness for the stove-baths, difficult to account for in a country so hot as theirs: but this appears to me to arise more from prejudice than the pleasure they find in them. The law of the Koran, which enjoins men a complete ablution after the conjugal act, is of itself a very powerful motive; and the gratification of their vanity in its observance is another not less efficacious: as for the women

men

on this occasion, that in Syria, as well as in Egypt, constant experience has proved that brandy distilled from common figs, or from the fruit of the sycamore tree, as well as that extracted from dates, and the fruit of the nopal, has a most immediate effect on the testicles, which it renders hard and painful the third or fourth day after it has been drank; and if the use of it be not discon-

men they have other motives; First, the bath is the only place in which they can make a parade of their luxury, and regale themselves with melons, fruits, pastry, and other delicacies. Secondly, they believe, as Prosper Alpinus has observed, that the bath gives them that *embonpoint* which passes for beauty. With respect to strangers, their opinions differ according to their tastes. Many merchants of Cairo are pleased with the baths, to others they are disagreeable. For my part, I found the bath produce in me a vertigo, and trembling at the knees, which lasted two days. I confess it is very extraordinary that a water absolutely scalding, and a profuse sweat, forced out by the convulsions of the lungs, as well as by the heat, should be considered as giving so much pleasure; nor do I envy the Turks either their opium, or their stoves, or their *too complaisant Massers!*

(These *Massers* are boys who knead the flesh, crack all the joints, scrape off the scurf, eradicate the superfluous hairs, rub the body gently, and are said to be subservient to the pleasures of the bather. T.)

tinued,

tinued, the diforder degenerates into a confirmed hydrocele.

Brandy made from dried raifins has not the
fame bad effect; it is always mixed with
annifeeds, and is very ftrong, being diftilled
no lefs than three times. The Chriftians of
Syria, and the Copts of Egypt, make great
ufe of it; the latter, efpecially, drink whole
bottles of it at their fupper: I imagined this
an exaggeration, but I have myfelf had ocular
proofs of its truth, though nothing could
equal my aftonifhment that fuch exceffes do
not produce inftant death, or, at leaft, every
fymptom of the moft infenfible drunken-
nefs.

The fpring, which in Egypt is the fummer
of our climates, brings with it malignant
fevers, which foon arrive at a crifis. A
French phyfician, who has had opportunities
to obferve a great number of them, has remarked, that the bark, given in the intermiffions,
in dofes of two or three ounces, has frequently
faved the patient at the laft extremity *(x)*.
As foon as the difeafe appears, the patient
muft be rigoroufly reftricted to a vegetable

(x) The next day he always adminifters a clyfter to
expel the bark.

acid

acid regimen; meat is prohibited, fish likewife, and above all, eggs; the latter are a fort
of poifon in Egypt.   In this country, as in
Syria, experience proves that bleeding is always more injurious than beneficial, even in
cafes where it appears to be moft neceffary:
the reafon of which is, that bodies nourifhed
with unwholefome aliments, fuch as green
fruits, raw vegetables, cheefe and olives, have,
in fact, but little blood, and a great quantity
of humours. The Egyptians are in general of
a bilious habit, as appears from their eyes and
their black eye-brows, their brown complexion, and meagre make.   Their habitual
malady is the cholic; and almoft all of them
frequently complain of a fournefs in the
throat, and an acid naufea; emetics and cream
of tartar are therefore very generally fuc-
cefsful.

The malignant fevers become fometimes
epidemic, in which cafe they are eafily
miftaken for the plague, of which I fhall
next fpeak.

Of the Plague.

Some perfons have attempted to eftablifh an opinion that the plague originates in Egypt; but this fuppofition, founded on vague prejudices, feems to be difproved by facts. The European merchants who have been fettled for many years at Alexandria, concur with the Egyptians in declaring that the plague never proceeds from the interior parts of the country (y), but firft makes its appearance, on the coaft, at Alexandria; from Alexandria it paffes to Rofetta, from Rofetta to Cairo, from Cairo to Damietta, and through the reft of the Delta. They further obferve, that it is invariably preceded by the arrival of fome veffel coming from Smyrna or Conftantinople; and that if the plague has been violent in one of thefe cities during

(y) Profper Alpinus, a Venetian phyfician, who wrote in 1591, fays alfo, that the plague never originates in Egypt; that it is brought from Greece, Syria, and Barbary; that the heats deftroy it, &c. See *Medicina Ægyptiorum,* p. 28.

the

the fummer, the danger is the greater for themfelves the following winter. It appears certain, that it really originates from Conftantinople, where it is perpetuated by the abfurd negligence of the Turks, which is fo great that they publicly fell the effects of perfons dead of that diftemper. The fhips which go to Alexandria never fail to carry furs and woollen cloths purchafed on thefe occafions, which they expofe to fale in the Bazar of the city, and thereby fpread the contagion. The Greeks who deal in thefe goods are almoft always the firft victims. By degrees the infection reaches Rofetta, and at length Cairo, following the ufual road by which the trade is carried on. As foon as it is confirmed, the European merchants fhut themfelves and their domeftics up in their *Kans*, and have no further external communication with the city. Their provifions, depofited at the gate of the Kan, are received there by the porter, who takes them up with iron tongs, and plunges them into a barrel of water provided for this purpofe. If it is neceffary to fpeak to any one, they always keep at fuch a diftance as to prevent touching with their clothes, or breathing on one another; by

3 which

which means they preferve themfelves from this dreadful calamity, unlefs by fome accidental neglect of thefe precautions. Some years ago, a cat which paffed by one of the terraces into the houfes of our merchants at Cairo, conveyed the plague to two of them, one of whom died.

It will eafily be imagined what a tirefome ftate of imprifonment this muft be : it continues for three or four months, during which time they have no other amufement than walking, in the evening, on the terraces, or playing at cards.

We obferve in the plague feveral very remarkable varieties. At Conftantinople it prevails during the fummer, and is greatly weakened, or entirely ceafes, in the winter. In Egypt, on the contrary, it is moft violent in winter, and infallibly ends in the month of June. This apparent contrariety may be explained on the fame principle. The winter deftroys the plague at Conftantinople, becaufe the cold there is very fevere, and the fummer revives it, becaufe the heat is very humid, on account of the feas, forefts, and adjacent mountains. In Egypt, the winter nourifhes the plague,

plague, becaufe it is mild and humid ; but the fummer deftroys it, becaufe it is hot and dry. It feems to act on it as on flefh meat, which it does not fuffer to corrupt. Heat is not prejudicial, but as it is combined with humidity *(z)*. Egypt is afflicted with the plague every fourth or fifth year, and the ravages it caufes would depopulate the country, were it not for the great numbers of ftrangers who refort thither from all parts of the empire, and in a great meafure repair its loffes.

In Syria the plague is much lefs common : five-and-twenty years have elapfed fince it has been known there. This arifes, no doubt, from the fmall number of veffels which come directly from Conftantinople. It is remarked likewife, that it does not naturalize itfelf fo eafily to that province. When brought from the Archipelago, or even from Damietta, into the harbours of Latakia, Saide, or Acre, it will not fpread : it rather chufes

---

(z) At Cairo, it is obferved, that the water-carriers, continually wet with the frefh water they carry in fkins upon their backs, are never fubject to the plague ; but in this cafe it is *lotion*, and not humidity.

preliminary

preliminary circumftances, and a more com-
plex route; but when it paffes directly from
Cairo to Damafcus, all Syria is fure to be in-
fected.

The doctrine of predeftination, and ftill
more the barbarifm of the government, have
hitherto prevented the Turks from attempting to guard againft this deftructive difeafe :
the fuccefs, however, of the precautions
taken by the Franks, has of late begun
to make fome impreffion on many of
them. The Chriftians of the country who
traffic with our merchants, would be difpofed to fhut themfelves up like them ;
but this they cannot do without permiffion from the Porte. It feems, indeed, as
if the Divan would at length pay fome
attention to this object, if it be true that
an edict was iffued laft year for the eftablifhment of a Lazaretto at Conftantinople,
and three others at Smyrna, Candia, and
Alexandria. The government of Tunis
adopted this wife meafure fome years ago :
but the Turkifh police is every where fo
wretched, that little fuccefs can be hoped
for from thefe eftablifhments, notwith-

VOL. I.   S   ftanding

ſtanding their extreme importance to com‐
merce, and the fafety of the Mediterranean
ſtates (a).

(a) The very laſt year afforded a proof of this, ſince
as violent a plague as ever was known, broke out there.
It was brought by veſſels coming from Conſtantinople,
the maſters of which corrupted the guards, and came
into port without performing quarantine.

CHAP. XVIII.

Defcriptive Sketch of Egypt refumed.

E G Y P T might ftill furnifh matter for many other obfervations; but as they are either foreign to my purpofe, or may be included in thofe which I fhall have occafion to make on Syria, I fhall purfue them no farther.

If the reader remembers my defcription of the nature and afpect of the country; if he figures to himfelf a flat plain, interfected with canals, under water during three months, marfhy and rank with vegetation for three others, and dufty and parched the remainder of the year: if he imagines a number of wretched mud-walled and brick villages, naked and fun-burnt peafants, buffaloes, camels, fycamore and date-trees thinly fcattered, lakes, cultivated fields, and vacant grounds of confiderable extent; and adds befides a fun darting his rays from an

S 2

azure

azure fky, almoft invariably free from clouds;
and winds conftantly blowing, but not always with the fame ftrength, he will have
formed a tolerably juft idea of the natural
afpect of this country. He may have judged
of its political ftate from the divifion of the
inhabitants into tribes, fects, and claffes;
from the nature of a government, which
neither refpects the perfon or property of its
fubjects; and from the abufes of an unlimited
power entrufted to a rude and licentious foldiery. He may, in fhort, have formed a juft
eftimation of the ftrength of this government,
by confidering its military eftablifhment,
and the character of its troops, by obferving that, throughout all Egypt and on its
frontiers, there is not a fingle fort nor re-
doubt, neither artillery nor engineers; and
that its whole navy confifts in twenty-eight
veffels and cayaffes of Suez, armed each
with four rufty fwivels, and manned by
failors who know not even the ufe of the
compafs.

From thefe facts the reader may judge
for himfelf what opinion he ought to form
of this country, which I may have reprefented

sented in a different point of view from some other writers *(b)*. He ought not to be astonished at this diversity; nothing can differ more than the judgments of travellers respecting the countries they have visited: one will frequently disparage what another has extolled; and describe as a Paradise what he who comes after him may consider as having no charms. They are particularly reproached with this contrariety of opinions, but it is in fact common to them and their critics, since it is founded in the very nature of things. Notwithstanding all our efforts, our judgments are much less directed by the real merits of objects, than by the impressions we receive, or carry with us in viewing them. Daily experience demonstrates that foreign ideas always obtrude themselves; and hence it is that the same country which appears beautiful to us at one moment, seems equally disagreeable at another. Besides that it is impossible to disengage ourselves from the prejudices of early habits. The inhabitant of the mountains dislikes the plain; the inhabitant of the plain is displeased with the mountains.

(*b*) See *De Maillet.*

S 3

The

The Spaniard wishes for a clear sky; the Dane prefers thick weather. We admire the verdure of our fields; the Swede is better pleased with the whiteness of his snow; and the Laplander, transported from his smoky hut, to the groves of Chantilly would die with heat and melancholy. Every man has his peculiar tastes, according to which he judges. To an Egyptian, I conceive that Egypt is, and always will be, the most beautiful country upon earth. But if I may be permitted to give my judgment, from what I have myself seen, I confess that I cannot entertain so high an opinion of it. I am willing to do justice to its extreme fertility, to the variety of its productions, and the advantages of its situation for commerce; I admit that Egypt is but little subject to the variations of weather, which occasion the failure of harvests with us; that the hurricanes of America are unknown there; and that the earthquakes which have laid waste Portugal and Italy in our days, are there extremely rare, though not without example *(c)*. I admit

(*c*) There was a very violent one, for instance, in the year 1112.

even.

even that the heat, which is fo infupportable
to Europeans, is no inconvenience to the natives; but I cannot be reconciled to the peftiferous fouthern blaft, the north-eaft winds,
which are conftantly the caufe of violent head-
achs, or thofe fwarms of fcorpions, gnats, and
efpecially flies, which are fo numerous, that it
is impoffible to eat without running the rifk of
fwallowing them. Befides, no country prefents fuch a famenefs of afpect. A boundlefs
naked plain; an horizon every where flat and
uniform *(d)*; date trees with flender and bare
trunks, or mud-walled huts on the caufeways,
are all it offers to the eye, which no where
beholds that richnefs of landfcape, that variety of objects, or diverfity of fcenery which
true tafte finds fo delightful. No country is
lefs picturefque, lefs adapted to the pencil of
the painter, or the defcriptions of the poet:
nothing can be feen of what conftitutes the
charm and beauty of their pictures; and it is
remarkable, that neither the Arabs, nor the
ancients make any mention of Egyptian poets.

(d) The reader may confult the views in Norden, in
which this is very confpicuous.

S 4   What

What indeed could an Egyptian fing on the reed of Gefner or Theocritus? He fees neither limpid ftreams, nor verdant lawns, nor folitary caves; and is equally a ftranger to vallies, mountain fides, and pendent rocks.

Thompfon could not there have known either the whiftling of the winds in the foreft, the rolling of thunder among the mountains, or the peaceful majefty of ancient woods: he could not have obferved the awful tempeft, nor the fweet tranquillity of the fucceeding calm. The face of nature, there eternally the fame, prefents nothing but well fed herds, fertile fields, a muddy river, a fea of frefh water, and villages which, rifing out of it, refemble iflands. Should the eye reach the horizon, we are terrified at finding nothing but favage deferts, where the wandering traveller, exhaufted with fatigue and thirft, fhudders at the immenfe fpace which feparates him from the world. In vain he implores heaven and earth: his cries, loft in the boundlefs plain, are not even returned by an echo; deftitute of every thing, and feparated from mankind, he perifhes in an agony of defpair,
amid

amid a gloomy defert, without even the con-
folation of knowing he has excited the fym-
pathifing tear. The contraft of this melancholy fcene, fo near, has probably given to the
cultivated fields of Egypt all their charms.
The barrennefs of the defert becomes a foil
to the plenty of the plains, watered by the
river; and the afpect of the parched fands,
fo totally unproductive, adds to the pleafures
the country offers. Thefe may have been
more numerous in former times, and might
revive under the influence of a well regulated
government: but at prefent, the riches of
nature produce not the fruits which might
be expected. In vain may travellers celebrate
the gardens of Rofetta and of Cairo. The
Turks are ftrangers to the art of gardening,
fo much cultivated by polifhed nations, and
defpife every kind of cultivation. Throughout the empire their gardens are only wild
orchards, in which trees are planted without
care or art, yet have not even the merit
of pleafing irregularity. In vain may they
tell us of the orange-trees and cedars,
which grow naturally in the fields. Accuftomed as we are to combine the ideas
of opulence and culture with thefe trees,
. fince

fince with us they are neceffarily connected
with them, we do not difcover the deception.
In Egypt, where they are frequent, and, as I
may fay, vulgar, they are affociated with
the mifery of the huts they cover, and recall only the idea of poverty and defolation.
In vain do they defcribe the Turk foftly re-
pofing under their fhade, and happy in
fmoking his pipe without reflection. Ignorance and folly, no doubt, have their enjoyments, as well as wit and learning; but, for
my own part, I confefs I could never bring
myfelf to envy the repofe of flaves, or to
dignify infenfibility with the name of happinefs. I fhould not even have been able to
conceive from whence could proceed the enthufiafm with which fome travellers have
extolled Egypt, had not experience revealed
to me the fecret motives.

S E C T. II.

Of the Exaggerations of Travellers.

It has long been remarked, that travellers
particularly affect to boaft of the countries
through

through which they themfelves have travelled, infomuch that the exaggeration of their
relations having been frequently difcovered,
we have been warned by a proverb, to be
on our guard againft their falfehoods *(e)*; but
the error ftill remains, becaufe the caufes
have not ceafed. Thefe in fact originate with
every one of us, and the reproach not unfrequently belongs even to thofe who make
it. For, let us obferve a traveller, newly
arrived from fome diftant country, and endeavouring to amufe the idlenefs and curiofity of the company around him. The
novelty of his relation procures him attention, which even extends to perfonal refpect.
He is loved becaufe he amufes, and becaufe
his pretenfions clafh not with thofe of others.
On his fide, he is foon fenfible that he ceafes
to be interefting, when he can no longer
raife new ideas. The neceffity of fupporting,
the defire even of increafing this power of
pleafing, induce him to beftow higher colouring on his pictures ; he paints the greateft
objects, that they may be the more ftriking ;
and his fuccefs encourages him to proceed.

(e) Multum mentitur qui multum vidit.

He

He catches the enthufiafm of his hearers, and, fhortly, a kind of emulation takes place between him and his auditors, by which he returns, in wondrous narrative, what he receives in admiration. The marvellous in what he has feen, is reflected, firft upon himfelf, and, by a ufual confequence, on thofe who have heard, and in their turn relate it. Thus does vanity, which pervades every thing, become one of the caufes of the propenfity we all have, either to believe, or recount ˙ prodigies. We have befides lefs defire to be inftructed than amufed, and it is from thefe reafons that tale-makers of every kind, have always held a diftinguifhed rank in the efteem of mankind, and in the clafs of writers.

There is alfo another caufe of the enthufiafm of travellers. Remote from the objects which have given us pleafure, the imagination takes fire; abfence again inflames defire, and the fatiety of furrounding enjoyments beftows a new charm on whatever is no longer within our reach. We regret a country from which we were often anxious to efcape; and pleafe ourfelves with the remembrance of places in which, were we there, we could

not

not bear to remain. Travellers who have only paſſed through Egypt, are not to be ranked in this claſs, as they have not time to loſe the illuſion of novelty; but this remark applies to whoever has made a long reſidence in the country. Our merchants know it; and have made a very juſt obſervation on this ſubject: they remark that thoſe among them, who have experienced the greateſt inconveniencies from reſiding in a foreign country, are no ſooner returned to France, than every thing diſagreeable is effaced from their memory; their recollection aſſumes cheerful colours, and in two years after, one would not imagine they had ever been there. " Do you ſtill think pro- " perly of us, and our ſituation," wrote one who ſtill reſides at Cairo to me lately? " Do " you retain juſt ideas of this place of " miſery (f); for we have experienced that

(f) No perſon has leſs reaſon than myſelf to be diſſatisfied with Egypt; I experienced from our merchants in that country the utmoſt generoſity and politeneſs; I never met with any diſagreeable accident, nor was even obliged to alight in reverence of the Mamlouks. It is true that, notwithſtanding it is held ſo diſgraceful, I always walked on foot in the ſtreets.

" all

" all thofe who return to Europe, fo far for-
" get them as to aftonifh us ?" Such general
and fuch powerful caufes would not have
failed to produce their ufual effect upon myfelf, had I not taken particular pains to
guard myfelf againft them, and to retain my
former impreffions, in order to give my defcriptions the only merit they can have, that
of truth. It is time now to proceed to objects more extenfively interefting; but, as the
reader would not pardon me fhould I quit
Egypt without mentioning the ruins and
the pyramids, I fhall content myfelf with
beftowing on them a few words.

CHAP.

C H A P. XIX.

Of the Ruins and the Pyramids.

I HAVE already explained how much the conftant difficulty of travelling in Egypt, which has increafed of late years, is unfavourable to refearches into antiquities. For want of means, and above all of favourable circumftances, we are reduced to be content with feeing what others have already feen, and to relate nothing but what they have already publifhed. For this reafon, I fhall not repeat what has been repeated more than once in Paul Lucas, Maillet, Sicard, Pocock, Greaves, Norden, and Niebuhr, and ftill more lately in the Letters of M. Savary. I fhall confine myfelf to a few general remarks.

The pyramids of Djiza are a ftriking example of the difficulty which I have already faid attends the making of obfervations. Though only four leagues diftant from Cairo, where the Franks refide, though they have been vifited by a crowd of travellers, their

2 true

true dimenfions are not yet known with certainty. Several times has their height been
meafured by geometrical methods, and each
operation has given a different refult *(g)*.
In order to decide this queftion, a new and
accurate menfuration fhould be undertaken by
perfons of known abilities. In the interim,
however, we may fafely affert that thofe are
miftaken who have affirmed the height of the
great pyramid is equal to the length of the
bafe, fince the angle at the vertex is fenfibly
too large. The knowledge of the true length
of this bafe appears to me the more interefting, as I am inclined to think it has fome
affinity with one of the fquare meafures of
the Egyptians; and if the dimenfions of the
ftones fhould be found frequently the fame,
we may poffibly from them deduce their other
meafures.

The difficulty of underftanding the defcription of the infide of the pyramid, has
been frequently complained of, and, in fact,
without being well verfed in the nature of

(g) To the lift of thefe differences, given by M. Savary, may be added a late menfuration, which affigns fix
hundred feet to each face of the Great Pyramid, and four
hundred and eighty feet for its perpendicular height.

3

plans

plans, it is not eafy to form any adequate idea from engravings. The beft method to convey fuch an idea of it, would bé to form of clay, or baked earth, a pyramid in minia- ture, in the reduced proportion, for inftance, of an inch to a toife. Such an imitation would be eight feet four inches at the bafe, and near feven and one half in height. By cutting it into two portions from top to bot- tom, it would be poffible to form the firft channel, which defcends obliquely, the gal- lery.which afcends in the fame manner, and the fepulchral chamber at the extremity. Norden would furnifh the beft defcription ; but fuch a model muft be executed by an artift accuftomed to this fort of work.

The ledge of rock on which the pyramids are built does not rife more than forty or fifty feet above the level of the plain. The ftone of which it confifts, is, as I have faid, white and calcareous, of a grain refembling that of the ftone known in fome provinces of France, by the name of *Rairie*. That of the pyramids is of a fimilar nature. It was ima- gined, at the beginning of the prefent century, on the authority of Herodotus, that the mate- rials of which they have been built had been

VOL. I, T brought

brought from a diftance; but travellers, obferving the refemblance I am fpeaking of,
think it more natural to conclude they were
taken from the rock itfelf; and, at this day,
the narrative of Herodotus is treated as a fable,
and fuch a removal of the ftones as an abfur-
dity. It has been calculated that the levelling
of the rock would furnifh nearly enough,
and the deficiency is fupplied by fuppofed
fubterranean cavities, which are magnified
at pleafure. But if the ancient opinion
have its improbabilities, the modern fyftem
is mere fuppofition. It is by no means
fufficient to fay : " it is incredible they fhould
" have tranfported whole quarries from fuch
" a diftance, and abfurd to multiply expen-
" ces to fo enormous an amount." In whatever relates to the opinions, and governments of ancient nations, it is difficult to
fay what is probable. However improbable therefore the fact in queftion may
feem, if we confider that the hiftorian who
relates it drew his materials from the original archives of the ancient Egyptians; that
he is remarkably accurate in every thing we
are able to verify; that the Lybic rock no
where prefents elevations fimilar to thofe
which

which are fuppofed, and that the fubterranean cavities remain ftill to be difcovered;
if we recollect the immenfe quarries which
extend from Saouadi to Manfalout, for the
fpace of five-and-twenty leagues; if we confider, in fhort, that the ftones extracted from
them, which are of the fame kind, could have
been intended for no other vifible purpofe *(b)*;
we fhall at leaft be tempted to fufpend our
judgment, until the fact be decided by better
evidence.

Other writers, in like manner, tired of the
opinion that the pyramids were tombs, have
converted them into temples or obfervatories. They confider it as abfurd to fuppofe
a wife and polifhed nation would think the
fepulchre of its king a matter of fo much importance, or that a prince would impoverifh
his people by forced labours, merely to en-
clofe a fkeleton of five feet in a mountain of
ftones; but I repeat it, we judge of the ancients improperly, when we make our own
opinions and cuftoms a ftandard of compa-

(b) I do not mean the pyramids of Djiza only, but
all of them in general. Some of them, fuch as thofe of
Bayamout, are neither founded on rocks, nor are there
any rocks near. See Pococke.

rifon,

rifon. The motives which influenced them, may appear to us extravagant, and poffibly may really be fo in the eye of reafon, without having been lefs powerful, or lefs efficacious. Befides, we muft engage in endlefs and idle contradictions of all hiftory, to fuppofe in them a wifdom conformable to our principles : we reafon too much from our own ideas, and do not fufficiently attend to theirs. But from whichever we reafon in the prefent difpute, we may affirm that the pyramids never can have been aftronomical obfervatories *(i)*, becaufe Mount Mokattam would have afforded a ftill more elevated fituation, and which bounds the former ; becaufe every elevated obfervatory is ufelefs in Egypt, where the country is very flat, and where the vapours hide the ftars for feveral degrees above the horizon ; becaufe it is impracticable to afcend to the top of the pyramids in general ; and becaufe it could not have been neceffary

(i) It has been alleged the pyramids are built fo as to correfpond with the four cardinal points ; but the ancients, in the greateft part of their monuments, have obferved this practice, and it was well adapted to tombs, which, from their ideas of a refurrection, Tartarus, Elyfium, &c. were connected with aftronomy.

to erect *eleven* obfervatories fo near each other as the eleven pyramids of different fizes, which may be feen from Djiza. From thefe reafons, we fhall be led to think that Plato, who firft fuggefted the idea in queftion, could only have fome particular cafes in view, or that he has in this inftance only his ordinary merit of an eloquent writer.

If, on the other hand, we weigh the teftimonies of the ancients, and local circumftances; if we obferve that near the pyramids there are thirty or forty monuments, which prefent rough outlines of the fame pyramidal form ; that this fterile fpot, remote from all cultivable land, poffeffes the qualities requifite for an Egyptian cemetery, and that near it was that of the whole city of Memphis, *the Plain of Mummies*, we fhall no longer doubt that the pyramids are only tombs. We fhall ceafe to wonder that the defpots of a fuperftitious people fhould have made it a point of importance and pride, to build for their fkeletons impenetrable habitations, when we are informed that, even before the time of Mofes, it was a dogma at Memphis, that fouls at the expiration of fix thoufand years, fhould return to the bo-

dies

dies they had quitted. It was for this reafon that fo much pains were taken to preferve
the body from putrefaction, and that endeavours were made to retain even its form, by
means of fpices, bandages, and farcophagi.
That which is ftill in the fepulchral chamber
of the great pyramid, is precifely of its natural dimenfions; and this chamber is fo obfcure and narrow *(k)*, that it never can have
contained more than one dead body. Attempts have been made to difcover fome
myftery in the fubterranean cavity which defcends perpendicularly within the pyramid,
forgetting that it was the uniform practice of
all antiquity to contrive communications with
the infide of their tombs, in order to perform, on certain days, prefcribed by their religion, the cuftomary ceremonies; fuch as
libations, and offerings of food to the deceafed.
We muft recur, therefore, to the ancient
opinion, antiquated as it may feem, that the
pyramids are tombs; and this hypothefis, favoured by a variety of circumftances, is ftill
more confirmed by their name, which, according to an analyfis conformable to every

(*k*) It is thirteen paces long by eleven wide, and
nearly of the fame height.

principle of etymology, I think I have difcovered to fignify *chamber*, or *cave* of the
dead (l).

(*l*) The word *pyramid*, is derived from the Greek
Πυραμις, Πυραμιδος ; but in the ancient Greek, the *v* was
pronounced *oo* ; we fhould therefore fay *pooramis*. When
the Greeks, after the Trojan war frequented Egypt, they
could not have in their language the name of thefe
prodigious edifices, which muft have been new to them ;
they muft have borrowed it from the Egyptians. *Pooramis*
then is not Greek, but Egyptian. Now there is little
doubt but the dialects of Egypt, which were various, had
a great analogy with thofe of the neighbouring countries,
fuch as Arabic and Syriac. In thefe languages it is certain the letter *p* is unknown ; but it is no lefs true, that
the Greeks, in adopting barbarous words, almoft always
changed them, and frequently confounded one found
with another, which refembled it. It is certain alfo, that
in the words we know, *p* is continually taken for *b*,
which very much refembles it. Now, in the dialect of
Paleftine, *bour* (בור) fignifies every excavation of the
earth, a *ciftern*, a *prifon* properly under ground, a *fepulchre*. (See *Buxtorf, Lexicon Hebr.*) There remains *amis*, in
which the final *s* appears to me a termination fubftituted
for *t*, which did not fuit the genius of the Greek tongue,
and which made the oriental (המת) *a-mit, of the dead, bour
a-mit, cave of the dead*; this fubftitution of the *s* for *t*,
has an example in *atribis*, well known to be *atribit*. The
learned may determine whether this etymology be not
equally plaufible with many others.

T 4   The

The great pyramid is not the only one which has been opened. There is another at *Sakara*, the infide of which appears conftructed in the fame manner. A few years ago, one of the Beys tried to open the third in fize of thofe that are at Djiza, to obtain the fuppofed treafure he imagined concealed there. He attempted this on the fame fide, and at the fame height at which the great one has been opened; but after forcing out two or three hundred ftones, with confiderable labour and expence, he relinquifhed his avaricious enterprize. The time when the greateft part of the pyramids were built is unknown, but that of the great one is fo evident, that it fhould never have been called in queftion. Herodotus attributes it to Cheops, with a detail of circumftances which prove his authors were well informed *(m)*. But Cheops, in his lift, which is the beft

(m) This prince, he tells us, reigned fifty years, twenty of which he employed in building the pyramids. The third part of the inhabitants of Egypt were employed, by forced fervice, in hewing, tranfporting, and raifing the ftones.

extant,

extant, is the second king after Proteus *(n)*, who was cotemporary with the Trojan war; whence it follows, that this pyramid was erected about one hundred and forty, or one hundred and sixty years after the building of Solomon's temple, or eight hundred and sixty years before Christ.

Destructive time, and the still more destructive hand of man, which have so defaced and destroyed all the other monuments of antiquity, have hitherto been able to effect but little against the pyramids. The solidity of their construction, and their enormous size, have secured them against every attempt, and seem to promise them an eternal duration. All travellers speak of them with enthusiasm, and enthusiasm they may well inspire. These artificial mountains are first discovered at ten leagues distance. They seem to retire in proportion as they are approached; and when still a league off, tower with such loftiness

---

(n) It is remarkable, that if we were to write the Egyptian name *Proteus*, as given by the Greeks, in *Phœnician* characters, we should make use of the same letters we pronounce *pharao*; the final *o* in the Hebrew is an *h*, which, at the end of words, frequently becomes *t*.

above

above our heads, that we imagine ourselves
at their feet; but when at length we reach
them, nothing can exprefs the various fenfa-
tions they infpire (o). Their ftupendous
height, the fteep declivity of their fides, their
prodigious furface, their enormous folidity,
the diftant ages they recall to memory, the
recollection of the labour they muft have
coft, and the reflection that thefe huge rocks
are the work of man, fo diminutive and feeble, who crawls at their feet, loft in wonder,

(o) I know nothing, at Paris, fo proper to give an idea
of the pyramids, as the *Hôtel des Invalides*, feen from the
Cours la Reine. The length of that building, being fix hundred feet, is precifely the fame as the bafe of the great pyramid; but to conceive their height and folidity, we muft
fuppofe the front I have mentioned to rife into a trian-
gle; the perpendicular of which fhould exceed the height
of the dome of that building by two thirds of the dome
itfelf, (it is three hundred feet high.) The fame furface muft be repeated on the four fides of the fquare, and
the whole mafs contained in them be fuppofed folid, and
offer to view nothing but an immenfe flope on every fide,
difpofed in fteps.

[The Englifh reader has only to fuppofe the vaft fquare
of *Lincoln's-inn-fields*, the dimenfions of which are the
exact bafe of the great pyramid, wholly filled up from
fide to fide, and gradually rifing in a pyramidal form,
to a height exceeding that of St. Paul's, by at leaft one
third. T.]

2   awe,

awe, humiliation, and reverence, altogether imprefs the mind of the fpectator in a manner not to be defcribed; but to this firft tranfport other fentiments foon fucceed. Elevated as we are with fo exalted a proof of the power of man, when we confider the purpofe for which thefe amazing works were intended, we cannot but view them with regret. We lament, that to conftruct a ufelefs fepulchre, a whole nation fhould have been rendered miferable for twenty years: we fhudder at the numberlefs acts of injuftice and oppreffion thefe tirefome labours muft have coft, in conveying, preparing, and piling up fuch an immenfe mafs of ftones; and we are inflamed with indignation at the tyranny of the defpots who enforced thefe barbarous works, a fentiment indeed which too frequently recurs on viewing the different monuments of Egypt. Thofe labyrinths, temples, and pyramids, by their huge and heavy ftructure, atteft much lefs the genius of a nation, opulent and friendly to the arts, than the fervitude of a people who were flaves to the caprices of their monarchs; and we are even inclined to pardon that avarice, which, by

violating

violating their tombs, has fruſtrated their idle hopes: we beſtow leſs pity on theſe ruins; and while the lover of the arts beholds with indignation, at Alexandria, the columns of her palaces ſawed into *mill-ſtones*, the philoſopher, after the firſt emotion, occaſioned by the deſtruction of every fine work, cannot ſuppreſs a ſmile at the ſecret juſtice of that deſtiny, which reſtores to the people what coſt them ſo much fruitleſs toil, and which renders the pride of unprofitable luxury ſubſervient to the meaneſt of neceſſities.

The happineſs of the people, rather than the preſervation of the ancient monuments of Egypt, ſhould certainly dictate the wiſh of ſeeing that country under the government of another nation; but were it only in the latter point of view, ſuch a revolution would ſtill be much to be deſired. Were Egypt poſſeſſed by a nation friendly to the fine arts, diſcoveries might be made there, which would make us better acquainted with antiquity than any thing the reſt of the world can afford us. Perhaps even books might be found. It is not above three years ago, that upwards of one hundred volumes, written in an unknown language,

3

language, were dug up near Damietta *(p)*, but immediately committed to the flames, by command of the Shaiks of Cairo. Indeed the Delta no longer affords any very interesting ruins, as they have been all deftroyed by the wants, or the fuperftition of the inhabitants. But the Said, which is lefs inhabited, and the edge of the defert, ftill lefs peopled, poffefs feveral yet untouched. We may hope to find them ftill more certainly in the Oafes, thofe iflands feparated from the world by an ocean of fand, where no traveller we know of, has ever penetrated fince the time of Alexander. Thefe countries, in which formerly were cities and temples, having never been fubject to the devaftations of the Barbarians, muft have preferved their monuments, and the rather as it is probable they are but thinly inhabited, or perhaps entirely deferted; and thefe monuments, buried in the fands, muft be preferved there, as a depofite for future generations. To a period lefs remote, poffibly than we imagine, we muft defer the gratification of our wifhes and our

(*p*) I have this fact from fome merchants of Acre, who told it me on the credit of a Marfeilles Captain, who, at that time was taking in a cargo of rice at Damietta.

hopes.

hopes. We may then be allowed to search
every part of the country, the banks of the
Nile, and the sands of Lybia. We may then
be permitted to open the small pyramid of
Djiza, the total demolition of which would
not cost fifty thousand livres (two thousand
pounds. It is probable too, that till that
period, we must remain ignorant of the signi-
fication of the hieroglyphics; though, in my
opinion, the means we at present possess
might be sufficient to explain them.

But enough of conjectures. It is now time
to proceed to the examination of another
country, the ancient and modern state of
which is not less interesting even than that
of Egypt.

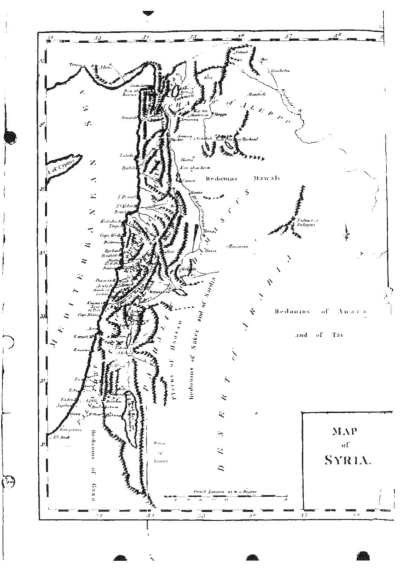

MAP
of
SYRIA.

TRAVELS

IN

EGYPT AND SYRIA.

STATE OF SYRIA.

CHAP. XX.

Geography and Natural History of Syria.

LEAVING Egypt by the Isthmus which separates Africa from Asia, and following the coast of the Mediterranean, we enter a second province of Turkey, known to us by the name of Syria. This name, which, like so many others, has been transmitted to us by the Greeks, is an abridgment of *Assyria*, which was first adopted by the Ionians who frequented those coasts, after the Assyrians of Niniveh had reduced that country to be a province of their empire *(a)*. The name of

(a) That is about the year 750 before Christ. This is the reason why Homer, who wrote a little before that time, no where uses this name, though he speaks of the inhabitants of the country, but employs the oriental word *aram*, changed into *arimean* and *erembos*.

Syria

Syria had not therefore fo extenfive a fignification as it has fince obtained. It compre-
hended neither Phœnicia nor Paleftine. The
prefent inhabitants, who, according to the
conftant practice of the Arabs, have not
adopted the Greek names, are ignorant of
the name of *Syria (b)*; inftead of which
they call it *Barr-el-Sham (c)*, which fignifies
country of the left; and is the name given to
the whole fpace contained between two lines
drawn, the one from Alexandretta to the
Euphrates, and the other from Gaza to the
defert of Arabia, bounded on the eaft by that
defert, and on the weft by the Mediterranean.
This name of country of the *left*, from its contraft with that of the *Yamin*, or country of the
right, indicates fome intermediate place, as a
common point, which muft be Mecca; and
from its allufion to the worfhip of the fun *(d)*

proves

(b) Geographers, however, fometimes write it *Souria*,
from the conftant change of the Greek upfilon into the
Arabic waw.

(c) *El-fham* alfo is the name of the city of Damafcus,
the reputed capital of Syria. I am at a lofs to difcover
why M. Savary has made it *el Shams*, or the *City of the Sun*.

(d) The ancient nations, who worfhipped the fun,
paid their homage at the moment of his rifing; their

faces

proves at once, an origin anterior to Mahomet, and the exiſtence, which is already certain, of this worſhip, in the temple of the Caaba.

S E C T. I.

General Appearance of the Country.

If we examine a map of Syria, we may obſerve that this country is in ſome meaſure only a chain of mountains, which diſtribute themſelves in various directions from one leading branch; and ſuch, in fact, is the appearance it preſents, whether we approach it from the ſide of the ſea, or by the immenſe plains of the deſert. We firſt diſcover, at a great diſtance, a clouded ridge, which runs north and ſouth, as far as the ſight extends; and, as we advance, diſtinguiſh the ſummits of mountains, which, ſometimes detached, and ſometimes united in

faces were therefore turned towards the eaſt. The north was on the *left*, the ſouth on their *right*, and the weſt behind them, called in the oriental languages, *acheron*, and *ataron*.

Vᴏʟ. I.   U   chains,

chains, uniformly terminate in one principal
line which overtops them all; we may follow this line, without interruption, from its
entry by the north, quite into Arabia. It
firſt runs cloſe to the ſea, between Alexandretta and the Orontes, and, after opening a
paſſage to that river, continues its courſe to
the ſouthward, quitting, for a ſhort diſtance,
the ſhore, and, in a chain of continued ſummits, ſtretches as far as the ſources of the
Jordan, where it ſeparates into two branches,
to encloſe, as it were, in a baſon, this river
and its three lakes. In its courſe, it detaches
from this line, as from a main trunk, an
infinity of ramifications, ſome of which loſe
themſelves in the deſert, where they form
various encloſed hollows, ſuch as thoſe of
Damaſcus and Hauran, while others advance
toward the ſea, where they frequently end in
ſteep declivities, as at Carmel, Nakoura, Cape
Blanco, and in almoſt the whole country between Bairout *(e)* and Tripoli of Syria; but
in general they gently terminate in plains,
ſuch as thoſe of Antioch, Tripoli, Tyre, and
Acre.

(e) The ancient Berytus.

SECT.

S E C T. II.

Of the Mountains.

These mountains, as they vary their levels
and situations, are also greatly changed in
their form and appearance. Between Alexandretta and the Orontes, the firs, larches,
oaks, box-trees, laurels, yews, and myrtles,
with which they abound, give them an air
of liveliness, which delights the traveller,
wearied with the melancholy nakedness of
the isle of Cyprus *(f)*. On some declivities
he even meets with cottages, environed with
fig-trees, and vineyards; and the sight of
these repays the fatigue he has endured on
a road which, by rugged paths, leads him
from the bottom of valleys to the tops of
hills, and from the tops of hills to the bot-
toms of valleys. The inferior branches,
which extend to the northward of Aleppo,
on the contrary, present nothing but bare

(f) All vessels which go to Alexandretta touch
at Cyprus, the southern part of which is a naked and
desolate plain.

rocks,

rocks, without verdure or earth. To the south of Antioch, and on the fea-coaft, the hill-fides are proper for the cultivation of tobacco, olives, and vines *(g)*; but, on the fide of the defert, the fummits and declivities of this chain are almoft one continued feries of white rocks. Towards Lebanon, the mountains are lofty, but are covered, in many places, with as much earth as fits them for cultivation by induftry and labour. There, amid the crags of the rocks, may be feen the no very magnificent remains of the boafted cedars *(h)*; but a much greater number of firs, oaks, brambles, mulberry-trees, figs, and vines. As we leave the country of the Druzes, the mountains are no longer fo high, nor fo rugged, but become fitter for tillage. They rife again to the fouth-eaft of Mount Carmel, are covered with woods, and afford very pleafant prof-

(*g*) Mount Cafius muft be excepted, which rifes above Antioch to a prodigious height. But Pliny furpaffes hyperbole, when he fays that, from its fummit, we may difcover at once both the morning's dawn and the evening twilight.

(*h*) There are now but four or five of thefe trees which deferve any notice.

2   pects;

pects; but as we advance toward Judea, they lose their verdure, their valleys grow narrower, they become dry and stoney, and terminate at the Dead Sea in a pile of desolate rocks, full of precipices and caverns *(i)*; while to the west of Jordan and the lake, another chain of rocks, still higher, and more rugged, presents a still more gloomy prospect, and announces, afar off, the entrance of the desert, and the end of the habitable lands.

A view of the country will convince us that the most elevated point of all Syria is Lebanon, on the south-east of Tripoli. Scarcely do we depart from Larneca, in Cyprus, which is thirty leagues distance, before we discover its summit, capped with clouds. This is also distinctly perceivable on the map, from the course of the rivers. The Orontes, which flows from the mountains of Damascus, and loses itself below Antioch ; the Kafmia, which, from the north of Balbec, takes its course towards Tyre; the Jordan,

---

(i) This is the place called the *Grottoes of Engaddi*, which have been a refuge for vagabonds in all ages. Some of them are capable of containing fifteen hundred men.

forced,

forced, by the declivities, toward the fouth,
prove that this is the higheft point. Next
to Lebanon, the moft elevated part of the
country is Mount Akkar, which becomes
vifible as foon as we leave Marra in the defert. It appears like an enormous flattened
cone, and is conftantly in view for two days
journey. No one has yet had an opportunity to afcertain the height of thefe mountains by the barometer; but we may deduce
it from another confideration. In winter their
tops are entirely covered with fnow, from
Alexandretta to Jerufalem; but after the
month of March it melts, except on Mount
Lebanon, where, however, it does not remain the whole year, unlefs in the higheft
cavities, and toward the north-eaft, where it
is fheltered from the fea winds, and the
rays of the fun. In fuch a fituation I faw
it ftill remaining, in 1784, at the very time
I was almoft fuffocated with heat in the
valley of Balbec. Now, fince it is well
known that fnow, in this latitude, requires an
elevation of fifteen or fixteen hundred fathom,
we may conclude that to be the height of
Lebanon, and that it is confequently much
                                            lower

lower than the Alps, or even the Pyrenees *(k)*.

Lebanon, which gives its name to the whole extensive chain of the Kesraouan, and the country of the Druzes, presents us every where with majestic mountains. At every step we meet with scenes in which nature displays either beauty or grandeur, sometimes singularity, but always variety. When we land on the coast, the loftiness and steep ascent of this mountainous ridge, which seems to enclose the country, those gigantic masses which shoot into the clouds, inspire astonishment and awe. Should the curious traveller then climb these summits which bounded his view, the wide extended space which he discovers becomes a fresh subject of admiration; but completely to enjoy this majestic scene, he must ascend the very point of Lebanon, or the *Sannin*. There, on every side, he will view an horizon without bounds; while, in clear weather, the sight is lost over the desert, which extends to the Persian

(k) Mount Blanc, the loftiest of the Alps, is estimated at two thousand four hundred fathom above the level of the sea; and the peak of Ossian, in the Pyrenees, at nineteen hundred.

U 4   Gulph,

Gulph, and over the sea which bathes the coasts of Europe. He seems to command the whole world, while the wandering eye, now surveying the successive chains of mountains, transports the imagination in an instant from Antioch to Jerusalem; and now approaching the surrounding objects, observes the distant profundity of the coast, till the attention, at length, fixed by distincter objects, more minutely examines the rocks, woods, torrents, hill-sides, villages, and towns; and the mind secretly exults at the diminution of things, which before appeared so great. He contemplates the valley obscured by stormy clouds, with a novel delight, and smiles at hearing the thunder, which had so often burst over his head, growling under his feet; while the threatening summits of the mountains are diminished till they appear only like the furrows of a ploughed field, or the steps of an amphitheatre; and he feels himself flattered by an elevation above so many great objects, on which pride makes him look down with a secret satisfaction.

When the traveller visits the interior parts of these mountains, the ruggedness of the roads,

roads, the fteepnefs of the defcents, the height of the precipices ftrike him at firft with terror; bat the fagacity of his mule foon relieves him, and he examines at his eafe thofe picturefque fcenes which fucceed each other to entertain him. There, as in the Alps, he travels whole days, to reach a place which was in fight at his departure; he winds, he defcends, he fkirts the hills, he climbs; and in this perpetual change of po-fition it feems as if fome magic power varied for him at every ftep the decorations of the fcenery. Sometimes he fees villages ready to glide from the fteep declivities on which they are built, and fo difpofed that the ter-races of one row of houfes ferve as a ftreet to the row above them. Sometimes he fees a convent ftanding on a folitary eminence, like Mar-Shaya, in the valley of the Tigris. Here is a rock perforated by a torrent, and become a natural arch, like that of Nahr-el-Leben *(1)*. There another rock, worn per-pendicular, refembles a lofty wall. Frequent-

(1) The river of milk, which falls into Nahr-el-Salib, called alfo the river of Bairout; this arch is upwards of one hundred and fixty feet long, eighty-five wide, and near two hundred high above the torrent.

ly

ly on the fides of hills he fees beds of ftones
ftripped and detached by the waters, rifing
up like artificial ruins. In many places, the
waters, meeting with inclined beds, have
undermined the intermediate earth, and
formed caverns, as at Nahr-el-kelb, near
Antoura : in others are formed fubterranean channels, through which flow rivulets for a part of the year, as at Mar-Elias-
el-Roum, and Mar-Hanna *(m)* ; but thefe

(m) Thefe fubterraneous rivulets are common throughout Syria ; there are fome near Damafcus, at the fources
of the Orontes, and at thofe of Jordan. That of Mar-
Hanna, a Greek convent, near the village of Shouair,
opens by a gulph called *El-balsua*, or the Swallower. It is
an aperture of about ten feet wide, fituated in the middle
of a hollow: at the depth of fifteen feet is a fort of firft bottom ; but it only hides a very profound lateral opening.
Some years ago it was fhut, as it had ferved to conceal a
murder. The winter rains coming on, the waters collected,
and formed a pretty deep lake ; but fome fmall ftreams pe-
netrating among the ftones, they were foon ftripped of the
earth which faftened them, and the preffure of the mafs of
water prevailing, the whole obftacle was removed with an
explofion like thunder ; and the re-action of the compreffed
air was fo violent, that a column of water fpouted up, and
fell upon a houfe at the diftance of at leaft two hundred
paces. The current this occafioned formed a whirlpool,
which fwallowed up the trees and vines planted in the
hollow, and threw them out by the fecond aperture.

picturefque

picturefque fituations fometimes become tra-
gical. From thaws and earthquakes rocks
have been known to lofe their equilibrium,
roll down upon the adjacent houfes, and
bury the inhabitants: fuch an accident happened about twenty years ago, and over-
whelmed a whole village near Mar-djordjos,
without leaving a fingle trace to difcover
where it formerly ftood. Still more lately,
and near the fame fpot, a whole hill fide,
covered with mulberries and vines, was detached by a fudden thaw, and fliding down the
declivity of the rock, was launched altogether, like a fhip from the ftocks, into the
valley. Hence arofe a whimfical, but reafon-
able, litigation, between the proprietor of the
original ground and the owner of the emigrated land ; the caufe was carried before the
tribunal of the Emir Youfef, who indemni-
fied both parties for their mutual loffes. It
might be expected fuch accidents would
difguft the inhabitants of thofe mountains ;
but befides that they are rare, they are com-
penfated by an advantage which makes them
prefer their habitations to the moft fertile
plains, I mean the fecurity they enjoy from the
oppreffions of the Turks. This fecurity is
                                    efteemed

efteemed fo valuable a blefling by the inhabitants, that they have difplayed an induftry on thefe rocks which we may elfewhere look for in vain. By dint of art and
labour they have compelled a rocky foil to
become fertile. Sometimes, to profit by the
water, they conduct it by a thoufand wind-
ings along the declivities, or ftop it by forming
dams in the valleys, while in other places, they
prop up ground, ready to crumble away, by
walls and terraces. Almoft all thefe mountains, thus laboured, prefent the appearance
of a flight of ftairs, or an amphitheatre, each
ftep of which is a row of vines or mulberry-
trees. I have reckoned from a hundred to a
hundred and twenty of thefe gradations on
the fame declivity, from the bottom of the
valley to the top of the eminence. While
amid thefe mountains, I forgot it was in
Turkey, or, if I recollected it, only felt
more fenfibly the powerful influence of even
the feebleft ray of liberty.

S e c t. III.

Structure of the Mountains.

If we examine the substance of these mountains, we shall find they consist of a hard calcareous stone, of a whitish colour, sonorous like free-stone, and disposed in strata variously inclined. This stone has almost the same appearance in every part of Syria ; sometimes it is bare, and looks like the peeled rocks on the coast of Provence : such, for instance, is that of the chain of hills on the north side of the road from Antioch to Aleppo, and that which serves as a bed to the upper part of the rivulet which passes by the latter city. Near Ermenaz, a village situated between Serkin and Kaftin, is a defile where the rocks exactly resemble those we pass in going from Marseilles to Toulon. In travelling from Aleppo to Hama, veins of the same rock are continually to be met with in the plain, while the mountains on the right present huge piles, which look like the ruins of towns and castles. The same stone, under a more regular form, likewise com-

poses

pofes the greater part of Lebanon, Anti-Lebanon, the mountains of the Druzes, Galilee, and Mount Carmel, and ftretches to the
fouth of the Lake Afphaltites. The inhabitants
every where build their houfes, and make
lime with it. I have never feen, nor heard
it faid, that thefe ftones contained any petrified fhells in the upper regions of Lebanon;
but we find, between Batroun and Djebail,
in the Kefraouan, at a little diftance from the
fea, a quarry of fchiftous ftones, the flakes
of which bear the impreffions of plants, fifh,
fhells, and efpecially the fea onion. The
bed of the torrent of Azkalan, in Paleftine,
is alfo lined with a heavy ftone, porous and
falt, which contains a great number of fmall
volutes and bivalves of the Mediterranean.
Pocock found a large quantity of them in the
rocks which border on the Dead Sea. Iron
is the only mineral which abounds here; the
mountains of the Kefraouan, and of the
Druzes, are full of it. Every fummer the
inhabitants work thofe mines, which are
fimply ochreous. Judea cannot be without
it, fince Mofes obferved, above three thoufand years ago, that its ftones were of iron.
There is a vague report, that there was an-
ciently

ciently a copper mine near Aleppo, but it muſt have been long ſince abandoned : I have been told likewiſe among the Druzes, that in the declivity of the hill I have mentioned, a mineral was diſcovered which produced both lead and ſilver ; but as ſuch a diſcovery would have ruined the whole diſtrict, by at-tracting the attention of the Turks, they made haſte to deſtroy every veſtige of it.

S E C T. IV.

Volcanos and Earthquakes.

The ſouth of Syria, that is, the hollow through which the Jordan flows, is a country of volcanos ; the bituminous and ſulphureous ſources of the Lake Aſphaltites, the lava, the pumice-ſtones thrown upon its banks, and the hot bath of Tabaria, demonſtrate that this valley has been the ſeat of a ſubterraneous fire which is not yet extinguiſhed. Clouds of ſmoke are often obſerved to iſſue from the lake, and new crevices to be formed up-on its banks. If conjectures in ſuch caſes were not too liable to error, we might ſuſ-

3   pect

pect that the whole valley has been formed
only by a violent finking of a country which
formerly poured the Jordan into the Mediterranean. It appears certain, at leaft, that
the cataftrophe of five cities, deftroyed by
fire, muft have been occafioned by the
eruption of a volcano, then burning. Strabo exprefsly fays *(n)*, " that the tradi-
" tion of the inhabitants of the country,
" (that is, of the Jews themfelves), was,
" that formerly the valley of the lake was
" peopled by thirteen flourifhing cities,
" and that they were fwallowed up by a
" volcano." This account feems to be confirmed by the quantities of ruins ftill found
by travellers on the weftern border. Thefe
eruptions have ceafed long fince, but earthquakes, which ufually fucceed them, ftill
continue to be felt at intervals in this country.
The coaft in general is fubject to them, and
hiftory gives us many examples of earthquakes, which have changed the face of
Antioch, Laodicea, Tripoli, Berytus, Tyre,
Sidon, &c. In our time, in the year 1759,
there happened one which caufed the greateft

(n) Lib. 16, p. 764.

ravages.

ravages. It is faid to have deftroyed, in the valley of Balbec, upwards of twenty thoufand perfons, a lofs which has never been re-paired. For three months, the fhocks of it terrified the inhabitants of Lebanon fo much as to make them abandon their houfes, and dwell under tents. Very lately (the 14th of December, 1783,) when I was at Aleppo, fo violent a fhock was felt, as to ring the bell in the houfe of the French conful. It is remarked in Syria, that earthquakes feldom happen but in winter, after the autumnal rains ; and this obfervation, conformable to that made by Docter Shaw in Barbary, feems to prove that the action of water on the dried earth has fome fhare in thefe convulfive motions. It may not be improper to remark, that the whole of Afia Minor is fubject to them in like manner.

S e c t. V.

Of the Locufts.

Syria, as well as Egypt, Perfia, and almoft all the fouth of Afia, is fubject to

Vol. I.   X   another

another calamity no lefs dreadful, I mean
thofe clouds of locufts, fo often mentioned
by travellers. The quantity of thefe infects
is incredible to all who have not themfelves
witneffed their aftonifhing numbers; the whole
earth is covered with them for the fpace of
feveral leagues. The noife they make in
browzing on the trees and herbage, may be
heard at a great diftance, and refembles that of
an army foraging in fecret. The Tartars themfelves are a lefs deftructive enemy than thefe
little animals; one would imagine, that fire
had followed their progrefs. Wherever their
myriads fpread, the verdure of the country
difappears, as if a covering had been removed;
trees and plants, ftripped of their leaves, and
reduced to their naked boughs and ftems,
caufe the dreary image of winter to fucceed
in an inflant, to the rich fcenery of the fpring.
When thefe clouds of locufts take their
flight, to furmount any obftacle, or to traverfe
more rapidly a defert foil, the heavens may
literally be faid to be obfcured by them.
Happily this calamity is not frequently repeated, for it is the inevitable forerunner of
famine, and the maladies it occafions. The
inhabitants of Syria have remarked, that

2   locufts

locusts are always bred by too mild winters, and that they conftantly come from the defert of Arabia. From this obfervation, it is eafy to conceive that, the cold not having been rigorous enough to deftroy their eggs, they multiply fuddenly, and, the herbage failing them in the immenfe plains of the defert, innumerable legions iffue forth. When they make their firft appearance on the frontiers of the cultivated country, the inhabitants ftrive to drive them off, by raifing large clouds of fmoke, but frequently their herbs and wet ftraw fail them ; they then dig trenches, where numbers of them are buried; but the two moft efficacious deftroyers of thefe infects, are the fouth or fouth-eafterly winds, and the bird called the *famarmar*. Thefe birds, which greatly refemble the woodpecker, follow them in large flocks, and not only greedily devour them, but kill as many as they can; they are therefore much refpected by the peafants, and nobody is ever allowed to fhoot them. As for the foutherly and fouth-eafterly winds, they drive with violence thefe clouds of locufts over the Mediterranean, where fuch quantities of them are drowned that, when

their

their carcafes are thrown on the fhore, they infect the air for feveral days, even to a great diftance.

We may reafonably prefume, that in fo extenfive a country as Syria, the quality of the foil is not every where the fame. In general the land of the mountains is harfh and ftoney; while that of the plains is fat and loamy, and exhibits every fign of the greateft fecundity. In the territory of Aleppo, towards Antioch, it refembles very fine brick-duft, or fpanifh fnuff. The waters of the Orontes, however, which traverfes this diftrict, are of a whitifh colour, which is occafioned by the nature of the lands towards its fource. Almoft every where elfe the earth is brown, and as fine as garden mold. In the plains, fuch as thofe of Hauran, Gaza, and Balbec, it is often difficult even to find a pebble. The winter rains occafion deep quagmires, and on the return of fummer, the heat produces, as in Egypt, large cracks in the earth feveral feet deep.

S E C T.

S e c t. VI.

Of the Rivers and Lakes.

The extravagant, or, if you will, the grand ideas which hiftory and travellers ufually give us of diftant objects, have accuftomed us to fpeak of the waters of Syria with a refpect which amufes our imagination. We are fond of faying the *river Jordan*, the *river Orontes*, the *river Adonis*. If, however, we wifh to preferve to words their proper fignification, we fhall hardly find in this country any other than *rivulets*. The channels of the Orontes and the Jordan, the two moft confiderable, are fcarcely fixty paces wide at their mouths *(o)*; the others do not merit to be mentioned. If the rains and melted fnow give them fome importance in winter, their courfe is only to be difcovered, during the remainder of the year, by the round ftones and fragments of rocks with which their

(o) The Jordan, it muft be owned, has confiderable depth, but if the Orontes were not impeded by fucceffive obftacles, it would be quite dry during the fummer.

X 3   beds

beds are filled. They are nothing but torrents and cafcades; and it may be conceived that, from the proximity of the mountains, among which they rife, to the fea, their waters have not time to collect in long valleys, fo as to form rivers. The obftacles oppofed by thefe mountains, in feveral places, at their iffue, have formed confiderable lakes, fuch as thofe of Antioch, Aleppo, Damafcus, Houla, Tabaria, and that which is honoured with the name of the Dead Sea, or Lake Afphaltites. All thefe lakes, except the laft, are of frefh water, and contain feveral fpecies of fifh, different from *(p)* thofe we are acquainted with.

Lake Afphaltites, alone, contains neither animal nor vegetable life. We fee no verdure on its banks, nor are fifh to be found within its waters; but it is not true that its exhalations are peftiferous, fo as to deftroy birds flying over it. It is very common to

(p) The lake of Antioch abounds particularly with eels, and a fort of red fifh of an indifferent quality. The Greeks, who keep a perpetual Lent, confume great quantities of them. Lake Tabaria is ftill richer; crabs, efpecially, are very numerous, but, as its environs are inhabited only by Mahometans, it is but little fifhed.

fee

fee fwallows fkimming its furface, and dipping for the water neceffary to build their nefts. The real caufe which deprives it of vegetables and animals is the extreme faltnefs of the water, which is infinitely ftronger than that of the fea. The foil around it, equally impregnated with this falt, produces no plants, and the air itfelf, which becomes loaded with it from evaporation, and which receives alfo the fulphureous and bituminous vapours, cannot be favourable to vegetation : hence the deadly afpect which reigns around this lake. The ground about it, however, is not marfhy, and its waters are limpid and incorruptible, as muft be the cafe with a diffolution of falt. The origin of this mineral is eafy to be difcovered ; for on the fouth-weft fnore, are mines of foffil falt, of which I have brought away feveral fpecimens. They are fituated in the fide of the mountains which extend along that border, and, for time immemorial, have fupplied the neighbouring Arabs, and even the city of Jerufalem. We find alfo on this fhore fragments of fulphur and bitumen, which the Arabs convert into a trifling article of commerce ; as alfo hot fountains, and deep

X 4

cre-

crevices, which are difcovered at a diftance,
by little pyramids built on the brink of them.
We likewife find a fort of ftone, which, on
rubbing, emits a noxious fmell, burns like
bitumen, receives a polifh like white alabaf-
ter, and is ufed for the paving of court-
yards. At intervals, we alfo meet with un-
fhapen blocks, which prejudiced eyes miftake
for mutilated ftatues, and which pafs with
ignorant and fuperftitious pilgrims, for monuments of the adventure of *Lot's Wife*,
though it is no where faid fhe was meta-
morphofed into ftone, like Niobe, but into
falt, which muft have melted the enfuing
winter.

Some naturalifts have been greatly embarraffed to find a difcharge for the waters which
the Jordan is continually pouring into the
lake, and have therefore been inclined to
fufpect it had a communication with the
Mediterranean; but, befides that we know
of no gulph to corroborate this fuppofition, it has been demonftrated, by accurate calculations, that evaporation is more
than fufficient to carry off the waters
brought by the river. It is, in fact, very
confiderable, and frequently becomes fenfible

fible to the eye, by the fogs with which the lake is covered, at the rifing of the fun, and which are afterwards difperfed by the heat.

S e c t. VII.

Of the Climate.

It is an opinion pretty generally received, that Syria is a very hot country; but it will be neceffary to make feveral diftinctions: firft, on account of the difference of latitude, which from one extremity to the other, is not lefs than fix degrees: fecondly, from the natural divifion of the country into low and flat, and high and mountainous, which divifion occafions a ftill more fenfible difference; for while Reaumur's thermometer ftands at twenty-five and twenty-fix degrees upon the coaft, it hardly rifes to twenty or twenty-one among the mountains *(q)*. In

(q) Along the coaft of Syria, and at Tripoli, in particular, the loweft degrees to which the thermometer falls in winter, are eight and nine degrees above the freezing point; (50 and 52 of *Fahrenheit's*) in fummer, in clofe apartments, it rifes from $25\frac{1}{2}$ to 26° (88 to 90). As for the barometer, it is remarkable that at the latter end of May, it fixes at 28 inches, and never varies till October.

winter,

winter, therefore, the whole chain of mountains is covered with fnow, while the lower
country is always free from it, or at leaft it
lies only for an inftant. We muft firft then
eftablifh two general climates; the one very
hot, which is that of the coaft, and the
interior plains, fuch as thofe of Balbec, Antioch, Tripoli, Acre, Gaza, Hauran, &c.
the other temperate, and almoft like our own,
which is the climate of the mountains, at
leaft at a certain height. The fummer of
1784 was reckoned, among the Druzes, one
of the hotteft they remembered, yet I never
found the heat to be compared to that I had
felt at Saide or Bairout.

In this climate, the order of the feafons is
nearly the fame as in the middle provinces
of France; the winter, which lafts from November to March, is fharp and rigorous.
Not a year paffes without fnow, and the earth
is frequently covered feveral feet deep with it
for months together; the fpring and autumn
are mild, and the fummer heat is abfolutely
infupportable. In the plains, on the contrary,
as foon as the fun returns to the equator, the
tranfition is rapid to oppreffive heats, which
continue to the end of October. But then
the

the winter is fo moderate, that the orange, date, banana, and other delicate trees, flourifh in the open air; and it appears equally extraordinary and picturefque to an European at Tripoli, to behold, under his windows, in the month of January, orange-trees loaded with flowers and fruit, while the lofty head of Lebanon is feen covered with ice and fnow. It muft neverthelefs be obferved that, in the northern parts, and to the eaft of the mountains, the winter is more rigorous, without the fummer being lefs hot. At Antioch, Aleppo, and Damafcus, there are feveral weeks of froft and fnow every winter; which arifes from the fituation of the country ftill more than the difference of latitude. For, in fact, all the plain to the eaft of the mountains is very high above the level of the fea, expofed to all the parching blafts of the north and north-eaft, and fcreened from the humid winds of the fouth and fouthweft. Befides, Antioch and Aleppo receive from the mountains of Alexandretta, which are within fight, an air which the fnow, that covers them fo long, muft necefsarily render very fharp.

Syria,

Syria, therefore, unites different climates under the fame fky, and collects, within a narrow compafs, pleafures and productions which nature has elfewhere difperfed at great diftances of times and places. With us, for inftance, feafons are feparated by months ; there we may fay they are only feparated by hours. If in Saide or Tripoli, we are incommoded by the heats of July, in fix hours we are in the neighbouring mountains, in the temperature of March; or, on the other hand, if chilled by the frofts of December, at Befharrai, a day's journey brings us back to the coaft, amid the flowers of May *(r)*. The Arabian poets have therefore faid, that " the " Sannin bears winter on his head, fpring " upon his fhoulders, and autumn in his " bofom, while fummer lies fleeping at his " feet." I have myfelf experienced the truth of this figurative obfervation, during the eight months I refided at the monaftery of Mar-Hanna *(s)*, feven leagues from Bairout. At the

(r) This is the practice of feveral of the inhabitants of this diftrict, who pafs the winter near Tripoli, while their houfes are buried under the fnow.

(s) Mar-Hanna el Shouair; i. e. St. John, near the village of Shouair. This monaftery is fituated in a ftoney valley,

the end of February, I left at Tripoli a variety
of vegetables which were in perfection, and
many flowers in full bloom. On my arrival
at Antoura *(t)*, I found the plants only beginning to shoot; and, at Mar-Hanna, every
thing was covered with snow. It had not
entirely left the Sannin till the end of April,
and, already, in the valley it overlooks, roses
had begun to bud. The early figs were past
at Bairout, when they were first gathered
with us, and the silk-worms were in cod,
before our mulberry-trees were half stripped.

To this advantage, which perpetuates enjoyments by their succession, Syria adds another, that of multiplying them by the variety
of her productions. Were nature assisted by
art, those of the most distant countries might
be produced within the space of twenty
leagues. At present, in spite of the barba-
rism of a government which is an enemy to
all industry and improvement, we are asto-

valley, which joins to that of *Nahr el Kelb,* or Torrent
of the Dog. The religious are Greek Catholics, of the
order of Saint Basil : I shall have occasion to speak of it
more amply.

(t) A house formerly belonging to the Jesuits, but
occupied at present by the Lazarists.

nished

nifhed at the variety this province affords.
Befides wheat, rye, barley, beans, and the
cotton plant, which is cultivated every where,
we find a multitude of ufeful and agreeable
productions, appropriated to different fituations. Paleftine abounds in fefamum, from
which oil is procured, and doura *(u)* as good
as that of Egypt *(x)*. Maize thrives in the
light foil of Balbec, and even rice is cultivated, with fuccefs, on the borders of the
marfhy country of Havula. They have lately
begun to plant fugar-canes in the gardens of
Saide and of Bairout, and they find them
equal thofe of the Delta. Indigo grows
without cultivating, on the banks of the Jordan, in the country of Bifan, and only requires care to make it of an excellent quality.
The hill-fides of Latakia produce tobacco,
which is the principal article of the commerce of that town with Damietta and Cairo.
This is now cultivated throughout all the
mountains. As for trees, the olive-tree of

(u) A fort of pulfe, fomething like lentils, which grows
in clufters, on a ftalk fix or feven feet high. It is the
holcus arundinaceus of Linnæus.

(x) I never faw any buck-wheat in Syria, and oats
are very rare. They feed their horfes with nothing but
rye and chaff.

Provence

Provence grows at Antioch, and at Ramla, to the height of the beech. The white mulberry tree conftitutes the wealth of the whole country of the Druzes, by the beautiful filks which are produced on it, while the vine, fupported on poles, or winding round the oaks, fupplies grapes which afford red and white wines that might rival thofe of Bordeaux. Before the ravages occafioned by the late troubles, there were, in the gardens of Yaffa, two plants of the Indian cotton-tree, which grew rapidly, nor has this town loft its lemons, its enormous citrons *(y)*, or its water-melons, which are preferable even to thofe of Broulos *(z)*. Gaza produces dates like Mecca, and pomegranates like Algiers; Tripoli affords oranges equal to thofe of Malta; Bairout figs like thofe of Marfeilles, and bananas not inferior to thofe of St. Domingo; Aleppo enjoys the exclufive advantage of producing piftachios; and Damafcus juftly boafts of poffeffing all the fruits known in our provinces. Its ftoney foil fuits equally the ap-

(y) I have feen fome which weighed eighteen pounds.

(z) Broulos on the coaft of Egypt, produces better water-melons than are found in the reft of the Delta, where the fruits in general are too watery.

ples

ples of Normandy, the plumbs of Touraine, and the peaches of Paris. Twenty forts of apricots are reckoned there, the ftone of one of which contains a kernel highly valued through all Turkey. In fhort, the cochineal plant, which grows on all that coaft, contains, perhaps, that precious infect in as high perfection as it is found in Mexico and St. Domingo *(a)*; and if we confider that the mountains of the Yemen, which produce fuch excellent coffee, are only a continuation of thofe of Syria, and that their foil and climate are almoft the fame *(b)*, we fhall be induced to believe that Judea, efpecially, might eafily cultivate this valuable production of Arabia.

With thefe numerous advantages of climate and of foil, it is not aftonifhing that Syria fhould

(a) It was long imagined that the infect of the cochineal was peculiar to Mexico; and the Spaniards, to fecure the exclufive poffeffion of it, have prohibited the exportation of the living cochineal, under pain of death; but M. Thierri, who fucceeded in bringing it away, in 1771, and carried it to Saint Domingo, found the nopals of that ifland contained it before his arrival. It feems as if nature fcarcely ever feparated infects from the plants appropriated to them.

(b) The fituation of the country of Yemen and Tahama is very fimilar to that of Syria. See M. Niebuhr *Voyage en Arabie.*

3   always

always have been efteemed a moft delicious country, and that the Greeks and Romans ranked it among the moft beautiful of their provinces, and even thought it not inferior to Egypt. In more modern times, alfo, a Pacha, who was acquainted with both thefe provinces, being afked to which he gave the preference, replied, " Egypt, without doubt, " is a moft beautiful farm, but Syria is a " charming country-houfe" *(c).*

S E C T.

(c) To complete the Natural Hiftory of Syria, it is proper to add that it produces all our domeftic animals, and, befides them, the buffalo and the camel, whofe utility is fo well known. We alfo find gazelles (antelopes) in the plains, which fupply the place of our roebucks; in the mountains are numbers of wild-boars, not fo large nor fo fierce as ours. The ftag and the deer are unknown there; the wolf and the real fox are very rare; but there is a prodigious quantity of the middle fpecies, named *Shacal* (jackall) which in Syria is called *wauwee*, in imitation of its howl; and in Egypt *dib*, or wolf. Thefe jackalls go in droves, and frequent the environs of the towns, where they feed on what carrion they can find. They never attack any body, but are always ready to fave themfelves by flight. Every evening they feem to give each other the watch-word, to begin howling, and their cries, which are very doleful, fometimes, laft a quarter of an hour. In unfrequented places there are alfo hyenas, in Arabic named *daba*, and ounces, im-

S e c t. VIII.

Qualities of the Air.

I muſt not forget to ſpeak of the qualities of the air and waters. Theſe elements preſent in Syria very remarkable phænomena. On the mountains, and in all the elevated plain which ſtretches to the eaſtward, the air is light, pure and dry; while on the coaſt, and eſpecially from Alexandretta to Yafa, it is

properly called tygers (in Arabic *nema*). Lebanon, the country of the Druzes, Nablous, Mount Carmel, and the environs of Alexandretta, are their principal haunts. But, in return, the country is free from lions and bears. Water fowl are very plentiful; land game is not ſo abundant, except in particular diſtricts. The hare and the large red partridge are the moſt common; rabbits, if there are any, are extremely ſcarce. The francolin, or attagen, is more numerous at Tripoli, and in the neighbourhood of Yafa. Nor ought we to omit obſerving that a ſpecies of the colibri (or humming-bird) ſtill exiſts in the territory of Saide. M. J. B. Adanſon, formerly interpreter in that city, who cultivates natural hiſtory with equal taſte and ſucceſs, met with one, which he made a preſent of to his brother the Academician. This, and the pelican are the only remarkable birds in Syria.

3   moiſt

moift and heavy; thus Syria is divided lengthways into two different diftricts, feparated by
the chain of mountains which alfo caufe their
diverfity; for thefe preventing, by their height,
the free paffage of the wefterly winds, force
the vapours which they bring from the fea to
collect in the valleys; and as air is light only
in proportion to its purity, thefe are unable
to rife above the fummits of this rampart.
The confequence is, that the air of the defert and the mountains, though fufficiently
wholefome for fuch as are in no danger of
pulmonary complaints, is hurtful to thofe
who are, and it is neceffary to fend fuch from
Aleppo to Latakia or Saide. This good property of the air on the coaft is, however, out-
weighed by more ferious bad ones, and it
may in general be pronounced unhealthy, as
it caufes intermittent and putrid fevers, and
thofe defluxions of the eyes, of which I have
fpoken in treating of Egypt. The evening
dews, and fleeping on the terraces, are found
much lefs hurtful in the mountainous and
interior parts of the country, as the diftance
from the fea is greater, which confirms what
I have already obferved upon that fubject.

SECT.

S e c t.   IX.

Qualities of the Waters.

The waters of this country have alfo a remarkable difference. In the mountains, that
of the fprings is light, and of a very good
quality; but in the plain, both to the eaft
and weft, if it has no natural or artificial
communication with the fprings, we find
nothing but brackifh water, which becomes
ftill more fo the nearer we approach the
defert, where there is not a drop of any
other. This inconvenience has rendered
rain fo precious to the inhabitants of the
frontiers, that they have in all ages taken
care to collect it in wells and caverns carefully
clofed: hence, among all ruins, cifterns are
the firft things we difcover.

The face of the heavens, in Syria, particularly on the coaft, and in the defert, is in
general more conftant and regular than in
our climates; rarely is the fun obfcured for
two fucceffive days. In the courfe of a whole'
fummer we fee few clouds, and ftill lefs
rain; which only begins about the end of
                                    October,

October, and then is neither long nor plentiful. The hufbandmen wifh for it to fow what they call their *winter* crop, that is, their wheat and barley *(d)*. In December and January, the rain becomes more frequent and heavier, and fnow often falls in the higher country. It fometimes rains alfo in March and April; and the hufbandman avails himfelf of it to fow his *fummer* crop of fefamum, doura, tobacco, cotton, beans, and water-melons. The remainder of the year is uniform, and drought is more frequently complained of than too much wet.

(d) The feed-time of the winter crop, called *Shetawia*, takes place, throughout Syria, only at the time of the autumnal rains, or toward the end of October. The time of reaping this crop varies according to the difference of fituation. In Palefine, and in the Hauran, they reap their wheat and barley from the end of April through the whole month of May. But as we advance toward the north, or afcend the mountains, the harveft does not begin till June and July.

The feed-time of the fummer crop, or *Saifia*, begins with the fpring rains, that is, in March and April; and their harveft is in the months of September and October.

The time of vintage, in the mountains, is about the end of September; the filk-worms hatch there in April and May, and begin to fpin in July.

SECT. X.

Of the Winds.

The winds in Syria, as in Egypt, are in
fome degree periodical, and governed by the
feafons. About the autumnal equinox the
north-weft wind begins to blow more frequently and ftronger. It renders the air dry,
ciear, and fharp; and it is remarkable that,
on the fea-coaft, it caufes the head-ach, like
the north-eaft wind in Egypt; and this more
in the northern than in the fouthern parts,
but never in the mountains. We may further remark, that it ufually blows three
days fucceffively, like the fouth and fouth-
eaft at the other equinox. It continues to
prevail till November, that is, about fifty
days, and its variations are generally toward
the eaft. Thefe winds are followed by the
north-weft, the weft, and fouth-weft, which
prevail from November to February. The
two latter are, to ufe the expreffion of the
Arabs, *the fathers of the rains.* In March
arife the pernicious winds from the fouthern
quarter, with the fame circumftances as in
Egypt;

Egypt; but they become feebler as we advance toward the north, and are much more fupportable in the mountains than in the flat country. Their duration, at each return, is ufually of four-and-twenty hours, or three days. The eafterly winds, which follow, continue till June, when a north wind fucceeds, with which veffels may go and return along all the coaft. At the fame feafon too, the wind varies through all the points, every day, paffing with the fun from the eaft to the fouth, and from the fouth to the weft, to return by the north, and recommence the fame circuit. At this time alfo a local wind, called the land-breeze, prevails along the coaft, during the night; it fprings up after fun-fet, lafts till fun-rifing, and reaches only two or three leagues out at fea.

The caufes of all thefe phænomena are problems well deferving the attention of natural philofophers. No country is better adapted to obfervations of this kind than Syria. It feems as if nature had there prepared whatever is neceffary to the ftudy of her operations. We, in our foggy climates, in the depth of vaft continents, are unable to purfue the great changes which happen in

Y 4   the

the atmofphere: the confined horizon which
bounds our view, circumfcribes alfo our
ideas. The field of our obfervation is very
limited; and a thoufand circumftances combine to vary the effects of natural caufes.
There, on the contrary, an immenfe fcene
opens before us, and the great agents of nature are collected in a fpace which renders
it eafy to watch their various operations.
To the weft is the vaft liquid plain of the
Mediterranean; to the eaft the plain of the
defert, no lefs vaft, but abfolutely dry; in
the midft of thefe two level furfaces, rife the
mountains, whofe fummits are fo many obfervatories, from whence the fight may difcern full thirty leagues. Four obfervers
might command the whole extent of Syria;
and from the tops of Cafius, Lebanon, and
Tabor, let nothing efcape them within that
boundlefs horizon. They might obferve how
the region of the fea, at firft unclouded, veils
itfelf with vapours; in what manner thefe
vapours form into groupes, and feparate, and
by a conftant mechanifm, afcend and rife
above the mountains; while, on the other
hand, the defert, invariably clear, never
produces clouds, and has only thofe it has

received from the fea. They might reply to the queftion of M. Michaelis *(e)*, " Whether the defert produces dews?" that the defert, containing no water, except in winter, after the rains, can only furnifh vapours at that period. On reviewing the valley of Balbec, burnt up with heat, whilft the head of Lebanon is hoary with ice and fnow, they would be fenfible of the truth of an axiom, which ought no longer to be difputed, *that the heat is greater in proportion as we approach the furface of the earth, and diminifhes as we remove from it* ; fo that it feems to proceed only from the action of the rays of the fun upon the earth. In fhort, they might fuccefsfully attempt the folution of the greateft part of meteorological problems.

(e) See the *Queftions* propofed by M. Michaelis to the travellers for the king of Denmark.

C H A P. XXI.

Obſervations on the Winds, Clouds, Rains, Fogs, and Thunder.

UNTIL this ſhall be undertaken by perſons capable of making ſuch experiments,
with all the accuracy ſo important a diſcuſſion merits, I ſhall ſubmit, in a few
words, ſome general ideas ſuggeſted by
my own obſervations. I have already mentioned the relation there is between the
winds and the ſeaſons; and have hinted
that the ſun, from the connection between
his annual progreſs, and their varieties, appears to be the principal agent. His action
on the atmoſphere which ſurrounds our
globe, ſeems to be the primary cauſe of all
the various motions in the upper regions of
the air. To conceive clearly how this is
effected, we muſt trace back theſe ideas to
their origin, and conſider the properties of
the element put in action.

First, the air, we know, is a fluid, all the
particles of which, naturally equal and moveable,

able, tend, like water, invariably to a level; fo that if we fuppofe a chamber fix feet fquare, every way, the air introduced into it will fill it equally. Secondly, another property of air is to be capable of dilatation or compreffion; that is, the fame quantity of it may occupy a greater or a lefs fpace. Thus, in the cafe of the chamber, were we to draw off two thirds of the air it contains, the remainder would replace it by expanfion, and ftill continue to fill its whole capacity; if inftead of drawing off the air, the quantity of it be doubled or tripled, the chamber will equally contain it; which is not the cafe with water.

This property of expanfion is more efpecially called into action by the prefence of fire; and as then the heated air contains in an equal fpace fewer particles than cold air, it becomes lighter, and rifes. If, for example, in the fuppofed chamber, you introduce a grate full of fire, the air affected by it will rife inftantly to the ceiling, and that which was near it will take its place. When this air is heated it will follow the firft, and a conftant current upwards, fupplied by the

influx

influx of the lateral air, be produced *(f)*; fo that the hotteft air will diffufe itfelf in the upper part of the room, and the lefs heated in the lower, each of them continuing to feek an equilibrium, agreeable to the general laws of fluidity *(g)*.

Let us now apply thefe obfervations to what paffes in the elements, on a larger fcale, and we fhall find they explain the greater part of the phænomena of the winds.

The atmofphere which furrounds the earth may be confidered as an ocean formed by a peculiar fluid, the bottom of which we occupy, and whofe furface is at an unknown height. From its primary law, that is, from its fluidity, this ocean has a conftant tendency to an equilibrium, and to remain ftagnant; but the fun, calling into action the law of expanfion, excites an agitation in it which keeps all its parts in a ftate of perpetual fluctuation. His rays, applied to the

---

(f) This is the mechanifm of chimneys and ftove-baths.

(g) There is befides this a continual effort of the rarefied air againft the obftacles by which it is confined; but this is of no confequence in the prefent cafe.

furface of the earth, have precifely the fame effect as the fire in the fuppofed chamber; they produce a degree of heat which dilates the contiguous air, and caufes it to rife towards the upper region. Were this heat equal throughout, the general procefs would be uniform; but it varies from an infinity of circumftances, which become the efficient caufes of the varieties we continually obferve.

Firft, it is certain that the earth is heated more or lefs in proportion as it is more or lefs expofed to the perpendicular rays of the fun. The heat is nothing at the poles, but exceffive under the line. For this reafon our climates are colder in winter and hotter in fummer; and for the fame reafon, likewife, the temperature may be very different in the fame place, and under the fame latitude, according as the country, inclining towards the north or fouth, prefents its furface more or lefs obliquely to the folar rays *(b)*.

(b) This is the reafon why, as Montefquieu has well obferved, Tartary, which is under the fame parallel as France and England, is infinitely colder than thefe countries.

Secondly,

Secondly, it is equally true that the furface of the water is lefs retentive of heat than that of the earth : the air over the fea, lakes, and rivers, therefore, will be lefs hot than that over the land in the fame latitude ; humidity is every where a principle of coolnefs, and hence a country covered with forefts, and abounding in moraffes, is colder than when thofe marfhy grounds are drained, and the forefts felled *(i)*.

A third confideration, not lefs important, is, that the heat diminifhes as we rife above the general plane of the earth. This is demonftrated by the obfervation, that the fummits of high mountains, even under the line, are covered with eternal fnows, which proves the conftant coldnefs of the upper region of the air.

If we now confider the combined effects of thefe different circumftances, we fhall find they account for the greateft part of the phænomena we are attempting to explain.

Firft, the air of the polar regions being colder and more denfe than that of the coun-

(i) This explains why ancient Gaul was much colder than modern France.

tries

tries near the equinoctial, its endeavour to preserve an equilibrium, inceffantly forces it from the poles towards the equator. And this reafoning is fupported by facts, fince the uniform obfervation of all navigators proves that the winds moft common in both hemifpheres proceed from that quarter of the horizon of which the pole occupies the center; that is to fay, from between the northweft and north-eaft. What is obferved on the Mediterranean, in particular, is perfectly analogous to this remark.

I have remarked, in fpeaking of Egypt, that the northerly winds are moft frequent in that fea, where they prevail nine months out of twelve. A very plaufible folution of this phenomenon may be given from the confideration that, the coaft of Barbary, ftruck powerfully by the rays of the fun, heats the furrounding air, the rarefaction of which caufes it to rife, and pafs into the interior part of the country, while that of the fea, meeting with lefs refiftance on that fide, immediately rufhes into its place; but being itfelf heated, follows the former current, till, by degrees, the Mediterranean lofes a great quantity of air. By this procefs, the air of Europe,

having

having no longer any fupport, diffufes itfelf
on that fide; and thus a general current is
eftablifhed. This will be the ftronger, in
proportion as the air of the north is colder,
and hence the greater impetuofity of the
winds in winter than in fummer; and it will
be more feeble as the air of the different
countries approaches nearer to an equilibrium; and hence thefe winds are more
moderate in the fine feafon, and in July
and Auguft terminate in a fort of general
calm, becaufe the fun then heats almoft
equally the whole hemifphere, even to the
pole. The uniform and conftant courfe
that the north-weft wind takes in June, is
caufed by the fun, which, advancing as far
as the parallel of Afouan, which is almoft
that of the Canaries, occafions, behind mount
Atlas, a conftant and regular wind. The periodical return of the eafterly winds, at the
time of each equinox, originates, no doubt,
from a fimilar caufe; but, in order to difcover
this, it would be neceffary to have a general
table of what paffes in other parts of the
continent; and here, I confefs, my fyftem
feems to fail me. I am ignorant, likewife,
of the reafon of that conftant duration

of

of *three days*, which we almoft always obferve in the foutherly and northerly winds,
whenever they blow at the time of the equinoxes.

Varieties are fometimes obfervable in the
fame wind, which arife from the nature of
the country. Thus, if a wind meets with
a valley, it follows that direction, like the
currents of the fea. And hence, doubtlefs,
it happens, that in the Adriatic Gulph fcarce
any but north-weft and fouth-eafterly winds
are known; fuch being the direction of this
arm of the fea. From a fimilar caufe, the
wind in the Red-fea blows conftantly from
the north or fouth; and the frequency of
the north-weft, or *Miftral,* in Provence, muft
arife from the currents of air, occafioned by
the Cevennes and the Alps, and which are
forced to follow the direction of the valley
of the Rhone.

But what becomes of the air thus attracted
by the coaft of Africa and the torrid zone?
This may be difpofed of in two different
ways.

Firft, the air, arrived under thefe latitudes,
forms there a great current, known by the
name of the Eaftern Trade-wind, that

extends, as is well known, from the Canaries to America *(k)*, which, when it has
reached, it seems to be broken by the
mountains of the continent: and thus diverted
from its original direction, it returns in an oppofite one, whence that wefterly wind which
prevails under the parallel of Canada, and
which, by this means, repairs the loffes of
the polar regions.

Secondly, The air which rufhes from the
Mediterranean upon Africa, rarefied there by
the heat, rifes into the fuperior region; but as it
cools at a certain height, the fpace it occupies is

(k) Dr. Franklin has thought, that the caufe of the
Eaftern Trade-wind has a connection with the diurnal
motion of the earth; but were it fo, why is not this
wind perpetual? Befides, how fhall we explain, on this
hypothefis, the two Monfoons of India, the fhiftings of
which conftantly follow the paffage of the fun over the
equinoctial line; that is, the wefterly and foutherly
winds prevail during the fix months the fun is in the
northern figns; and the eafterly and northerly winds,
during the fix months he is in the fouthern. Does not
this prove, that all the varieties of the winds depend
folely on the action of the fun upon the atmofphere?
The moon too, which has fo great an effect upon the
ocean, may alfo produce fome on the winds; but the
influence of the other planets feems a chimæra fuited
only to the aftrology of the ancients.

infinitely

infinitely reduced by condenfation. It may be alleged, that having recovered its weight, it fhould defcend; but befides that, on returning towards the earth, it becomes again heated, and confequently expands, it experiences a powerful and continued effort of the inferior air which fupports it. Thefe two *ftrata*, of the fuperior air refrigerated, and the inferior air dilated, maintain a perpetual ftruggle with each other. If the equilibrium be loft, the fuperior, obeying the law of gravity, may rufh into the inferior region, even to the earth. To accidents of this nature we muft afcribe thofe fudden torrents of frozen air, known by the name of hurricanes and fqualls, which feem to fall from heaven, and produce, in the warmeft feafons, and the hotteft regions of the earth, the cold of the polar circles. If the furrounding air refifts, their duration is limited to a fhort time; but when they fall in with currents already eftablifhed, they encreafe their violence, and become tempefts, which laft feveral hours. Thefe tempefts are dry when the air is pure; but when it is loaded with clouds, they are attended with a deluge of rain and hail, which the cold air conden-

fes

fes in its fall. It may also happen that a continued fall of water shall accompany the rupture, increased by the surrounding clouds, attracted to the same vortex; and hence will result those columns of water, known by the name of *Typhons* and *water-spouts (1)*. These water-spouts are not unusual on the coast of Syria, towards Cape Wedjh and Mount Carmel; and it is observed that they are most frequent at the equinoxes, and in a stormy sky, obscured by clouds.

Mountains of a certain height often afford examples of this descent of refrigerated air from the upper region. When their summits are covering with snow, at the approach of winter, impetuous torrents of wind, called by mariners *snow winds*, rush down from them. They then say, *the mountains are defending themselves*, because these winds blow on you, in whatever direction you approach them. The gulphs of Lyons and Alexandretta are remarked frequently to furnish instances of this kind of winds.

On the same principles we may explain the phænomena of those winds of the coast, vul-

(1) Dr. Franklin has explained them in the same manner.

garly

garly called *land breezes*. It is obferved by
mariners, that, in the Mediterranean, they
blow from the land during the night, and
in the day from the fea; the caufe of which
is, that the air, rarefied by the heat of the
day, and condenfed by the coldnefs of the
night, rufhes alternately from the land to the
fea, and the fea to the land. Thus, in Syria,
the fide of Lebanon which faces the fea,
being heated by the fun during the day, and
efpecially towards noon, the air, on its declivity, being rarefied, and lofing its relative
equilibrium with that of the fea, is forced
upwards; but the new air, which takes its
place, becoming heated, likewife, foon follows
it, until, by this fucceffion, a current is formed
fimilar to that we obferve in the funnels of
a ftove or chimney *(m)*. When the fun fets,
this action ceafes, the mountain cools, the
air condenfes, and, condenfing, becomes
heavier, and falls down again, thus forming
a torrent which rufhes along the declivity to
the fea. The current ceafes in the morning, on the fun's return, and the fame round

(m) This is often fenfible to the eye; but it is rendered ftill more evident by approaching a filk thread or a
piece of down to the funnels.

Z 3

is

is repeated. This wind does not advance above two or three leagues into the fea, becaufe the impulfe of its fall is gradually deftroyed by the refiftance of the mafs of air into which it enters. The extent of the land breeze is in proportion to the height and fteepnefs of this declivity. It reaches further at the foot of Lebanon, and the northern chain of eminences, becaufe the mountains in that quarter are loftier, fteeper, and nearer to the fea; and there are often violent and fudden fqualls at the mouth of the Kafmia (*n*), where the deep valley of Bekaa collecting the air in its narrow channel, propels it as from a funnel. Thefe winds do not extend fo far on the coaft of Paleftine, becaufe the mountains there are not fo lofty, and between them and the fea there is a plain of four or five leagues; and at Gaza, and on the coaft of Egypt, they are never known, becaufe that country has no declivity proper to caufe them. In fhort, they are every where ftronger in fummer, and feebler in winter, becaufe in the latter feafon the heat and rarefaction are lefs confiderable.

(*n*) Thefe fqualls are fo violent, that they fometimes overfet boats; as I was once very near experiencing myfelf.

This

This comparative ſtate of the air of the
ſea, and that of continents, is the cauſe of a
phenomenon long ſince obſerved, viz. the
general property of all land, and eſpecially
mountains, to attract clouds. Whoever has
viſited different ſea coaſts, cannot but have
remarked that clouds continually ariſe at ſea,
and regularly direct their courſe towards the
land, and eſpecially the higheſt mountains.
Some philoſophers have aſcribed this to an
attractive virtue ; but beſides that, this *occult
quality* is as unintelligible as the ancient *horror of a vacuum*, the mechanical cauſe of that
phenomenon may be explained by material
agents ; I mean the law of the equilibrium of
fluids, by which the heavier air forces the
lighter upwards ; for continents, when under the ſame parallel, and of like elevation,
being always more heated than ſeas, a conſtant current of air muſt take place, and
drive the clouds from the ſea towards the
land. This direction will be the more conſtant, the more the mountains are heated.
If the vapours meet with a flat and level
country, they will glide over it without
falling, becauſe the land being equally heated, there is nothing to condenſe them.

This

This is the reafon why it never, or but very rarely, rains, in fummer, in Egypt, or the deferts of Arabia and Africa. The air of thefe countries being heated and rarefied, raifes the clouds, and, as it is the nature of all vapour to be elevated by hot air, they continue to float in the middle region, where the prevailing current carries them towards the higher parts of the continent, which perform, in fome meafure, as I have already faid, the office of a chimney. Being then at a greater diftance from the furface of the earth, which is the great receptacle of heat, they are refrigerated and condenfed, till their particles collect into rain or fnow. In winter, the effects vary with circumftances. During that feafon, when the fun is remote from the countries we are fpeaking of, the earth being lefs heated, the air in general affumes a temperature more nearly approaching to that of the high mountains; it becomes colder and more denfe; the vapours are no longer elevated to the fame height; the clouds are formed lower down; and frequently fall quite to the earth, and are called fogs. At this period, accumulated by the wefterly winds, and by the abfence of the currents which

carry

carry them off in fummer, they are compelled to fall upon the plains, and hence the folution of the problem *(o)*: " The " evaporation being more confiderable in " fummer than in winter, why are there " more clouds, fogs, and rains in winter " than in fummer?" Hence alfo we are able to explain another appearance obfervable both in Egypt and Palefline *(p)*, " that if " there be a continual and gentle rain, it will " fall rather in the night than in the day." In thefe countries, it is generally obferved that clouds and fogs approach the earth at night, and rife from it in the day, becaufe the prefence of the fun always excites a degree of heat fufficient to raife them; I have often experienced the truth of this at Cairo, in the months of July and Auguft, 1783. At funrife, we frequently had a fog, the thermometer being at feventeen degrees *(q)*; two hours after, the thermometer being at twenty,

(o) See Chap. IV.

(p) I have obferved this in Paleftine, in the months of November, December, and January, 1784 and 1785. The temperature of the plain of Paleftine, efpecially towards Gaza, is nearly the fame with that of Egypt.

(q) By Reaumur's fcale, (anfwering to 70 of Fahrenheit's).

or,

or, perhaps, twenty-four degrees, the fky was covered with fcattered clouds driving to the fouth. On my return from Suez, about the fame time, that is, between the 24th and 26th of July, we had no fog during the two nights we paffed in the defert; but on arriving, at break of day, in fight of the valley of Egypt, I obferved it covered with a body of vapours which had the appearance of a ftagnant lake. As the day came on, they began to move and rife, and, before eight o'clock in the morning, they had left the ground, and the air only fhewed fome fcattered clouds, which took their courfe along the valley. The following year, being among the Druzes, I obferved nearly fimilar phænomena. Firft, about the end of June, there was formed a chain of clouds, to be attributed, no doubt, to the over-flowing of Egypt by the Nile (r), and which, in fact, proceeded from that quarter, and were paffing to the north-eaft (s). After this firft

(r) It is not fuperfluous to obferve that the Nile, at that period, caufes a current along the whole coaft of Syria, which extends from Gaza to Cyprus.

(s) This appears to me to be the column of clouds mentioned by Baron de Tott. I have alfo obferved the multineis of the horizon of Egypt, of which he fpeaks.

irruption,

irruption, towards the end of July, and in August, there was a fecond feafon of clouds. Every day, towards eleven o'clock, or about noon, the fky was overcaft, the fun was often invifible the whole afternoon, the *fannin,* or fummit of Lebanon, was capped with clouds, and many of them, afcending the declivities, remained among the vineyards and the pines, and I was frequently fo enveloped in a white, humid, warm and opake mift, as not to be able to fee four paces before me. About ten or eleven at night, the fky grew clear, the ftars appeared, and the remainder of the night was very fine; the fun rofe fhining, and, towards noon, the like appearances returned in the fame circle. This repetition puzzled me the more, as I could not conceive what became of all this quantity of clouds. Part of them, it is true, paffed the chain of the Sannin; thefe I might fuppofe had proceeded to Anti-Lebanon, or the defert; but what was to become of that portion which was paffing along the declivity, at the moment the fun fet, for there was neither dew nor rain into which they could be refolved? To difcover the caufe of this, I

afcended

afcended feveral mornings fucceffively, at
day-break, a neighbouring eminence, and
there, looking down upon the valley, and the
fea, diftant, in an oblique line, about five
leagues, I examined attentively the ftate of
the atmofphere. I at firft perceived nothing
but a body of vapours which veiled the
waters; and the horizon, towards the fea, appeared to me very thick, while on the fide
of the mountains it was quite clear. As the
fun enlightened that part, I difcovered clouds
by the reflection of his rays; thefe at firft
feemed to me very low; but, as the heat en-
creafed, they feparated, and rofe higher, and
continually proceeding towards the mountain, continued there the remainder of the
day, as I have defcribed. From hence I
concluded that the clouds I faw, thus mount-
ing, formed a great part of thofe which
were on the declivities in the evening, and
which, not being able to rife fufficiently
high, had been feized by the cold air, and
thrown back on the fea, by the land breeze;
I imagined that they were retained there the
whole night, till the fea breeze, getting up,
drove them back upon the mountain, and
hurried

hurried part of them over the fummit, to fall on the other fide in dews, or to moiften the parched air of the defert.

I have faid that thefe clouds conveyed no dews; and I have frequently remarked that there were fewer when the fky was clouded, than when the heavens were clear. But the dew is at all times lefs abundant on thefe mountains, than on the coaft, and in Egypt, which may be eafily explained, by fuppofing that the air is not able to elevate to that height the excefs of humidity with which it is loaded; for the dew, as is well known, is the excefs of humidity which the heated air raifes in vapour during the day, and which, condenfing by the coolnefs of the evening, falls down again in greater or lefs abundance, according to the vicinity of the country to the fea *(t)*. Hence the exceffive

(*t*) This refolves a queftion propofed to me at Yafa; viz. " Why one fweats more at Yafa, on the borders of " the fea, than at Ramla, which is at three leagues dif- " tance up the country ?" The reafon is, that the air of Yafa, being faturated with humid particles, imbibes the emanations of the body but flowly, while at Ramla, the air being more dry, abforbs them fafter. For this reafon, alfo, the breath is vifible in winter, in our climates, and not in fummer.

dews

dews in the Delta, which are lefs confiderable in the Thebais, and the defert, as I am well affured; and if the moifture does not fall when the heavens are obfcured, it is from its affuming the form of clouds, or being intercepted by them.

In other cafes, the fky being ferene, we fee the clouds fometimes difperfe and diffolve, like fmoke; at others, form in an inftant, and from a fmall fpeck, become of a prodigious fize. This is particularly obfervable at the fummit of Lebanon, and mariners have experienced that, the appearance of a cloud, on this peak, is an infallible prefage of a wefterly wind. At fun-fet, I have often obferved thefe light clouds adhering to the fides of the rocks of Nahr-el-Kelb, and augmenting fo rapidly, that in an hour the valley was quite full of them. The inhabitants fay, they are the vapours of the valley itfelf; but this valley being all ftone, and without water, it is impoffible they fhould be exhalations from that; it is more natural to fuppofe them vapours of the atmofphere, which, condenfed at the approach of night, fall in an imperceptible rain, and caufe the mift which is then obferved. Fogs
are

are explicable on the fame principles.   There
are none in the hot countries diftant from
the fea, nor during the fummer droughts;
for, in thefe cafes, the air has no furplus of
humidity.   But they appear after the autumnal rains, and, even in fummer, after
heavy fhowers, becaufe the earth has then
imbibed matter for evaporation, and acquired
a degree of coolnefs fufficient to caufe a condenfation of the vapours.   In our climates,
they always begin in the meadows, in preference to tilled ground.   We frequently obferve, at the fetting of the fun, a fheet of
fmoke, forming on the grafs, which foon increafes in extent and height.   The reafon
of this is, that humid and cool places con-
denfe the falling vapours fooner than thofe
which are dry and dufty.

A variety of other obfervations might be
made on the formation and nature of thefe
vapours, which though, in reality, the fame,
are called fogs, when they reft on the ground,
and clouds, when they rife into the air.   By
confidering their various properties, we fhall
perceive they are governed by the laws of
combination, diffolution, precipitation, and
faturation; of which modern phyfics, under

the

the appellation of chemiftry, is employed in developing the theory. But to treat of them, in this place, I fhould be under a neceffity of entering into details which would lead me too far from my fubject. I fhall confine myfelf, therefore, to one concluding obfervation, relative to thunder.

Thunder is known in the Delta as well as in Syria; but with this difference, that in the Delta, and the plain of Paleftine, it is extremely rare in fummer, and more frequent in winter; while in the mountains, on the contrary, it is more common in fummer, and very feldom heard in winter. In both thefe countries, it happens ofteneft in the rainy feafon, or about the time of the equinoxes, efpecially the autumnal one; it is further remarkable, that it never comes on from the land-fide, but always from the fea. The ftorms which fall on the Delta and Syria conftantly come from the Mediterranean (u).

Thefe

(u) I do not know what paffes in this refpect in Upper Egypt: as for the Delta, it appears that it fometimes receives clouds and thunder from the Red Sea. On the day that I left Cairo, (September 26th, 1783,) as night was coming on, a ftorm appeared in the fouthcaft,

These storms, in general, happen either in the evening or morning, and rarely in the middle of the day (x); they are accompanied with violent showers, and sometimes with hail; which, in an hour's time, render the country full of little lakes. These circumstances, and, above all, this perpetual connection of clouds with thunder, may suggest the following remarks.

If thunder is constantly attended with clouds, and they are absolutely necessary to its existence, it must be caused by some of their elements. But in what manner are clouds formed? By the evaporation of water. How is this evaporation effected? By the presence of the element of fire. Water

east, which soon produced several claps of thunder, and ended by a violent fall of hail, as large as the largest fort of peas. It continued ten or twelve minutes; and my companions and I had time enough to collect a quantity of hail-stones, sufficient to fill two large glasses, and could say that we had drank iced water in Egypt. It is proper to add that it was at the time when the southerly monsoon begins to blow on the Red-Sea.

(x) M. Niebuhr has also observed, at Moka and Bombay, that storms always proceed from the sea.

Vol. I. A a of

of itfelf is not volatile ; fome agent is neceffary to raife it ; this agent is fire ; and hence,
as has been already obferved, " evaporation
" is always in proportion to the heat applied
" to water." Each particle of water is rendered volatile by a particle of fire, and, unqueftionably, alfo, by a particle of air combined with it. This combination may be
regarded as a neutral falt, and, comparing it
with nitre, we may fay the water in it reprefents the alkali, and the fire the nitrous acid.
The clouds, thus compofed, float in the atmofphere until they meet with fomething
which feparates their conftituent parts. If,
from any caufe, thefe particles are fuddenly
difunited, a detonation is the confequence,
accompanied, as in nitre, with explofion and
light. The igneous matter, and the air,
being inftantly diffipated by the fhock, the
water which was combined with them, reftored to its natural gravity, falls precipitately
from the height to which it had been elevated ; and hence the violent fhowers which
follow loud claps of thunder, and which
happen, generally, at the end of ftorms, the
igneous matter being then expended. Sometimes

times the particles of fire being combined with the air only, it melts like nitre; and this it is, doubtlefs, which produces thofe lightnings, when no thunder is heard, called fires of the horizon *(feux d'horizon) (y)*. But is this igneous matter diftinct from the electric? Does it obferve peculiar laws and affinities in its combinations and detonations? This is what I fhall not take upon me to examine. Thefe refearches are not fuited to a narrative of travels: I ought to confine myfelf to facts; and the few explanatory remarks I have added, though they were naturally fuggefted by them, have already led me too far from my fubject.

(y) Shooting ftars feem alfo to be a particular combination of igneous matter. The Maronites of Mar-Elias affured me that one of thefe ftars falling, three years ago, on two mules of the convent, killed them both, making an explofion like the report of a piftol, and leaving no more traces than thunder.

A a 2   CHAP.

C H A P. XXII.

Of the Inhabitants of Syria.

SYRIA, as well as Egypt, has undergone
revolutions which have confounded the different races of its inhabitants. Within two
thousand five hundred years, we may reckon
ten invasions, which have introduced into that
country a succession of foreign nations. First,
the Assyrians of Nineveh, who, passing the
Euphrates, about the year 750 before the
Christian æra, within sixty years, obtained
possession of almost the whole country lying
to the north of Judea. Next the Chaldeans, or
Babylonians, who, having destroyed the power
on which they were dependent, succeeded, as
by hereditary right, to its possessions, and completed the conquest of Syria, except only
the Isle of Tyre. The Chaldeans were followed by the Persians, under Cyrus, and the
Persians, by the Macedonians, under Alexander. It then seemed as if Syria was about to
cease being subject to foreign powers, and that
it would obtain a distinct and independent government,

vernment, according to the natural right of every country; but the people, who found in the Seleucidæ only cruel defpots and oppreffors, feeing themfelves reduced to the neceffity of bearing fome yoke, preferred the lighteft; and Syria, yielding to the arms of Pompey, became a province of the Roman empire.

Five centuries after, when the fons of Theodofius divided their immenfe patrimony, this country changed the capital to which it was to appertain, without changing its mafters, and was annexed to the empire of Conftantinople. Such was its fituation when, in the year 622, the Arabian tribes, collected under the banners of Mahomet, feized, or rather laid it wafte. Since that period, torn to pieces by the civil wars of the Fatmites, and the Ommiades, wrefted from the Caliphs by their rebellious governors, taken from them by the Turkman foldiery, invaded by the European crufaders, retaken by the Mamlouks of Egypt, and ravaged by Tamerlane and his Tartars, it has at length fallen into the hands of the Ottoman Turks, who have been its

mafters

mafters for two hundred and fixty-eight years.

Thefe viciffitudes have introduced into the country diftinct tribes of inhabitants, as various as the revolutions it has undergone, fo that the people of Syria muft not be confidered as one fingle nation, but rather as a mixture of different nations.

They may be divided into three principal claffes.

Firft, The pofterity of the people conquered by the Arabs, that is, the Greeks of the Lower Empire.

Secondly, The pofterity of the Arabian conquerors.

Thirdly, The prefent ruling people, the Ottoman Turks.

Of thefe three claffes, the former muft be again fubdivided, in confequence of feveral diftinctions which have taken place among them. The Greeks then muft be divided into,

Firft, Greeks proper, vulgarly called *Schifmatics*, or feparated from the Romifh communion.

Secondly, Latin Greeks, re-united to that communion.

Thirdly,

Thirdly, Maronites, or Greeks of the sect of the Monk Maron, formerly independent of the two communions, but at present united to the latter.

The Arabs must be divided into,

First, The proper descendents of the conquerors, who have greatly intermixed their blood, and are considerably the most numerous.

Secondly, The Motoualis, distinguished from these by their religious opinions.

Thirdly, The Druzes, distinct likewise, from the same reason.

Fourthly, The Ansarians, who are also descended from the Arabs.

To these people, who are the cultivators and settled inhabitants of Syria, must still be added three other wandering tribes, or pastors, viz. the Turkmans, the Curds, and the Bedouin Arabs.

Such are the different races dispersed over the country, between the sea and the desert, from Gaza to Alexandretta.

In this enumeration, it is remarkable that the ancient inhabitants have no remaining representative; their distinguishing character is lost and confounded in that of the Greeks,

who,

who, in fact, by a continued refidence from
the days of Alexander, have had fufficient
time entirely to take place of the ancient
people; the country alone, and a few traits
of manners and cuftoms, preferve the veftiges
of diftant ages.

Syria has not, like Egypt, refufed to adopt
the foreign races. They all become equally
naturalized to the country. The features and
complexion are governed by nearly the fame
laws there as in the fouth of Europe, with
the differences only which naturally refult
from the nature of the climate. Thus the
inhabitants of the fouthern plains are more
fwarthy than thofe of the northern, and thefe,
more fo than the inhabitants of the mountains. In Lebanon, and the country of the
Druzes, the complexion does not differ from
that in our provinces in the middle of France.
The women of Damafcus and Tripoli are
greatly boafted for their fairnefs, and even the
regularity of their features; but we muft take
this praife on truft, fince the veil, which they
perpetually wear, allows no perfon to make
nice obfervations. In feveral diftricts, the
women are lefs fcrupulous, without being
lefs chafte. In Paleftine, for example, you

may

may fee married women almoft uncovered;
but want and fatigue have robbed the countenance of all its charms; their eyes alone
are almoft every where beautiful; and the
long drapery, which forms their general drefs,
permits the body freely to difplay its fhape:
it is fometimes without elegance, but its
proportions at leaft are no way injured. I do
not recollect having feen in Syria, nor even in
Egypt, two perfons crooked or deformed. It
is true they are ftrangers to thofe tight-laced
waifts, which are fo much admired among
us: they are in no eftimation in the eaft;
and the young women, affifted by their
mothers, very early ftudy, even fuperftitious
receipts, to acquire an *embonpoint*: happily,
Nature, by refifting our caprices, has fet
bounds to our fingularities, for we do not
perceive in Syria, where the fhape is not confined, that the body becomes any larger than
in France, where it is fo tightly laced.

The Syrians are, in general, of a middling
ftature, and are, as in all warm countries,
lefs corpulent than the inhabitants of the
north.   We find, however, in the cities,
fome individuals whofe amplitude of belly
proves that the influence of diet is able, in
a certain

a certain degree, to counterbalance that of climate.

Syria has no difeafe peculiar to itfelf, but the pimple of Aleppo, which I fhall notice when I come to fpeak of that city. The diforders prevalent here are dyfenteries, inflammatory and intermittent fevers, which are the confequences of the bad fruit which the people greedily devour. The fmallpox is fometimes very fatal; but the general and moft frequent illnefs is the cholic, the caufes of which are very evident, when we confider that every body eats to excefs of unripe fruit, raw vegetables, honey, cheefe, olives, ftrong oil, four milk, and ill-fermented bread. Thefe are the ufual food of all the inhabitants; and the acid juices they contain produce crudities, naufea, and even frequent vomitings of bile. Accordingly, the firft prefcription in almoft all diforders is an emetic, which method of treatment, however, is only known to the European phyficians. Bleeding, as I have already faid, is neither neceffary, nor very ufeful. In imminent cafes, cream of tartar and tamarinds have the moft certain fuccefs.

The general language of Syria is the
Arabic

Arabic tongue. M. Niebuhr reports, upon hearfay, that the Syriac is ftill ufed in fome villages of the mountains ; but, though I interrogated, on this fubject, feveral monks, who are perfectly well acquainted with the country, I have not been able to learn any thing like it. I have been told only that, in the towns of Maloula and Sidnaia, near Damafcus, they fpeak a dialect fo corrupted, that it is difficult to be underftood. But this difficulty proves nothing, fince, in Syria, as in all the Arabian countries, the dialects vary at every place. The Syriac may be, therefore, regarded as a dead language ; for the Maronites, who have preferved it in their liturgy, and in their mafs, underftand very little of it, while they recite them. We may affert the fame of the Greek. Among the monks and fchifmatic priefts, there are very few who have any knowledge of it, unlefs they have made it their particular ftudy in the iflands of the Archipelago : befides, we know that the modern Greek is fo corrupted, that it would no more enable a man to underftand Demofthenes, than the Italian to read Cicero. The Turkifh language is only ufed, in Syria, by the military, perfons

in

in office, and the Turkman hordes *(a)*. Some of the natives learn it, as the Turks learn Arabic, to facilitate their dealings with ftrangers : but the pronunciation and accent of thefe two languages have fo little analogy that they always continue foreign to each other. The Turks, habituated to a nafal and pompous profody, are rarely able to imitate the harfh founds and ftrong af- pirations of the Arabic. This tongue abounds fo in harfh vowels and guttural confonants that, on hearing it fpoken for the firft time, you would imagine they were gargling their throats. On this account it is difagreeable and difficult to all Europeans ; but fuch is the power of habit that, when we complain to the Arabs of its afperity, they accufe us of a want of ear, and retort the charge upon our languages ; among which they give the preference to the Italian ; and they compare, with fome reafon, the French to the Turkifh, and the Englifh to the Per- fian. In the dialects of their own we find

---

(a) At Alexandretta, and Beilam, which is conti- guous, they fpeak Turkifh ; but they muft be regarded as frontiers of Caramania, where Turkifh is the vulgar tongue.

almoft

almoft the fame difference. The Arabic of
Syria is much harfher than that of Egypt;
the pronunciation of the profeffors of the
law at Cairo is efteemed a model of facility
and elegance. But, according to the obfervation of M. Niebuhr, that of the inhabitants of the Yemen, and the fouthern coaft,
is infinitely fofter, and gives a fluency to the
Arabic, of which he could not have thought
it fufceptible. Attempts have been made
to eftablifh an analogy between the climates
and the pronounciation of languages; it has
been faid, for inftance, that the inhabitants
of the north fpeak more with their lips
and teeth than thofe of the fouth. This
may be juft when applied to fome parts of
our continent; but, to decide univerfally,
we muft make more circumftantial and extenfive obfervations. We fhould not too haftily pronounce thefe general decifions concerning languages and their different characters; becaufe we are always naturally led to
judge from our own, and, confequently, from
a prejudice of habit extremely inimical to
juft reafoning.

Among the different inhabitants of Syria
I have mentioned, fome are difperfed, indif-
ferently,

ferently, over every part of the country, others confine themselves to particular spots, which it will be neceffary to determine.

The Greeks proper, the Turks, and the Arabian peafants, belong to the former clafs, with this difference, that the Turks refide only in the towns where they are in poffeffion of the military employments, and the offices of the magiftracy, and where they exercife the arts. The Arabs and the Greeks inhabit the villages, and form the clafs of hufbandmen in the country, and the inferior people in the towns. The part of the country which contains the moft Greek villages is the Pa-chalic of Damafcus.

The Greeks of the Romifh communion, who are much lefs numerous than the fchif-matics, are all retired within the towns, where they cultivate the arts and commerce. The protection of the Franks, procured them, in the late war, a decided fuperiority in trade, wherever there are European fettle-ments.

The Maronites form a national body, which occupies, almoft exclufively, the whole country comprifed between Nahr-el-kelb (the river of the Dog) and Nahr-el-bared
(the

(the cold river), from the fummit of the mountains on the eaſt, to the Mediterranean on the weſt.

The Druzes border upon them, and extend from Nahr-el-kelb to the neighbourhood of Sour, (Tyre) between the valley of Bekaa and the fea.

The country of the Motoualis formerly included the valley of Bekaa, as far as Sour: but this people, of late years, have undergone, a revolution which has reduced them almoſt to nothing.

As for the Anſarians, they are diſperſed throughout the mountains, from Nahr-akkar as far as to Antakia; they are diſtinguiſhed into different tribes, ſuch as the Kelbia, the Kadmouſia, the Shamſia, &c.

The Turkmans, the Curds, and the Bedouins, have no fixed habitations, but are perpetually wandering with their tents and herds, in limited diſtricts, of which they look upon themſelves as the proprietors. The Turkman hordes generally encamp on the plain of Antioch; the Curds in the mountains between Alexandretta and the Euphrates; and the Arabs ſpread over the whole

whole frontier of Syria, adjacent to their deferts, and even the plains of the interior part of the country, as thofe of Paleftine, Bekaa, and Galilee.

To form more diftinct ideas of thefe different claffes, let us confider more circumftantially what is peculiar to each of them.

.

CHAP.

C H A P. XXIII.

Of the paſtoral, or wandering Tribes of Syria.

S E C T. I.

Of the Turkmans.

THE Turkmans are of the number of thoſe Tartar hordes, who, on the great revolutions of the empire of the Caliph, emigrated from the eaſtward of the Caſpian ſea, and ſpread them-ſelves over the vaſt plains of Armenia and Aſia Minor. Their language is the ſame with that of the Turks, and their mode of life nearly ſimi-lar to that of the Bedouin Arabs. Like them, they are paſtors, and conſequently obliged to travel over immenſe tracts of land to pro-cure ſubſiſtence for their numerous herds. But there is this difference, that the countries frequented by the Turkmans being rich in paſturage, they can feed more cattle on them, and are therefore leſs diſperſed than

Vᴏʟ. I.   B b   the

the Arabs of the defert. Each of their
Ordous, or camps, acknowledges a Chief,
whofe power is not determined by fixed
laws, but governed by cuftom and circumftances. It is rarely abufed, becaufe the
fociety is compact, and the nature of their
fituation maintains fufficient equality among
its members. Every man able to bear arms
is anxious to carry them, fince on his individual force depend both his perfonal fafety,
and the refpect paid him by his companions.
All their property confifts in cattle, that is
camels, buffaloes, goats, and efpecially fheep.
They live on milk, butter, and meat, which
are in great abundance among them, and
the furplus of which they fell in the towns
and the neighbouring country, for they are
almoft able alone to fupply the butcheries.
In return, they take arms, clothes, money,
and corn. Their women fpin wool, and
make carpets, the ufe of which is immemorial in thefe countries, and confequently indicates their manner of living to have been
always the fame. As for the men, their
whole occupation confifts in fmoking, and
looking after their flocks. Perpetually on
horfe-

horſe-back, with their lances on their ſhoul-
ders, their crooked ſabres by their ſides, and
their piſtols in their belts, they are expert
horſemen and indefatigable ſoldiers. They
have frequent differences with the Turks,
who dread them; but as they are divided
among themſelves, and form ſeparate camps,
they do not aſſume that ſuperiority which
their combined forces would enſure them.
The Pachalics of Aleppo and Damaſcus, which
are the only parts of Syria they frequent, may
be computed to contain about thirty thouſand wandering Turkmans. A great number of
theſe tribes paſs, in ſummer, into Armenia and
Caramania, where they find graſs in greater a-
bundance, and return to their former quarters
in the winter. The Turkmans are reputed Muſ-
ſulmen, and generally bear the diſtinguiſhing
mark, circumciſion. But they trouble themſelves very little about religion, and they have
neither the ceremonies, nor the fanaticiſm of
ſedentary nations. As for their manners, to
deſcribe them accurately, it would be neceſſary to have lived among them. They have,
however, the reputation of not being robbers, like the Arabs, though they are neither
leſs generous, nor leſs hoſpitable than they;

and

and when we confider that they live in plenty, without being rich, and are inured to
war, and hardened by fatigue and danger,
we may prefume they are equally removed
from the ignorance and fervility of the peafants, and the corruption and felfifhnefs of
the inhabitants of the towns.

S E C T.   II.

Of the Curds.

The Curds are another national body, the
divided tribes of which are equally difperfed
over the Lower Afia, and have extended
themfelves very widely, efpecially within the laft hundred years. Their original
country is the chain of mountains from
whence iffue the different branches of the
Tigris, which, furrounding the upper part
of the great Zab, paffes to the fouthward, as
far as the frontiers of the Irak-adjami, or
Perfian Irak *(a)*. In modern geography, it

(a) *Adjam* is the Arabic name for the Perfians. The
Greeks were acquainted with it, and expreffed it by *Ache-
men-ides.*

is known by the name of *Curd-eſtan*. This
country is mentioned in the moſt ancient tra-
ditions and hiſtories of the eaſt, in which it is
made the ſcene of ſeveral mythological events.
The Chaldean Beroſus, and the Armenian
Maribas, cited by Moſes Chorenenſis, aſſert
that it was in the mountains Gord-ouæi *(b)*,
that Xiſuthrus landed after eſcaping from the
deluge; and the local circumſtances which
they add, prove, what was otherwiſe ſufficiently evident, that *Gord* and *Curd* are the ſame.
Thoſe were the ſame Curds who are mentioned by Xenophon under the denomination
of *Card-uchi*, and who oppoſed the retreat
of the Ten Thouſand. This hiſtorian ob-
ſerves that, though ſhut in on all ſides by the
Perſian empire, they had conſtantly braved
the power of the *Great King*, and the arms
of his *Satraps*. They have changed but little
in their modern ſtate; for, though, in appearance, tributaries to the Porte, they pay
very little reſpect to the orders of the Grand
Signior, or his Pachas. M. Niebuhr, who
travelled in theſe countries in 1769, reports,
that in their mountains they are ſubject to a

(b) Strabo, lib. 11. ſays, that the Niphates, and its
chain of mountains, are called *Gordouæi*.

ſort

fort of feodal government, which appears to me fimilar to that we obferve among the Druzes. Each village has its chief, and the whole nation is divided into different and independent factions. The difputes infeparable from this ftate of anarchy have detached from the nation a great number of tribes and families, which have adopted the wandering life of the Turkmans and Arabs.

Thefe are difperfed in the Diarbekir, and over the plains of Arzroum, Erivan, Sivas, Aleppo and Damafcus: all their tribes united are eftimated to exceed one hundred and forty thoufand *tents*, that is, one hundred and forty thoufand armed men. Like the Turkmans, thefe Curds are paftors and wanderers; but differ from them in fome particular cuftoms. The Turkmans give their daughters a marriage dower: the Curds receive a premium for them. The Turkmans pay no refpect to that antiquity of extraction which we call nobility: the Curds honour it above every thing. The Turkmans do not fteal: the Curds are almoft every where looked upon as plunderers; on which account, they are much dreaded in the neighbourhood of Aleppo, and of Antioch, where

they

they occupy, under the name of Bagdafhlia, the mountains to the eaſt of Beilam, as far as near Kles. In this Pachalic, and in that of Damaſcus, their number exceeds twenty thouſand tents and huts; for they have alſo fixed habitations. They are reputed Mahometans; but they never trouble themſelves about religious rites or opinions. Several of them, diſtinguiſhed by the name of Yazdia, worſhip *Shaitan*, or Satan, that is, the genius who is the *enemy* (of God). This notion, eſpecially prevalent in the Diarbekir, and the frontiers of Perſia, is a relic of the ancient ſyſtem of the *good* and *evil principles*, which, varied according to the ſpirit of the Perſian, Jewiſh, Chriſtian, and Mahometan doctrines, has continually prevailed in theſe countries. Zoroaſter is generally conſidered as its author; but, long before his time, Egypt acknowledged Oroſmades and Arimanius, under the names of Oſiris and Typhon. It is no leſs an error, likewiſe, to ſuppoſe, that this dogma was not propagated prior to the reign of Darius Hyſtaſpes, ſince Zoroaſter, who taught it, flouriſhed in Media, and was cotemporary with Solomon.

Language

Language is the principal indication of the confanguinity of nations. That of the Curds is divided into three dialects. It has neither the afpirations nor the gutturals of the Arabic; and I am affured that it does not refemble the Perfian; fo that it muft be an original language. Now, if we confider the antiquity of the people who fpeak it; and that we know they are related to the Medes, Affyrians, Perfians, and even the Parthians *(c)*, we may be allowed to con-jecture, that a knowledge of this tongue might throw fome light on the ancient hif-tory of thefe countries. There is no known dictionary of it; but it would be no diffi-cult matter to form one. If the government of France fhould think proper to offer en-couragements to the Dragomans, or to the mif-fionaries of Aleppo, the Diarbekir, or Bag-dad, proper perfons might foon be found to accomplifh fuch an undertaking *(d)*.

S E C T.

(c) " On the Tigris," fays Strabo, lib. 16, " are " many places belonging to the Parthians, whom the " ancients called Carduchi."

(d) The Emprefs of Ruffia has lately given orders to Doctor Pallas to make a collection of all the languages fpoken

SECT. III.

Of the Bedouin Arabs.

A third wandering people in Syria, are the Bedouin Arabs, whom we have already found in Egypt. Of thefe I made but a flight mention in treating of that province, becaufe, having only had a tranfient view of them, without knowing their language, their name fuggefted but few ideas to my mind ; but having been better acquainted with them

fpoken in the Ruffian empire ; and thefe refearches muft extend even to the Cuban and Georgia ; and, perhaps, to Curdeftan. When this collection is completed, it will be neceffary to reduce all the alphabets of thefe languages to one ; for this diverfity of Arabic, Armenian, Georgian, Iberian, and Tartarian alphabets is a great obftacle to the advancement of fcience. This will, perhaps, appear impoffible to many perfons ; but, from fome experiments of the fame nature, which I have myfelf made, I think I may venture to pronounce it not only practicable, but eafy. It is fufficient to be well acquainted with the elements of fpeech, to be able to clafs the vowels and confonants of all the alphabets. It is proper alfo to obferve here, that the firft book of every nation is the dictionary of its language.

in

in Syria; having even made a journey to one of their camps, near Gaza, and lived feveral days among them, I am now able to treat of them with more minutenefs and accuracy.

In general, when fpeaking of the Arabs, we fhould diftinguifh whether they are cultivators, or paftors; for this difference in their mode of life occafions fo great a one in their manners, and genius, that they become almoft foreign nations, with refpect to each other. In the former cafe, leading a fedentary life, attached to the fame foil, and fubject to regular governments, the focial ftate in which they live, very nearly refembles our own. Such are the inhabitants of the Yemen; and fuch, alfo, are the defcendants of thofe ancient conquerors, who have either entirely, or in part, given inhabitants to Syria, Egypt, and the Barbary ftates. In the fecond cafe, having only a tranfient intereft in the foil, perpetually removing their tents from one place to another, and under fubjection to no laws, their mode of exiftence is neither that of polifhed nations, nor of favages; and, therefore, more particularly merits our attention. Such are the

Bedouins,

Bedouins, or inhabitants of the vaſt deſerts
which extend from the confines of Perſia, to
Morocco. Though divided into independent
communities, or tribes, not unfrequently
hoſtile to each other, they may ſtill be conſidered as forming one nation. The reſemblance of their language is a manifeſt token
of this relationſhip. The only difference
that exiſts between them is, that the African
tribes are of a leſs ancient origin, being
poſterior to the conqueſt of theſe countries
by the Caliphs, or ſucceſſors of Mahomet;
while the tribes of the deſert of Arabia, properly ſo called, have deſcended by an unin-
terrupted ſucceſſion from the remoteſt ages;
and it is of theſe I mean more eſpecially to
treat, as being more immediately connected
with my ſubject. To theſe the orientals are
accuſtomed to appropriate the name of Arabs,
as being the moſt ancient, and the pureſt
race. The term *Bedaoui* is added as a ſyno-
nimous expreſſion, ſignifying, as I have obſerved, inhabitant of the *Deſert*; and this
term has the greater propriety, as the word
Arab, in the ancient language of theſe countries, ſignifies a ſolitude or deſert.

It

It is not without reafon that the inhabitants of the defert boaft of being the pureft
and the beft preferved race of all the Arab
tribes : for never have they been conquered,
nor have they mixed with any other people,
by making conquefts; for thofe by which
the general name of Arabs has been rendered
famous, really belong only to the tribes of the
Hedjaz, and the Yemen; thofe who dwelt
in the interior parts of the country, never
emigrated at the time of the revolution effected by Mahomet; or if they did take any
part in it, it was confined to a few individuals, detached by motives of ambition. Thus
we find the prophet, in his Koran, continually ftiling the Arabs of the defert rebels, and
infidels; nor has fo great a length of time
produced any very confiderable change. We
may affert they have, in every refpect, retained their primitive independence and fimplicity. Every thing that ancient hiftory has
related of their cuftoms, manners, language,
and even their prejudices, is almoft minutely
true of them to this day; and if we confider, befides, that this unity of character,
preferved through fuch a number of ages,
ftill fubfifts, even in the moft diftant fituations,

tions, that is, that the tribes moſt remote from each other preſerve an exact reſemblance, it muſt be allowed, that the circumſtances which accompany ſo peculiar a moral ſtate, are a ſubject of moſt curious enquiry.

In Europe, and eſpecially in its more civilized and improved countries, where we have no examples of wandering people, we can ſcarcely conceive what can induce men to adopt a mode of life ſo repugnant to our ideas. We even conceive with difficulty what a deſert is, or how it is poſſible for a country to have inhabitants, if it be barren; or why it is not better peopled, if it be capable of cultivation. I have been perplexed, myſelf, with theſe difficulties, as well as others; for which reaſon, I ſhall dwell more circumſtantially on the facts which will furniſh us with their explanation.

The wandering and paſtoral life led by ſeveral Aſiatic nations, ariſes from two çauſes. The firſt is, the nature of the ſoil, which, being improper for cultivation, compels men to have recourſe to animals, which content themſelves with the wild herbage of the earth. Where this herbage is
but

but thin, a fingle animal will foon confume the produce of a great extent of ground, and it will be neceffary to run over large tracts of land. Such is the cafe of the Arabs in the defert of Arabia, properly fo called, and in that of Africa.

The fecond caufe muft be attributed to habit, fince the foil is cultivable, and even fertile, in many places ; fuch as the frontiers of Syria, the Diarbekir, Natolia, and the greateft part of the diftricts frequented by the Curds and Turkmans. But it appears to me that thefe habits are only the effect of the political ftate of the country, fo that the primary caufe of them muft be referred to the government itfelf. This opinion is fupported by daily facts ; for as often as the different hordes and wandering tribes find peace and fecurity, and a poffibility of pro-curing fufficient provifions, in any diftrict, they take up their refidence in it, and adopt, infenfibly, a fettled life, and the arts of cul-tivation. But when, on the contrary, the tyranny of the government drives the in-habitants of a village to extremity, the pea-fants defert their houfes, withdraw with their families into the mountains, or wander in the

the plains, taking care frequently to change
their place of habitation, to avoid being furprifed. It often happens even that individuals,
turned robbers, in order to withdraw themfelves from the laws, or from tyranny, unite
and form little camps, which maintain themfelves by arms, and, increafing, become new
hordes, and new tribes. We may pronounce, therefore, that in cultivable countries, the wandering life originates in the
injuftice or want of policy of the government ; and that the fedentary and cultivating
ftate is that to which mankind is moft naturally inclined.

With refpect to the Arabs, they feem efpecially condemned to a wandering life, by
the very nature of their deferts. To paint
to himfelf thefe deferts, the reader muft
imagine a fky almoft perpetually inflamed, and without clouds, immenfe and boundlefs plains, without houfes, trees, rivulets,
or hills, where the eye frequently meets nothing but an extenfive and uniform horizon,
like the fea, though in fome places the
ground is uneven and ftoney. Almoft invariably naked on every fide, the earth prefents nothing but a few wild plants, thinly
                              fcattered,

scattered, and thickets, whose solitude is rarely disturbed but by antelopes, hares, locusts, and rats. Such is the nature of nearly the whole country, which extends six hundred leagues in length, and three hundred in breadth, and stretches from Aleppo to the Arabian sea, and from Egypt to the Persian gulph.

It must not, however, be imagined that the soil in so great an extent is every where the same; it varies considerably in different places. On the frontiers of Syria, for example, the earth is in general fat and cultivable, nay, even fruitful. It is the same also on the banks of the Euphrates; but in the internal parts of the country, and towards the south, it becomes white and chalky, as in the parallel of Damascus; rocky, as in the Tih, and the Hedjaz; and a pure sand, as to the eastward of the Yemen. This variety in the qualities of the soil is productive of some minute differences in the condition of the Bedouins. For instance, in the more sterile countries, that is those which produce but few plants, the tribes are feeble, and very distant; which is the case in the desert of Suez, that of the Red Sea, and the interior

of

of the Great Defert, called the Najd. Where the foil is more fruitful, as between Damaf- cus and the Euphrates, the tribes are more numerous, and lefs diftant from each other; and, laftly, in the cultivable diftricts, fuch as the Pachalics of Aleppo, the Hauran, and the neighbourhood of Gaza, the camps are frequent and contiguous. In the former cafe, the Bedouins are merely paftors, and fubfift only on the produce of their herds, and on a few dates, and flefh meat, which they eat, either frefh, or dried in the fun, and reduced to a powder. In the latter, they fow fome land, and add cheefe, barley, and even rice, to their flefh and milk.

If we examine the caufes of the fterility and uncultivated ftate of the Defert, we fhall find it is principally to be attributed to the ab- fence of fountains and rivers, and, in general, to the want of water. This want of water itfelf is occafioned by the nature of the country, which being flat, and deftitute of mountains, the clouds glide over its heated furface, as I have already remarked is the cafe with Egypt. They never reft there but in winter, when the coldnefs of the atmo- fphere hinders them from rifing, and condenfes

them into rain. The nakednefs of this country is alfo another caufe of drought, fince the
air is for that reafon more eafily heated, and
compels the clouds to rife. It is probable
that a change of climate might be effected,
if the whole defert were planted with trees;
as for example, with pine trees.

The confequence of the winter rains is,
that in thofe parts where the foil is good, as
on the frontiers of Syria, a cultivation takes
place very fimilar to that of even the interior parts of the province; but as thefe
rains neither produce fprings, nor conftant
rivulets, the inhabitants are expofed to the
inconvenience of wanting water the whole
fummer. To remedy this it is neceffary to
have recourfe to art, and to form wells, refervoirs, and cifterns, in which they collect
their annual fupplies: fuch works require
money and labour, and are, after all, expofed to a variety of accidents. War may
deftroy in one day, the labour of many
months, and the refources of the year. A
drought, which is but too common, may
caufe the failure of a crop, and reduce the inhabitants even to a total want of water. It is
true, that by digging it is almoft every where

to

to be found, at from fix to twenty feet depth, but this water is brackifh, as in all the defert of Arabia and Africa *(e)*; it alfo frequently dries up, when thirft and famine fucceed; and, if the government does not lend its aid, the villages are deferted. It is evident that agriculture muft be very precarious in fuch a country, and that under a government like that of the Turks, it is fafer to lead a wandering life, than to refide in a fixed habitation, and rely for fubfiftence on agriculture.

In thofe diftricts where the foil is ftoney and fandy, as in the Tih, the Hedjaz, and the Najd, thefe rains make the feeds of the wild plants fhoot, and revive the thickets, ranunculas, wormwood, and kali. They render the lower grounds marfhy, which then produce reeds and grafs; and the plain affumes a tolerable degree of verdure. This is the feafon of abundance both for the herds and their mafters; but on the return of the

(*e*) This faline quality is fo inherent in the foil, that it impregnates even the plants. All thofe of the defert abound in alkali, and Glauber's falt; but it is remarkable that this falt diminifhes as we approach the mountains, where it is fcarcely fenfible.

heats,

heats, every thing is parched up, and the
earth, converted into a grey, and fine duft,
prefents nothing but dry ftems, as hard as
wood, on which neither horfes, oxen, nor
even goats can feed. In this ftate the Defert
would become uninhabitable, and muft be
totally abandoned, had not nature formed
an animal no lefs hardy and frugal than the
foil is fterile and ungrateful; I mean the
camel. No creature feems fo peculiarly
fitted to the climate in which it exifts. We
cannot doubt but the nature of the one
has been adapted to that of the other by fome
difpofing intelligence. Defigning the camel to
dwell in a country where he can find little
nourifhment, Nature has been fparing of her
materials in the whole of his formation.
She has not beftowed on him the plump
flefhinefs of the ox, horfe, or elephant; but,
limiting herfelf to what is ftrictly neceffary,
fhe has given him a fmall head without ears,
at the end of a long neck without flefh. She
has taken from his legs and thighs every
mufcle not immediately requifite for motion;
and, in fhort, has beftowed on his withered
body only the veffels and tendons neceffary to
connect its frame together. She has furnifhed

nifhed him with a ftrong jaw, that he may grind the hardeft aliments; but left he fhould confume too much, fhe has contracted his ftomach, and obliged him to chew the cud. She has lined his foot with a lump of flefh, which, fliding in the mud, and being no way adapted to climbing, fits him only for a dry, level, and fandy foil, like that of Arabia : fhe has evidently deftined him like-wife to flavery, by refufing him every fort of defence againft his enemies. Deftitute of the horns of the bull, the hoof of the horfe, the tooth of the elephant, and the fwiftnefs of the ftag, how can the camel refift or avoid the attacks of the lion, the tyger, or even the wolf? To preferve the fpecies, therefore, Nature has concealed him in the depth of the vaft deferts, where the want of vegetables can attract no game, and whence the want of game repels every voracious animal. Tyranny muft have expelled man from the habitable parts of the earth, before the camel could have loft his liberty. Become domeftic, he has ren-dered habitable the moft barren foil the world contains. He alone fupplies all his mafter's wants. The milk of the camel nourifhes the family of the Arab, under the varied forms

of

of curds, cheefe, and butter; and they often
feed upon his flefh.   Slippers and harnefs are
made of his fkin, and tents and clothing of his
hair.   Heavy burthens are tranfported by his
means; and when the earth denies forage to
the horfe, fo valuable to the Bedouin, the fhe
camel fupplies that deficiency by her milk, at
no other coft, for fo many advantages, than
a few ftalks of brambles or wormwood, and
pounded date kernels.   So great is the importance of the camel to the defert, that were it
deprived of that ufeful animal, it muft infallibly lofe every inhabitant.

Such is the fituation in which nature has
placed the Bedouins, to render them a race
of men equally fingular in their phyfical and
moral character.   This fingularity is fo ftriking, that even their neighbours, the Syrians,
regard them as extraordinary beings; efpecially
thofe tribes which dwell in the depths of the
deferts, fuch as thofe of Anaza, Kaibar, Tai,
and others, which never approach the towns.
When, in the time of Shaik Daher, fome of
their horfemen came as far as Acre, they excited the fame curiofity there, as a vifit from
the favages of America would among us.
Every one viewed with furprife thefe men,
                                                            who

who were more diminutive, meagre, and fwarthy, than any of the known Bedouins. Their withered legs had no calves, and appeared to confift merely of tendons. Their bellies feemed fhrunk to their backs, and their hair was frizzled almoft as much as that of the negroes. They, on the other hand, were no lefs aftonifhed at every thing they faw; they could neither conceive how the houfes and minarets could ftand erect, nor how men ventured to dwell beneath them, and always on the fame fpot; but, above all, they were in an ecftafy at beholding the fea, nor could they comprehend what that *defert of water* could be. They were told of mofques, prayers, and ablutions; but they afked what thofe meant, and enquired who Mofes, Jefus Chrift, and Mahomet, were; and why, fince the inhabitants were not of feparate tribes, they followed different leaders?

We may imagine, that the Arabs of the frontiers are not fuch novices; there are even feveral fmall tribes of them, who, living in the midft of the country, as in the valley of Bekaa, that of the Jordan, and in Paleftine, approach nearer to the condition of the peafants; but thefe are defpifed by the others,

who

who look upon them as baſtard Arabs, and *Rayas*, or ſlaves of the Turks.

In general, the Bedouins are ſmall, meagre, and tawny; more ſo, however, in the heart of the deſert, than on the frontiers of the cultivated country; but they are always of a darker complexion than the neighbouring peaſants. They alſo differ among themſelves in the ſame camp; and I have remarked, that the Shaiks, that is, the rich, and their attendants, were always taller, and more corpulent, than the common claſs. I have ſeen ſome of them above five feet five and ſix inches high; though, in general, they do not exceed five feet two inches. This difference can only be attributed to their food, with which the former are ſupplied more abundantly than the latter *(f)*. It may, likewiſe, be affirmed, that the lower claſs of Bedouins live in a ſtate of habitual wretchedneſs and famine. It will appear almoſt incredible to us, but it is an undoubted fact, that the quantity of food uſually conſumed by the

_____

(f) The effects of this are equally evident in the Arabian and Turkman camels; for theſe latter, dwelling in countries rich in forage, are become a ſpecies more robuſt and fleſhy than the former.

greateſt

greateſt part of them, does not exceed ſix ounces a day. This abſtinence is moſt remarkable among the tribes of the Najd, and the Hedjaz. Six or ſeven dates ſoaked in melted butter, a little freſh milk, or curds, ſerve a man a whole day; and he eſteems himſelf happy, when he can add a ſmall quantity of coarſe flour, or a little ball of rice. Meat is reſerved for the greateſt feſtivals; and they never kill a kid but for a marriage or a funeral. A few wealthy and generous Shaiks alone can kill young camels, and eat baked rice with their victuals. In times of dearth, the vulgar, always half famiſhed, do not diſdain the moſt wretched kinds of food; and eat locuſts, rats, lizards, and ſerpents, which they boil on briars. Hence are they ſuch plunderers of the cultivated lands, and robbers on the high-roads : hence, alſo, their delicate conſtitution, and their diminutive and meagre bodies, which are rather active than vigorous. It may be worth while to remark, that their evacuations of every kind, even perſpiration, are extremely ſmall; their blood is ſo deſtitute of ſeroſity, that nothing but the greateſt heat can preſerve its fluidity. This, however,

does

does not prevent them from being tolerably healthy, in other refpects, for maladies are lefs frequent among them than among the inhabitants of the cultivated country.

From thefe facts, we are by no means juftified in concluding, that the frugality of the Arabs is a virtue purely of choice, or even of climate. The extreme heat in which they live, unqueftionably facilitates their abftinence, by deftroying that activity which cold gives to the ftomach. Their being habituated alfo to fo fparing a diet, by hindering the dilatation of the ftomach, becomes doubtlefs a means of their fupporting fuch abftemioufnefs; but the chief and primary caufe of this habit, is with them, as with the reft of mankind, the neceffity of the circumftances in which they are placed, either from the nature of the foil, as I have before explained, or that ftate of fociety in which they live, and which I fhall now proceed to examine.

I have already faid, that the Bedouin Arabs are divided into tribes, which conftitute fo many diftinct nations. Each of thefe tribes appropriates to itfelf a certain tract of land; in this they do not differ from cultivating nations, except that their territory
requires

requires a greater extent, in order to furnish
subliftence for their herds throughout the
year. Each of thefe tribes is collected in one
or more camps, which are difperfed through
the country, and which make a fucceffive
progrefs over the whole, in proportion as it is
exhaufted by the cattle; hence it is, that
within a great extent a few fpots only are
inhabited, which vary from one day to another; but as the entire fpace is neceffary
for the annual fubfiftence of the tribe, whoever encroaches on it is deemed a violator
of property; this is with them the law of
nations. If, therefore, a tribe, or any of
its fubjects, enter upon a foreign territory,
they are treated as enemies, and robbers, and
a war breaks out. Now, as all the tribes
have affinities with each other by alliances
of blood, or treaties, leagues are formed,
which render thefe wars more or lefs general. The manner of proceeding, on fuch
occafions, is very fimple. The offence made
known, they mount their horfes, and feek
the enemy; when they meet, they enter
into a parley, and the matter is frequently
made up; if not, they attack either in fmall
bodies, or man to man. They encounter
each

each other at full fpeed, with fixed lances,
which they fometimes dart, notwithftanding
their length, at the flying enemy; the victory is rarely contefted; it is decided by the
firft fhock, and the vanquifhed take to flight
full gallop over the naked plain of the defert. Night generally favours their efcape
from the conqueror. The tribe which has
loft the battle ftrikes its tents, removes to
a diftance, by forced marches, and feeks an
afylum among its allies. The enemy, fatif-
fied with their fuccefs, drive their herds
farther on, and the fugitives foon after return to their former fituation. But the
flaughter made in thefe engagements frequently fows the feeds of hatreds which
perpetuate thefe diffenfions. The intereft of
the common fafety has, for ages, eftablifhed
a law among them, which decrees that the
blood of every man who is flain muft be
avenged by that of his murderer. This vengeance is called *Tar*, or retaliation; and the
right of exacting it devolves on the neareft
of kin to the deceafed. So nice are the
Arabs on this point of honour, that if any one
neglects to feek his retaliation, he is dif-
graced for ever. He, therefore, watches every
opportunity

opportunity of revenge : if his enemy perifhes from any other caufe, ftill he is not fatisfied, and his vengeance is directed againft the neareft relation. Thefe animofities are tranf-mitted, as an inheritance, from father to children, and never ceafe but by the extinction of one of the families, unlefs they agree to facrifice the criminal, or *purchafe the blood* for a ftated price, in money or in flocks. Without this fatisfaction, there is neither peace, nor truce, nor alliances between them, nor fometimes, even between whole tribes: *There is blood between us*, fay they, on every occafion ; and this expreffion is an infur-mountable barrier. Such accidents being neceffarily numerous in a long courfe of time, the greater part of the tribes have ancient quarrels, and live in an habitual ftate of war ; which, together with their way of life, renders the Bedouins a military people, though they have made no great progrefs in war as an art.

Their camps are formed in a kind of irregular circle, compofed of a fingle row of tents, with greater or lefs intervals. Thefe tents, made of goat or camels hair, are black or brown, in which they differ from thofe

of

of the Turkmans, which are white. They are ftretched on three or four pickets, only five or fix feet high, which gives them a very flat appearance; at a diftance, one of thefe camps feems only like a number of black fpots; but the piercing eye of the Bedouin is not to be deceived. Each tent, inhabited by a family, is divided, by a curtain, into two apartments, one of which is appropriated to the women. The empty fpace within the large circle ferves to fold their cattle every evening. They never have any intrenchments; their only advanced guards and patroles are dogs; their horfes remain faddled, and ready to mount on the firft alarm; but, as they are utter ftrangers to all order and difcipline, thefe camps, always eafy to furprife, afford no defence in cafe of an attack: accidents, therefore, very frequently happen, and cattle are carried off every day; a fpecies of marauding war in which the Arabs are very experienced.

The tribes which live in the vicinity of the Turks, are ftill more accuftomed to attacks and alarms; for thefe ftrangers, arrogating to themfelves, in right of conqueft, the property of the whole country, treat the
Arabs

Arabs as rebel vaffals, or as turbulent and
dangerous enemies. On this principle, they
never ceafe to wage fecret or open war
againft them. The Pachas ftudy every occafion to harafs them. Sometimes they
conteft with them a territory which they
had let them, and at others demand a tribute
which they never agreed to pay. Should a
family of Shaiks be divided by intereft or
ambition, they alternately fuccour each party,
and conclude by the deftruction of both.
Frequently too they poifon or affaffinate thofe
chiefs whofe courage or abilities they dread,
though they fhould even be their allies. The
Arabs, on their fide, regarding the Turks as
ufurpers and treacherous enemies, watch every
opportunity to do them injury. Unfortunately,
their vengeance falls oftener on the innocent
than the guilty. The harmlefs peafant generally fuffers for the offences of the foldier. On
the flighteft alarm, the Arabs cut their harvefts,
carry off their flocks, and intercept their
communication and commerce. The peafant
calls them thieves, and with reafon ; but the
Bedouins claim the right of war, and, perhaps,
they alfo are not in the wrong. However
this may be, thefe depredations occafion a
mifunderftanding

misunderstanding between the Bedouins and
the inhabitants of the cultivated country,'
which renders them mutual enemies.

Such is the external situation of the Arabs.
It is subject to great viciffitudes, according to
the good or bad conduct of their chiefs.
Sometimes a feeble tribe raises and aggran-
dizes itself, whilst another, which was powerful, falls into decay, or perhaps is entirely annihilated ; not that all its members perish, but
they incorporate themselves with some other ;
and this is the consequence of the internal
constitution of the tribes. Each tribe is composed of one or more principal families, the
members of which bear the title of Shaiks,
i. e. chiefs or lords.   These families have a
great resemblance to the Patricians of Rome,
and the nobles of modern Europe.   One of
the Shaiks has the supreme command over
the others.   He is the general of their little
army, and sometimes assumes the title of *Emir*,
which signifies Commander and Prince.   The
more relations, children, and allies he has, the
greater is his influence and power.   To these
he adds particular adherents, whom he studi-
ously attaches to him, by supplying all their
wants.   But besides this, a number of small
                                        families,

families, who, not being ſtrong enough to live independent, ſtand in need of protection and alliances, range themſelves under the banners of this chief. Such an union is called *kabila*, or tribe. Theſe tribes are diſtinguiſhed from each other by the name of their reſpective chiefs, or by that of the ruling family; and when they ſpeak of any of the individuals who compoſe them, they call them the *children* of ſuch a chief, though they may not be all really of his blood, and he himſelf may have been long ſince dead. Thus they ſay, *Beni Temin, Oulad Tai,* the children of Temin and of Tai. This mode of expreſſion is even applied, by metaphor, to the names of countries: the uſual phraſe for denoting their inhabitants, being to call them *the children of ſuch a place.* Thus the Arabs ſay, *Oulad Maſr,* the Egyptians; *Oulad Sham,* the Syrians: they would alſo ſay, *Oulad Franſa,* the French; *Oulad Moſkou,* the Ruſſians, a remark which is not unimportant to ancient hiſtory.

The government of this ſociety is at once republican, ariſtocratical, and even deſpotic, without exactly correſponding with any of theſe forms. It is republican, inaſmuch as

the people have a great influence in all affairs, and as nothing can be tranfacted without the confent of a majority. It is arifto-
cratical, becaufe the families of the Shaiks
poffefs fome of the prerogatives which every
where accompany power; and, laftly, it is
defpotic, becaufe the principal Shaik has an
indefinite and almoft abfolute authority,
which, when he happens to be a man of
credit and influence, he may even abufe; but
the ftate of thefe tribes confines even this
abufe to very narrow limits; for if a chief
fhould commit an act of injuftice, if, for
example, he fhould kill an Arab, it would be
almoft impoffible for him to efcape punifhment; the refentment of the offended party
would pay no refpect to his dignity; the law
of *retaliation* would be put in force: and,
fhould he not pay the blood, he would be
infallibly affaffinated, which, from the fimple and private life the Shaiks lead in their
camps, would be no difficult thing to effect.
If he haraffes his fubjects by feverity, they
abandon him, and go over to another tribe.
His own relations take advantage of his mif-
conduct to depofe him, and advance themfelves to his ftation. His fubjects com-
municate

municate too eafily with each other to render it poffible for him to divide their interefts,
and form a faction in his favour ; nor can
he have any refource in foreign troops;
for how is he to pay them, fince he receives no kind of taxes from the tribe ; the
wealth of the greater part of his fubjects being limited to abfolute neceffaries, and his
own confined to very moderate poffeffions,
and thofe too loaded with great expences ?

The principal Shaik in every tribe, in fact,
defrays the charges of all who arrive at or
leave the camp. He receives the vifits of the
allies, and of every perfon who has bufinefs
with them. Adjoining to his tent is a large
pavillion for the reception of all ftrangers
and paffengers. There are held frequent
affemblies of the Shaiks and principal men,
to determine on encampments and removals,
on peace and war; on the differences with
the Turkifh governors and the villages; and
the litigations and quarrels of individuals.
To this crowd, which enters fucceffively, he
muft give coffee, bread baked on the afhes,
rice, and fometimes roafted kid or camel ; in
a word, he muft keep open table ; and it is
the more important to him to be generous,
as this generofity is clofely connected with

matters

matters of the greateſt conſequence. On the
exerciſe of this depend his credit and his
power. The famiſhed Arab ranks the libe-
rality which feeds him before every virtue,
nor is this prejudice without foundation ; for
experience has proved that covetous chiefs
never were men of enlarged views : hence
the proverb, as juſt as it is brief, *A cloſe fiſt,
a narrow heart*. To provide for theſe expences, the Shaik has nothing but his herds,
a few ſpots of cultivated ground, the profits
of his plunder, and the tribute he levies on
the high roads, the total of which is very
inconſiderable. The Shaik, with whom I
reſided in the country of Gaza, about the
end of 1784, paſſed for one of the moſt
powerful of thoſe diſtricts ; yet it did not
appear to me that his expenditure was greater
than that of an opulent farmer. His perſonal effects, conſiſting in a few peliſſes, carpets, arms, horſes, and camels, could not be
eſtimated at more than fifty thouſand livres
(a little above two thouſand pounds) ; and
it muſt be obſerved that in this calculation,
four mares of the breed of racers, are valued at
ſix thouſand livres (two hundred and fifty
pounds), and each camel at ten pounds ſter-
ling. We muſt not therefore, when we ſpeak
of

of the Bedouins, affix to the words *Prince*
and *Lord*, the ideas they ufually convey; we
fhould come nearer the truth by comparing
them to fubftantial farmers, in mountainous
countries, whofe fimplicity they refemble in
their drefs, as well as in their domeftic life and
manners. A Shaik, who has the command of
five hundred horfe, does not difdain to faddle
and bridle his own, nor to give him his barley and chopped ftraw. In his tent, his wife
makes the coffee, kneeds the dough, and fu-
perintends the dreffing of the victuals. His
daughters, and kinfwomen wafh the linen,
and go with pitchers on their head, and veils
over their faces, to draw water from the foun-
tain. Thefe manners agree precifely with the
defcriptions in Homer, and the hiftory of Abra-
ham, in Genefis. But it muft be owned
that it is difficult to form a juft idea of them
without having ourfelves been eye-witneffes.

The fimplicity, or, perhaps, more properly,
the poverty, of the lower clafs of the Bedouins, is proportionate to that of their chiefs.
All the wealth of a family confifts of move-
ables, of which the following is a pretty exact
inventory. A few male and female camels, fome
goats and poultry; a mare, and her bridle and
faddle; a tent, a lance fixteen feet long, a

D d 3   crooked

crooked fabre, a rufty mufket, with a flint,
or matchlock; a pipe, a portable mill, a pot
for cooking, a leathern bucket, a fmall coffee roafter, a mat, fome clothes, a mantle of
black woollen, and a few glafs or filver rings,
which the women wear upon their legs and
arms; if none of thefe are wanting, their
furniture is complete. But what the poor
man ftands moft in need of, and what he
takes moft pleafure in, is his mare; for
this animal is his principal fupport. With
his mare the Bedouin makes his excurfions
againft hoftile tribes, or feeks plunder in the
country, and on the highways. The mare
is preferred to the horfe, becaufe fhe does not
neigh (*), is more docile, and yields milk,
which, on occafion, fatisfies the thirft, and
even the hunger of her mafter.

Thus confined to the moft abfolute neceffaries of life, the Arabs have as little induftry
as their wants are few; all their arts confift
in weaving their clumfy tents, and in making
mats, and butter. Their whole commerce

(*) This ftrange affertion may be found in other
authors. M. Chenier, in his *Recherches Hiftoriques fur les
Maures*, Vol. III. page 139, affirms mares do not neigh,
Mares in Europe, however, certainly neigh, as every
body knows, or may know.

only

only extends to the exchanging camels, kids, ftallions, and milk; for arms, clothing, a little rice or corn, and money, which they bury. They are totally ignorant of all fcience; and have not even any idea of aftronomy, geometry, or medicine. They have not a fingle book; and nothing is fo uncommon, among the Shaiks, as to know how to read. All their literature confifts in reciting tales and hiftories, in the manner of the Arabian Nights Entertainments. They have a peculiar paffion for fuch ftories; and employ in them almoft all their leifure, of which they have a great deal. In the evening, they feat themfelves on the ground, at the door of their tents, or under cover, if it be cold, and there, ranged in a circle, round a little fire of dung, their pipes in their mouths, and their legs croffed, they fit a while in filent meditation, till, on a fudden, one of them breaks forth with, *Once upon a time*— and continues to recite the adventures of fome young Shaik, and female Bedouin: he relates in what manner the youth firft got a fecret glimpfe of his miftrefs; and how he became defperately enamoured of her; he minutely defcribes the

lovely

lovely fair, extols her black eyes, as large and soft as those of the gazelle; her languid and empaſſioned looks, her arched eye-brows, reſembling two bows of ebony: her waiſt ſtreight, and ſupple as a lance; he forgets not her ſteps, light as thoſe of the *young filley*, nor her eye-laſhes, blackened with *kohl*, nor her lips painted blue, nor her nails, tinged with the golden coloured *henna*, nor her breaſts, reſembling two pomegranates, nor her words, ſweet as honey. He recounts the ſufferings of the young lover, *ſo waſted with deſire and paſſion, that his body no longer yields any ſhadow.* At length, after detailing his various attempts to ſee his miſtreſs, the ob-ſtacles on the part of the parents, the invaſions of the enemy, the captivity of the two lovers, &c. he terminates, to the ſatisfaction of the au-dience, by reſtoring them, united and happy, to the paternal tent, and by receiving the tribute paid to his eloquence, in the *Ma ſha allah* he has merited *(h)*. The Bedouins have likewiſe their love ſongs, which have more ſentiment and nature in them than

(h) An exclamation of praiſe, equivalent to *admirably well!*

thoſe

thofe of the Turks, and inhabitants of the towns; doubtlefs, becaufe the former, whofe manners are chafte, know what love is; while the latter, abandoned to debauchery, are acquainted only with enjoyment.

When we confider how much the condition of the Bedouins, efpecially in the depths of the defert, refembies, in many refpects, that of the favages of America, we fhall be inclined to wonder why they have not the fame ferocity; why, though they fo often experience the extremity of hunger, the practice of devouring human flefh was never heard of among them; and why, in fhort, their manners are fo much more fociable and mild. The following obfervations appear to me to contain the true folution of this difficulty.

It feems, at firft view, that America, being rich in pafturage, lakes, and forefts, is more adapted to the paftoral mode of life than to any other. But if we confider, that thefe forefts, by affording an eafy refuge to animals, protect them more furely from the power of man, we may conclude, that the favage has been induced to become a hunter, inftead of a fhepherd, by the nature of the country.

country. In this ſtate, all his habits have
concurred to give him a ferocity of character. The great fatigues of the chace
have hardened his body; frequent and extreme hunger, followed by a ſudden abundance of game, has rendered him voracious.
The habit of ſhedding blood, and tearing
his prey, has familiarized him to the ſight
of death and ſufferings. Tormented by
hunger, he has deſired fleſh; and finding it
eaſy to obtain that of his fellow creature,
he could not long heſitate to kill him to ſatisfy the cravings of his appetite. The firſt
experiment made, this cruelty degenerates
into a habit; he becomes a cannibal, ſan-
guinary and atrocious; and his mind acquires all the infenſibility of his body.

The ſituation of the Arab is very different.
Amid his vaſt naked plains, without water,
and without foreſts, he has not been able,
for want of game, or fiſh, to become either
a hunter or a fiſherman. The camel has
determined him to a paſtoral life, the manners of which have influenced his whole
character. Finding, at hand, a light, but
conſtant and ſufficient nouriſhment, he has
acquired the habit of frugality. Content
with

with his milk and his dates, he has not de-
fired flefh ; he has fhed no blood: his hands
are not accuftomed to flaughter, nor his ears
to the cries of fuffering creatures, he has
preferved a humane and fenfible heart.

No fooner did the favage fhepherd become
acquainted with the ufe of the horfe, than
his manner of life muft confiderably change.
The facility of paffing rapidly over extenfive
tracts of country, rendered him a wanderer.
He was greedy from want; and became a
robber from greedinefs ; and fuch is, in fact,
his prefent character.　A plunderer, rather
than a warrior, the Arab poffeffes no fan-
guinary courage ; he attacks only to defpoil;
and, if he meets with refiftance, never thinks
a fmall booty is to be put in competition
with his life.　To irritate him, you muft
fhed his blood, in which cafe he is found to
be as obftinate in his vengeance as he was
cautious in avoiding danger.

The Arabs have often been reproached
with this fpirit of rapine; but, without
wifhing to defend it, we may obferve, that
one circumftance has not been fufficiently attended to, which is, that it only takes place
towards reputed enemies, and is confequent-

ly

ly founded on the acknowledged laws of almoſt all nations. Among themſelves they
are remarkable for a good faith, a diſintereſt-
edneſs, a generoſity which would do honour
to the moſt civilized people. What is there
more noble than that right of aſylum ſo re-
ſpeded among all the tribes? A ſtranger,
nay, even an enemy, touches the tent of the
Bedouin, and, from that inſtant, his perſon
becomes inviolable. It would be reckoned a
diſgraceful meanneſs, an indelible ſhame, to
ſatisfy even a juſt vengeance at the expence
of hoſpitality. Has the Bedouin conſented
to eat bread and ſalt with his gueſt, nothing
can induce him to betray him. The power
of the Sultan himſelf would not be able
to force a refugee *(i)* from the protedion
of a tribe, but by its total extermination.
The Bedouin, ſo rapacious without his camp,
has no ſooner ſet his foot within it, than he
becomes liberal and generous. What little
he poſſeſſes he is ever ready to divide. He
has even the delicacy not to wait till it is

(i) The Arabs diſcriminate their gueſts, into gueſt
moſtadjir, or *imploring protedion*; and gueſt *matnoub*,
who ſets up his tent in a line with theirs; that is, who becomes naturalized.

aſked:

afked: when he takes his repaft, he affects to feat himfelf at the door of his tent,
in order to invite the paffengers; his generofity is fo fincere, that he does not look
upon it as a merit, but merely as a duty:
and he, therefore, readily takes the fame liberty with others. To obferve the manner
in which the Arabs conduct themfelves
towards each other, one would imagine that
they poffeffed all their goods in common.
Neverthelefs, they are no ftrangers to property; but it has none of that felfifhnefs
which the increafe of the imaginary wants
of luxury has given it among polifhed nations. It may be alleged, that they owe
this moderation to the impoffibility of greatly multiplying their enjoyments; but, if it
be acknowledged, that the virtues of the
bulk of mankind are only to be afcribed to
the neceffity of circumftances, the Arabs, perhaps, are not for this lefs worthy our efteem.
They are fortunate, at leaft, that this neceffity fhould have eftablifhed among them a
ftate of things, which has appeared to the
wifeft legiflators as the perfection of human
policy: I mean, a kind of equality in
the partition of property, and the variety
of

of conditions. Deprived of a multitude of enjoyments, which nature has lavifhed upon other countries, they are lefs expofed to temptations which might corrupt and de-bafe them. It is more difficult for their Shaiks to form a faction to enflave and im-poverifh the body of the nation. Each individual, capable of fupplying all his wants, is better able to preferve his cha-racter, and independence; and private po-verty becomes at once the foundation and bulwark of public liberty.

This liberty extends even to matters of religion. We obferve a remarkable difference between the Arabs of the towns and thofe of the defert; fince, while the former crouch under the double yoke of political and re-ligious defpotifm, the latter live in a ftate of perfect freedom from both : it is true that on the frontiers of the Turks, the Bedouins, from policy, preferve the appearance of Ma-hometanifm; but fo relaxed is their obfer-vance of its ceremonies, and fo little fervor has their devotion, that they are generally confidered as infidels, who have neither law nor prophets. They even make no difficulty in faying that the religion of Mahomet was

not

not made for them ; " for," add they, " how
" shall we make ablutions who have no
" water ? How can we bestow alms, who
" are not rich ? Why should we fast in the
" Ramadan, since the whole year with us is one
" continual fast ? and what necessity is there
" for us to make the pilgrimage to Mecca,
" if God be present every where ?" In short,
every man acts and thinks as he pleases, and
the most perfect toleration is established
among them. Nothing can better describe,
or be a more satisfactory proof of this than
a dialogue which one day passed between
myself and one of their Shaiks, named Ah-
med, son of Bahir, chief of the tribe of
Wahidia. " Why," said this Shaik to me,
" do you wish to return among the Franks ?
" Since you have no aversion to our manners ;
" since you know how to use the lance,
" and manage a horse like a Bedouin, stay
" among us. We will give you pelisses, a
" tent, a virtuous and young Bedouin
" girl, and a good blood mare. You shall
" live in our house."—" But do you not
" know," replied I, " that, born among the
" Franks, I have been educated in their re-
" ligion ? In what light will the Arabs view
an

" an infidel, or what will they think of an
" apoftate?"—" And do not you yourfelf
" perceive," faid he, " that the Arabs live
" without troubling themfelves either about
" the Prophet, or the *Book* (the Koran)?
" Every man with us follows the direction
" of his confcience.   Men have a right to
" judge of actions, but religion muft be left
" to God alone."—Another Shaik, conver-
fing with me, one day, addreffed me, by miftake, in the cuftomary formulary, " Liften,
" and pray for the Prophet."   Inftead of the
ufual anfwer, *I have prayed*, I replied, with
a fmile, *I liften*.   He recollected his error,
and fmiled in his turn.   A Turk of Jerufalem, who was prefent, took the matter up
more ferioufly : " O Shaik," faid he, " how
" canft thou addrefs the words of the true
" believers to an infidel ?"   " The tongue is
" *light*," replied the Shaik, " let but the
" heart be *white* (pure); but you, who
" know the cuftoms of the Arabs, how
" can you offend a ftranger with whom
" we have eaten bread and falt ?"——Then,
turning to me, " All thofe tribes of Frank-
" eftan, of whom you told me that they
" follow   not   the   law   of   the   Prophet,
" are

" are they more numerous than the mufful-
" men ?" " It is thought," anfwered I, " that
" they are five or fix times more numerous,
" even including the Arabs."—" God is juft,"
returned he, " he will weigh them in his
" balance *(k)*."

It

(k) M. Niebuhr relates in his *Defcription de l'Arabie*,
tome II. page 208, Paris edition, that, within the laft
thirty years, a new religion has fprung up in the Najd,
the principles of which are analogous to the difpofition
of mind I have been defcribing. " Thefe prin-
" ciples," fays that traveller, " are, that God alone
" fhould be invoked and adored, as the author of all
" things; that we fhould make no mention of any
" prophet in praying, becaufe that too nearly re-
" fembles idolatry : that Mofes, Jefus Chrift, Maho-
" met, &c. were in truth great men, whofe actions
" are edifying; but that no book was ever infpired by
" the angel Gabriel, or any other celeftial fpirit. In
" fhort, that vows made in the time of imminent
" danger are neither meritorious nor obligatory. I
" do not know," adds M. Niebuhr, " how far we
" may truft the veracity of the Bedouin who told
" me this. Perhaps it was his peculiar way of think-
" ing ; for the Bedouins, though they call themfelves
" Mahometans, in general, care very little about either
" Mahomet or the Koran."

The authors of this new fect were two Arabs, who,
having travelled, in confequence of fome commercial
affairs, into Perfia and Malabar, reafoned on the di-

It muſt be owned, that there are few po-
liſhed nations whoſe morality is, in general,
ſo much to be eſteemed as that of the Bedouin Arabs; and it is worthy of remark
that the ſame virtues are equally to be found
in the Turkman hordes, and the Curds.
It is ſingular, alſo, that it ſhould be among
theſe that religion is the freeſt from exterior forms, inſomuch that no man has ever
ſeen, among the Bedouins, the Turkmans,
or Curds, either prieſts, temples, or regular
worſhip.   But it is time to continue the
deſcription of the other tribes of the inhabitants of Syria, and to direct our attention
to a ſocial ſtate, very different from that we
are now quitting, to the ſtate of a cultivating
and ſedentary people.

verſity of religions they had ſeen, and thence deduced this general toleration.   One of them, named
Abd-el-Waheb, in 1760, erected an independent ſtate
in the Najd; the other, called Mekrami, Shaik of
Nadjeran, had adopted the ſame opinions; and, by
his valour, raiſed himſelf to conſiderable power in thoſe
countries.   Theſe two examples render ſtill more probable a conjecture I have already mentioned, That
nothing is more eaſy than to effect a grand political
and religious revolution in Aſia.

END OF THE FIRST VOLUME.

Printed in Great Britain
by Amazon

44849380R00248